RESCUING
Wayward Children

D1467966

OTHER BOOKS AND AUDIO BOOKS
BY LARRY BARKDULL:

Priesthood Power: Blessing the Sick and Afflicted

RESCUING
Wayward Children

LARRY BARKDULL

Covenant Communications, Inc.

Cover image: *Black Lamb* © Del Parson.

Cover design copyrighted 2009 by Covenant Communications, Inc.

Published by Covenant Communications, Inc.
American Fork, Utah

Copyright © 2009 by Barkdull Publishing LLC

All rights reserved. No part of this book may be reproduced in any format or in any medium without the written permission of the publisher, Covenant Communications, Inc., P.O. Box 416, American Fork, UT 84003. This work is not an official publication of The Church of Jesus Christ of Latter-day Saints. The views expressed within this work are the sole responsibility of the author and do not necessarily reflect the position of The Church of Jesus Christ of Latter-day Saints, Covenant Communications, Inc., or any other entity.

Printed in U.S.A.
First Printing: May 2009

14 13 12   10 9 8 7 6

ISBN 13: 978-1-59811-733-2
ISBN 10: 1-59811-733-5

To Charlaine Thompson, our dear, longtime friend

Author's Note

Many people have contributed their stories to this book. In most cases they asked that their names and the names of their loved ones remain anonymous. Therefore, to accommodate their wishes, all names and locations have been changed.

TABLE *of* CONTENTS

INTRODUCTION

In terms of your happiness, in terms of the matters that make you proud or sad, nothing—I repeat, nothing—will have so profound an effect on you as the way your children turn out.

—President Gordon B. Hinckley[1]

IMAGINE YOURSELF AS THE LEADER of a people who have been at war for decades trying to avoid extinction at the hands of an overwhelming foe. Then, in addition to your military duties, you're given the task of combing through a thousand years of history to compile a record never to be read by anyone in your generation except for your son. You're writing this record wholly for a future generation—people who have been converted to Jesus Christ by your writings and who will prepare the earth for His Second Coming. To that end, you are allowed to see the future as if you lived in it. As you write this book, you come to understand that future generation better than most people who would live in it, so well, in fact, that you can glean parallel incidents from your present history and apply them to that future people.

It is safe to say that few prophets knew us better than Mormon. Given his extraordinary mandate and visionary gift, we might conclude that he never wrote one word of the Book of Mormon to teach history; rather, he wrote the book to convince all men "Jew and Gentile that JESUS is the CHRIST, the ETERNAL GOD."[2] He wrote the Book of

---

1 Gordon B. Hinckley, "Great Shall be the Peace of Thy Children," *Ensign,* November 2000, 50.
2 Book of Mormon title page.

Mormon to teach us the fullness of the gospel and to prepare us for the coming of the Lord. Furthermore, he includes clear instruction within the pages of the Book of Mormon to liken the book's teachings unto ourselves.[3] So, if you were Mormon, and if you were to take a long, prophetic view of latter-day parenting challenges, and if you were to see an epidemic of waywardness, what lessons would you draw from history to instruct and give hope to those future parents?

Mormon chose powerful examples, one of which was the story of Alma and his son. To set up this story, he related an important incident of the Nephite "pioneers," whom the Lord had delivered and brought to the land of promise, Zarahemla. These stalwart people, who had sacrificed so much to establish their Zion, were raising children who did not believe as their parents had. Here is how Mormon described these children of the next generation:

> Now it came to pass that there were many of the rising generation that could not understand the words of king Benjamin, being little children at the time he spake unto his people; and they did not believe the tradition of their fathers.
>
> They did not believe what had been said concerning the resurrection of the dead, neither did they believe concerning the coming of Christ.
>
> And now because of their unbelief they could not understand the word of God; and their hearts were hardened.
>
> And they would not be baptized; neither would they join the church. And they were a separate people as to their faith, and remained so ever after, even in their carnal and sinful state; for they would not call upon the Lord their God.[4]

This frightening account of children abandoning their parents' beliefs and following paths of carnality and sin resonates in too many Latter-day Saint families today. Mormon continued by demonstrating

---

3 See 1 Nephi 19:23.
4 Mosiah 26:1–4.

that no set of parents, not even the king of the land or the prophet of God, is safe from the effects of the plague of waywardness: "Now the sons of Mosiah were numbered among the unbelievers; and also one of the sons of Alma was numbered among them, he being called Alma, after his father."[5] Clearly, Satan can reach into any family and attempt to snatch away any of our innocent children.

Of course, when this happens to us, we feel grief-stricken. President James E. Faust said, "The depth of the love of parents for their children cannot be measured. It is like no other relationship. It exceeds concern for life itself. . . . The grief of a parent over a rebellious child is almost inconsolable."[6] Parents of wayward children may feel isolated, ashamed, and guilty. And they often internalize and personalize the child's bad behavior. "What did I do wrong? Why didn't I see this coming?" These parents groan under the weight of apparent scriptural indictments, such as the following:

> And again, inasmuch as parents have children in Zion, or in any of her stakes which are organized, that teach them not to understand the doctrine of repentance, faith in Christ the Son of the living God, and of baptism and the gift of the Holy Ghost by the laying on of the hands, when eight years old, the sin be upon the heads of the parents. . . . And they shall also teach their children to pray, and to walk uprightly before the Lord.[7]

Perhaps worst of all, they feel helpless to change things. Because the children have their own agency, parents often feel limited in their efforts to remedy the situation. Should they employ tough love and risk destroying the relationship, or should they silently watch and mourn and risk losing the child completely? Where are the answers? Is there a way to change things?

The scriptures give us the answers we seek. In particular, they offer insight on three powerful principles parents of wayward children can use in overcoming the challenges they face.

---

5 Mosiah 27:8.

6 James E. Faust, "Dear Are the Sheep That Have Wandered," *Ensign,* May 2003.

7 D&C 68:25, 28.

First, perspective. The Fall renders us significantly impotent. We constantly feel sin beckoning us, and we cannot escape the realities of corruption, aging, disease, and opposition. Mortality is a hard experience for our children and for us.

Second, grace. We cannot make it alone. The Fall is an impossible situation without divine intervention. Only Jesus Christ can give us the strength to persevere, to overcome, and to do good works.

Third, strength. Strength to do what? When Nephi's brothers bound him, he did not pray that the Lord eliminate his circumstances; rather, he prayed to draw upon the power of the Atonement for strength to change his circumstances. Nephi knew that he had limited power, but he also knew that the Lord had infinite power.

For a parent to become an agent of change and capable of acting in the strength of the Lord, he must come to understand the eternal perspective offered by the plan of redemption, exercise intense faith in Jesus Christ, and courageously implement the redemptive power of His Atonement. The gospel teaches us this powerful truth: every effort that we make to increase our own level of sanctification has a direct redeeming effect on those for whom we are praying. In other words, the redeemed do the redeeming; the sanctified do the sanctifying. The gospel of Jesus Christ holds the spiritual solution for spiritual waywardness. We will discuss this idea in detail and with supporting evidence throughout this book.

Of course, nothing trumps agency, and no guarantee can ever be made that a child will ultimately choose to turn from a life of waywardness. Nevertheless, these principles are so powerful that prophets have used very little qualifying language in making sweeping promises. For example, Joseph Smith said, "When a seal is put upon the father and mother, it secures their posterity, so that [their children] cannot be lost, but will be saved by virtue of the covenant of their father and mother."8 In addition, on February 9, 2008, in a worldwide leadership training meeting, President Boyd K. Packer confirmed such doctrine, saying that we could count on the promises of the prophets—that though our children may seem lost today, they are not permanently lost. If they are sealed to us in the temple, and

---

8 Alma P. Burton, ed., *Discourses of the Prophet Joseph Smith,* 151.

if we keep our temple covenants, they will return after they have received the Lord's correction.[9]

Certainly it is possible for anyone to sin away from salvation; nevertheless, the Atonement has a much greater reach than we might imagine. Such optimism from the prophets for eventual success should kindle hope within any parent's despairing heart. These empowering principles and promises should be good news for parents. Rather than languishing in hopelessness while watching children die spiritually, parents can employ the sanctifying principles found in the plan of redemption and expect miracles to happen.

And miracles do happen!

The plan of redemption is a living, breathing, practical reality, and parents of the covenant have access to it to save their spiritually sick children. The mountain of evidence is astounding. Again, while nothing can interfere with a child's freedom of choice, the Lord has promised that in His own due time—even if that time extends into the next life—He will tailor-make conversion opportunities for every wayward child, just as he did for Alma, the sons of Mosiah, Paul, and others.

Because redemption is only possible through the gospel of Jesus Christ, this book examines the spiritual solution that the prophets and scriptures have set forth to give parents perspective, spiritual tools, and hope. It may be helpful to consider the following questions in relation to each of these areas of focus in order to understand just how they can assist us as parents in our quest to help our children find salvation.

Perspective

1. What kind of a world do our children live in?
2. What is their true divine nature?
3. What kind of adversity do they face in these latter days?
4. Who are we as parents in the latter days, and what is our divine appointment?
5. Is a child's waywardness really a reflection of our failing of Heavenly Father's trust?

---

9 See Boyd K. Packer, "The Proclamation on the Family," Worldwide Leadership Training Meeting, February 11, 2008.

Spiritual Tools

1. What are the great qualities—*gifts*—that we can develop by working with our wayward children, and how do these benefits equip us for our eternal calling?
2. How do we become partners with heavenly beings in the redemption process?
3. What are the redemptive skills taught as the "heart" of the gospel message?
4. How do we gain power to become saviors on Mount Zion (In other words, how can we learn to sanctify ourselves first so that we might be empowered to rescue others)?
5. How can we access the saving power of the priesthood and temple ordinances?
6. How can we gain the power of Zion's *oneness?*

Hope

1. What are the prophets' promises to parents concerning wayward children?
2. Are the prophets' promises really true? If victory is the Lord's goal and spiritual rescue His work and glory, then do we have the patience and faith to let the Lord work through us?

This book is not a clinical treatise. The science of psychology is certainly beneficial for changing behavior, which this book heartily endorses, but that science is not an antidote for *spiritual* sickness, which is epidemic in the Church. President Boyd K. Packer reminded the Saints in three different general conferences that "true doctrine, understood, changes attitudes and behavior. The study of the doctrines of the gospel will improve behavior quicker than a study of behavior will improve behavior."[10]

Consider these questions: If your son had a broken leg, would you take him to the bishop? Or if your daughter had a behavioral or emotional problem, would you take her to a medical doctor? Specialists in each science effect certain types of healings. For instance,

10 Boyd K. Packer, "Do Not Fear," *Ensign,* May 2004, 79.

psychiatrists and psychologists effect behavioral and emotional healing; if a child's waywardness has a behavioral or emotional dimension, one would consider taking him to a psychiatrist or psychologist. Following that reasoning, spiritual specialists effect spiritual healing; if a child has a spiritual sickness, we should enlist the aid of a spiritual specialist, such as a bishop, home teacher, or a youth or quorum leader. Of course, the child's parents should be at the top of the list. In each area of healing expertise, information and training are needed. Medical doctors, psychiatrists, and psychologists study for years before they are equipped to practice their art. Just so, if parents are to become spiritual specialists, they must apply themselves to the curriculum of the scriptures and the teaching of the prophets. While this book does *not* attempt to teach medical or psychological skills, it does attempt to introduce parents to principles that will help them develop the spiritual skills needed to rescue their spiritually sick children.

A psychologist in Utah shared his experience:

> When our teenage son abandoned the Church and fell into a life of alcohol, drugs, and wanton sex, my wife and I were devastated. My reaction was to apply the principles of psychology to change the boy, but I soon discovered that this situation was beyond my training. I had never felt so disempowered. I had always thought that I could handle even the most difficult behavioral situations with my science, but as I watched my son free-fall into spiritual oblivion, I felt absolutely helpless.
>
> [Then], my wife [proposed] a solution. She had no professional training for this, but she was a student of the scriptures—the very thing she needed to be. . . . My wife's solution was this: "We will pray and fast for our son. Then we will go to the temple twice a month, instead of once, and we will put his name on the prayer rolls in faith."
>
> [At the time] that struck me as a disappointing answer. I thought, *We are dealing with an urgent, complicated situation, for goodness sake; it calls for an*

urgent, complicated answer, not all this Sunday School stuff. Our son is dying, and all you can come up with are pat answers? Prayer, fasting, temple attendance—give me a break! I didn't say this out loud, of course. For the sake of our marriage, I agreed to do as my wife recommended, but I held onto my psychology books, just in case.

Over time, my wife extended more love to our son. Together, we prayed, fasted, and upped our temple attendance. She found promises from the prophets and kept copies in her nightstand. She searched the scriptures for spiritual remedies. Despite our effort, things went from bad to worse. On several occasions, I picked up my son from jail. He would [also] bring home his [immoral] friends, who helped themselves to our food. He became belligerent and cursed at us when he didn't get his way. But through it all, my wife urged patience, faith, and perseverance.

And then it happened. My wife and I had been praying for the Lord to send our son a *conversion opportunity*—not something that would interfere with his agency and force him out of his destructive lifestyle, but something that would provide him perspective and a clear choice. One night, in a drunken stupor, he had an accident that threatened his life. In a miraculous way, he was spared. The situation was so miraculous that it defied explanation. He knew that this was not *luck*. . . . Heavenly Father had given him a second chance, and he knew it. That experience opened the door. His accident involved immediate medical treatment. Lying in bed, recovering, he was willing to talk about the spiritual implications of his actions. Now I could use my skills as a psychologist to discuss his behavior and emotional problems. Now all the sciences came together to heal our son.

Although his complete spiritual recovery is still a work in progress, and although sometimes we feel that we are taking baby steps, we know that our son's direction has turned 180 degrees and hope is on the horizon. I am convinced that my wife's and my spiritual efforts opened the door for the Lord to offer our son a choice to change. And our boy took it. Looking back, I recognize other, more subtle invitations that he'd dismissed. But this invitation finally worked. Truly, the Lord extends His hand all the day long. I no longer resist my wife's simple *Sunday School* answers. We search the scriptures with more purpose; we pray, fast and attend the temple with more purpose; we hold family home evening and attend to our callings with more purpose. In the beginning, I had wanted to do something to change my son. But I had it all turned around. The Lord's way is not man's way. Spiritual healing requires another tactic. I learned that I had to change myself first, then an opportunity would come to my son. What a discovery! Now I feel as though I am finally developing spiritual skills in proportion to the skills that I developed for my profession. With so much at stake, I am willing to pay the price.

The purpose of this book is *not* to explore psychological causes of or antidotes for waywardness in children. Marriage and family therapists are qualified to write such things, and their exceptional science is one that parents should consider employing. Rather, the purpose of this book is to focus our perspective on the unique conditions of the latter days that directly affect parenting, the tools that are available to us by applying gospel principles, the scriptural insights that speak to divine attention and intervention, and the prophetic promises about the outcome.

The scriptures, which were written for our day, contain powerful principles that, if obeyed, can turn each of us into a savior on Mount Zion in the similitude of the Savior of the world. We learn that the plan of salvation is just that: *a plan to save.* Said another way, within the plan of salvation is a personal plan of salvation for each of us and each of our children. However, though we can *help* save God's children, we must realize that we, personally, cannot save them. Only the Lord can do that if they are willing to let Him.

Imagine that you have just been called to be the Young Women's president or a bishop, and you have stewardship over several girls who have gone astray. You are concerned about them, but you do not take their choice of waywardness personally. You face the challenge knowing that God has called you to work with these girls at this very time and because of this very situation. Your calling is a trust. Due to that perspective, though you might feel overwhelmed, you know that Heavenly Father prepares and qualifies those whom He calls. To help rescue these girls, you have one of two choices: (1) You can stay up nights, wring your hands, worry, and blame yourself for your shortcomings and their decisions, or (2) Put all your energy into personal sanctification so that you can better participate in the Father's plan of salvation for these girls. You are aware of the gap between your ability and the enormity of the challenge, and that realization drives you to your knees to plead for grace—that principle of power which requires you to give your best effort and thus qualifies you for Christ's promise that He will make up the difference. Without His grace, you can never do the work that is reserved for Gods.

Parents should adopt this attitude and let go of the paralyzing feelings of failure. We are involved in a carefully orchestrated trust, which was foreseen and provided for in the Atonement. We, personally, were prepared for and will be strengthened to accomplish our part in that trust. In accomplishing our mission, we do not have to create a plan of salvation; we simply need to increase our spiritual capacity to better participate in God's plan, as He reveals it to us. We are not alone; we are partners! Through the sealing ordinances of the temple, special powers are given to parents that tether a child to them. Harnessing that power is the quest of a lifetime and an important step in assuming the work of God. We are novices, and God understands that we are getting on-the-job training. Therefore He provides for us the principle of grace. Despite our weaknesses and failings, God is ultimately in control. Our children are being worked on by the Greatest Powers in the universe, and these Beings never consider failure as an option. They are very good at what they do—*the best!* They are the ones who extend the promises and effect the miracles.

They understand timing, circumstances, and relationships.

We partner with God by means of our covenants, and He allows us to vitalize His plan of salvation for our wayward children by means of our personal sanctification. The highest level of sanctification comes through temple worship, and this is where we receive many of our answers. The more we learn about covenants, the priesthood, and the ordinances of that priesthood, the more His power is infused into our lives. Then the gospel becomes a tool rather than a culture. The power of the temple ordinances is greater than any of us understands. Eventually, such power will bring a wayward child home.

So how do we harness this power? How do we partner with God through our covenants? If Sunday School answers seem too simple, then we need to understand that, amazingly, the gospel is simple. In explaining how easy it was to harness the power of the Liahona, Alma said, "O my son, do not let us be slothful because of the *easiness of the way;* for so was it with our fathers; for so was it prepared for them, that if they would look they might live; even so it is with us. The way is prepared, and if we will look we may live forever."[11] Imagine, salvation by just looking with faith. Nephi reminds us that great healings often pivot on simple, faith-filled actions: "[The Lord] sent fiery flying serpents among [the Israelites]; and after they were bitten he prepared a way that they might be healed; and the labor which they had to perform was to look; and because of the simpleness of the way, or the easiness of it, there were many who perished."[12] Again, they weren't looking to the right source in faith. Are we like the apostate Israelites who looked beyond the mark[13]—do we look for a sophisticated, scientific solution when God's answer is so simple and easy?

Is it really that easy? The solution, yes; the effort, not necessarily. The common blessing that every parent of a wayward child receives is insight into becoming like God. And that may take years. One parent wrote in desperation, "How long does a parent go on trying to provide guidance to a wayward child? I mean, at what age am I to stop being concerned—after the child has turned 18? 21? 25? 28? 30? 50?" Good question. The prophets have indicated that our responsibility extends

11 Alma 37:46; emphasis added.
12 1 Nephi 17:41.
13 See Jacob 4:14.

beyond this life into the next. Much as the Savior never gives up on us, we, as saviors on Mount Zion, must never give up on our charges. Can we interfere with agency? Of course not. But love, acceptance, prayer, and all other efforts to reclaim must be ongoing. The Book of Mormon provides good insight on how we must persevere.

Alma's first attempt to reach the people of Ammonihah resulted in failure. The reason was one that is all too familiar for parents of wayward children: "Now Satan had gotten great hold upon the hearts of the people of the city of Ammonihah; therefore they would not hearken unto the words of Alma."[14] Alma's reaction is equally familiar to us: "And it came to pass that while he was journeying thither, [Alma was] weighed down with sorrow, wading through much tribulation and anguish of soul, because of the wickedness of the people."[15] Then comes the lesson: "It came to pass while Alma was thus weighed down with sorrow, behold an angel of the Lord appeared unto him." Alma was not alone! A loving Father in Heaven was watching and aware of Alma all along, and He sent an angel. The angel commanded Alma to return and try again. And Alma returned *speedily*.[16] We know the result. The spiritual giant Amulek was converted, and ultimately Alma and Amulek's efforts yielded an amazing harvest of converted souls. This is one of the greatest accounts of salvation found in scripture. Why? Because Alma *never* gave up and was willing to sanctify himself so that he could better fulfill his part in God's plan of salvation.

Although this book is written primarily for parents, these principles also apply to children, Church leaders, friends, and family members who are struggling to rescue wayward parents, siblings, or others in their charge. The powerful principles in the plan of salvation are within the reach of anyone willing to exert the effort. Is there a need? A survey of any ward in the Church or a perusal of recent conference talks should provide the answer. Spiritual waywardness is epidemic. *You are not alone!* In fact, you are in good company. Some of the best parents who ever lived have struggled with wayward children. Perhaps it is not a curse after all; maybe it is a trust. Nevertheless, this epidemic was foretold in the scriptures, and a

---

14 Alma 8:9.

15 Alma 8:14.

16 See Alma 8:14–18.

remedy was prescribed. Once parents become acquainted with these redemptive principles, miracles often happen.

The divine resources available to us are amazingly expansive, the vast body of confirming evidence of eventual success overwhelming. Therefore, to discount the Lord's power to reclaim, even from incredible distances, or to minimize the power the Lord has placed within our reach is to disparage the redeeming power of the infinite and universal Atonement of Jesus Christ. With God's help, we can make a difference.

And absolutely, there is hope.

Section 1

PERSPECTIVE

Chapter 1
A Very Wicked World

*You face so much evil . . . I do not know that there was
ever a time in the history of the world when there was greater evil
in the world than there is today.*

—*President Gordon B. Hinckley*[17]

ALMOST WITHOUT EXCEPTION, PARENTS OF wayward children describe "life before waywardness" as living in a bubble. Then, when their child is caught up is some difficulty, the parents became acutely aware of their surroundings. Few of us think it can happen to our family. We read the scriptures and hear the prophets talk about extreme conditions, but somehow we feel insulated—until it hits home.

If you are the parent of a wayward child and have felt the associated pain and guilt, maybe you should step back and go a little easier on yourself. This world is a hard place; in fact, it is one of the *hardest* places. Because we have the inherent ability to acclimate to our environment, we get used to conditions and imagine them as *normal.* That might be how we see our life in this world. But it is not the case.

In this chapter we will discuss the unique and disturbing situation of our world in the last days. The intention is to provide perspective and not to shock or discourage. While it is true that we live in a very wicked world, it is also true that these conditions were foreseen and overcome by our benevolent Savior. Nevertheless, it is difficult to defend ourselves if we do not know the enemy and his strategy. So,

---

17 Gordon B. Hinckley, "Inspirational Thoughts," *Ensign,* September 2007, 7.

for a few pages, let us put our day in perspective; then we will spend the rest of the book examining the hopeful and attainable solution to our modern problems.

It's true that we live in a day when our youth are under attack and that *no one* is exempt from the influences of the adversary. This is illustrated in the following heartbreaking story:

> Our community in Idaho is predominantly LDS, and we are in the greenbelt of Mormonism. People move here from all over the United States to escape the wickedness and to give their children a fighting chance to grow up clean and safe. I wonder if such a place exists anymore. [Our daughter] Lisa began using drugs when she was twelve and in grade school. She started with alcohol and tobacco and progressed to street drugs such as marijuana and cocaine. By the time we realized that she was using drugs, she was already in the early stages of addiction. When we did our first intervention on her, she was in the late stage of addiction and her chances of recovery were not very good. By the time she was a young adult we had already spent tens of thousands of dollars on treatment, wiping out my . . . precious resources.
>
> Lisa's addiction caused untold suffering for our family. After the second intervention, Lisa remained sober for four years, but after her third failed marriage, she began to use again and has never stopped. She has done jail time and destroyed her health, she cannot keep a job, and she has damaged or destroyed most of the important relationships in her life. Drug addicts end up dead, in jail, insane, or—with great effort—they overcome and recover. That is our hope.
>
> Amazingly, Lisa is still alive, and at the moment she is not in jail. With such bleak prospects, some people ask me what keeps us going. The answer is [that] as long as Heavenly Father doesn't give up on her, neither will we. While we are wiser and no longer

enable her addiction, pay her bills, bail her out of jail, or do anything to contribute to her addiction, we are ever hopeful and will never lead her to believe that she is not loved and not a valued member of this family. We are not angry with her. We do not judge her. We do not condemn her. We do not lecture or belittle her. We just patiently and tenaciously love her, and pray and wait for yet another opportunity to help her.

And if the next opportunity is not successful, we will wait for another. If she chooses to go into treatment again, we will be there. If she suffers tragedy, we will be there. If she turns to us for anything, we will be there. Just as the Savior said about leaving the ninety and nine to search after the one lost sheep, we will never give up on Lisa. We are assured that sometime, somewhere, there will be another opportunity to help her, and we are doing all we can to prepare ourselves to be ready when that day comes. That is [the cause of] our faith and our peace.

Our world is far from normal. What we and our children face these days is an exception to history. This is the place where the war that began in heaven plays out—a war of gargantuan proportions and eternal and universal implications—a clash of titans, if you will. "And there was war in heaven: Michael and his angels fought against the dragon; and the dragon fought and his angels, And prevailed not; neither was their place found any more in heaven. And the great dragon was cast out, that old serpent, called the Devil, and Satan, which deceiveth the whole world: he was cast out into the earth [this earth!], and his angels were cast out with him."[18]

Here on this earth we are experiencing the continuing conflict between the two greatest powers in the universe. It's a fight to the death, so to speak. We know the outcome, of course, but in the meantime, we are caught in the middle of a war that only a god can win. And there are casualties—billions of them. This world seems to be a frontline of

---

18 Revelation 12:7–9.

a cosmic battle where sides have been drawn . . . again. One side is for the "Eternal God of all other gods"[19] and His Christ; the other side is for Lucifer, the usurper and impostor, the one who would wrest the kingdom from the Father and proclaim himself God.[20]

Once we align ourselves with Christ and Heavenly Father, the true God, we are at enmity[21]—enemies—with the devil, and he will use every resource at his disposal to injure and destroy us, including targeting our children. There is no mercy in him, only eternal hatred. Once, in the distant past, we helped defeat him, and he remembers. That fact alone should cause us to shudder; it should summon our constant vigilance to "watch and pray always lest [we] enter into temptation; for Satan desireth to have [us]."[22] So why should we be surprised when Satan aims for us, ambushes our children, and does so ruthlessly?

When our children are attacked, we can take some comfort in knowing that other righteous parents have suffered from the artillery launched by Satan toward their children: Adam and Eve; Isaac and Rebekah; Jacob and Rachel; Lehi and Sariah; Alma the Elder and his wife; King Mosiah and his wife; even Joseph and Lucy Mack Smith had a problem child (William). Clearly, no family is immune.

Therefore, when we feel the war intrude upon our family, a proper perspective may help. A gospel perspective tells us that we do not face a typical enemy, for even the worst tyrants that have ever lived are tame compared with the master tyrant to whom they surrendered their agency. A gospel perspective tells us that our world is more wicked even than other telestial worlds.[23] A gospel perspective tells us that both our circumstances and our adversary are extraordinary. And finally, a gospel perspective opens our eyes to see things as they really are, and to see our children and ourselves for who we really are. Such perspective, then, directs us to the only Power upon whom we may draw strength to assist in God's work of redemption.

---

19 D&C 121:32.
20 See D&C 29:36.
21 See Moses 4:21.
22 3 Nephi 18:18.
23 See Moses 7:36.

COSMIC PERSPECTIVE

In theater, when the curtains are drawn back, we are suddenly exposed to an entirely new perspective. Enoch too experienced this drawing back of the Lord's curtains. In a vision of visions, the Lord began by parting the veil and showing Enoch some of the workmanship of His hands. Of course, Enoch was awestruck. Struggling for comparatives, he exclaimed, "And were it possible that man could number the particles of the earth, yea, millions of earths like this, it would not be a beginning to the number of thy creations; *and thy curtains are stretched out still.*"[24]

In that cosmic view of the universe, which could only be facilitated by the power of God, Enoch saw "millions of earths like this."[25] Then, as he wondered at all of it, he saw the Lord weeping. How could this be? Why, in the midst of the grandeur of eternity, would the Great Creator of the universe weep? So Enoch asked, and the Lord responded with an answer that should give every parent in Zion cause to tremble: "Among all the workmanship of mine hands there has not been so great wickedness as among thy brethren."[26]

Interpreted narrowly, the Lord's answer might be thought to reference only Enoch's generation. This was the generation that preceded the great flood, which, by all accounts, was a generation so wicked that it warranted divine destruction, a generation that some have suggested was destroyed because its children no longer had a chance to grow up without being overwhelmed by the sin that abounded everywhere. But because Enoch was enjoying a sweeping view of the ages, we might interpret the Lord's statement as including the generations of this earth, including those in the last days.

In that view, we latter-day parents begin to realize that our children are at terrible risk. Enoch saw that our day would be much like his—a day defined by gross wickedness. In fact, our day would equal the depravity achieved by the people in the days of Noah: "But as it was in the days of Noah, so it shall be also at the coming of the Son of Man."[27] The message is clear: Enoch's "brethren," who

24 Moses 7:30; emphasis added.
25 Moses 7:30
26 Moses 7:36.
27 JS—Matthew 1:41.

would live upon this earth across the ages of time, would sink to one of the lowest levels in all the universe, and, scripturally, we speculate that perhaps some of the worst circumstances are here and now. As Brigham Young said, "We are inhabitants of a world of sin and sorrow; pain and anguish, every ill that can be heaped upon intelligent beings in a probation we are heirs to. I suppose that God never organized an earth and peopled it that was ever reduced to a lower state of darkness, sin and ignorance than this. I suppose this is one of the lowest kingdoms that ever the Lord Almighty created."[28]

Speaking of the evils facing our youth in "epidemic proportions," President Boyd K. Packer, said, "These are days of great spiritual danger for our youth." Continuing, he stated that he knew of no time when worse things were so widely accepted in the world, not even in the time of Sodom and Gomorrah. While evil was localized then, he pointed out, it is now spread across the world.[29] Sodom and Gomorrah and the world of Noah are examples of civilizations whose wickedness became so oppressive that it strangled agency and overwhelmed children before they could make informed choices. Such conditions demand extermination for the merciful sake of the children.

THE IMPACT OF OUR WORLD'S WICKEDNESS ON THE HOSTS OF HEAVEN
Evidence that our world and situation are extraordinary can be found in a further reading of Enoch's vision. After the Lord explained that the wickedness on this earth is unique, he stated, "The whole heavens shall weep over them, even all the workmanship of mine hands."[30]

The events that transpire on this earth are viewable by all of heaven. The powers of darkness that prevail upon this earth, and the enemy that has combined against us, have corrupted all flesh "in the presence of all the hosts of heaven—Which causeth silence to reign, and all eternity is pained."[31] Have you ever witnessed something so abhorrent that speech fails you? So shocking that you cannot summon a response to a scene that is so grossly depraved and contrary to the order of heaven? What you are viewing "causeth silence to reign."

---

28   George D. Watt, ed., *Journal of Discourses,* Volume 10, 175.
29   Boyd K. Packer, "One Pure Defense," CES Devotional, February 6, 2004.
30   Moses 7:37.
31   D&C 38:11–12.

Such may be the case with those who dwell in the eternal realm. With jaw-dropping disbelief, they are evidently sickened to the point of silence. Apparently, the awful wickedness that occurs on this world rouses profound anxiety among the angels of God who await "the great command to reap down the earth, to gather the tares that they may be burned."[32] There can be no other divine reaction; there never has been. Only the patience and mercy of God stay certain retribution for the sake of his elect.[33]

Clearly, the hosts of heaven are keenly aware of us and watch with heightened interest. And they have good reason. It was here that their Savior came to work out the universal Atonement to make all the inhabitants of God's created worlds "begotten sons and daughters unto God."[34] Moreover, this world is destined to be crowned with glory, and with the presence of God the Father,[35] and will belong to Christ[36] and His Saints,[37] which suggests that this earth—presently one of the lowest and darkest objects in the heavens—will be exalted and become one of the highest and most brilliant luminaries in the universe, a significant celestial kingdom where Christ shall dwell. We might note with interest here the chiasmic law of opposites:[38] "the first shall be last, and the last shall be first."[39]

Extremes, therefore, define our earth. Some of the worst acts of wickedness and some of the greatest acts of righteousness have been and are being played out on this planet. The salvation of the universe depends on the outcome of the events that happen here. This should tell us something about our children and ourselves. We—our children and us—have strengths beyond our imagination, and over time the Lord will help us remember and then employ our abilities to do the work of redemption among those who are temporarily deceived or wounded in this benighted world.

---

32 D&C 38:12.
33 See JS—Matthew 1:20.
34 D&C 76:24.
35 See D&C 88:19–20.
36 See D&C 130:9.
37 See D&C 103:7.
38 See 2 Nephi 2:11.
39 D&C 29:30.

THE LURES OF SATAN

Nephi's vision of the latter days is chilling:

> And it came to pass that I saw among the nations of the Gentiles the formation of a great church.
>
> And the angel said unto me: Behold the formation of a church which is most abominable above all other churches, which slayeth the saints of God, yea, and tortureth them and bindeth them down, and yoketh them with a yoke of iron, and bringeth them down into captivity.
>
> And it came to pass that I beheld this great and abominable church; and I saw the devil that he was the founder of it.
>
> And I also saw gold, and silver, and silks, and scarlets, and fine-twined linen, and all manner of precious clothing; and I saw many harlots.
>
> And the angel spake unto me, saying: Behold [all these] are the desires of this great and abominable church.
>
> And also for the praise of the world do they destroy the saints of God, and bring them down into captivity.[40]

In the language of war, Nephi describes an organized effort within the confines of the nations of the Gentiles, where we live, to slay the Saints. The sole purpose of the "great and abominable church"—for it truly is a consuming religion to its founder and its adherents—is to torture, bind down, yoke "with a yoke of iron," and bring "down into captivity" the covenant people. To accomplish this "slaying," the devil dangles bait like a fisherman dangles a lure. Although the older and wiser can sometimes recognize these lures for what they are, the young and inexperienced are often, tragically, the most fascinated by simple lures and are drawn close and caught.

---

40 1 Nephi 13:4–9.

Because of this, the devil's tackle holds an impressive arsenal of lures—if he can't catch us with one, he will simply change lures and keep trying. According to Nephi's vision, the following lures can tempt all of us given a certain level of complexity of context or greater cunning on Satan's part.

- The pursuit of wealth
- Fashion and materialism
- Sexual sin of every variety
- Peer acceptance and popularity

Whether or not these lures are employed singly or in combination, or whether or not they are chosen or imposed upon us, the devil's intention is the same—"to destroy the saints of God, and to bring them down into captivity." With some degree of confidence, then, we can retrace a child's wayward footsteps—by his choice or by his victimization—to his being hooked by one of these lures.

Is Satan's strategy working to deceive and destroy even the very elect?[41] Evidently better than he had hoped. He has made us to "bow down with grief, sorrow, and care, under the most damning hand of murder, tyranny, and oppression." He has "strongly riveted the creeds of the fathers, who have inherited lies, upon the hearts of the children, and filled the world with confusion," which condition of wickedness and confusion has been "growing stronger and stronger, and is now the very mainspring of all corruption, and the whole earth groans under the weight of its iniquity. It is an iron yoke, it is a strong band; they are the very handcuffs, and chains, and shackles, and fetters of hell." Satan has been so successful that even he is astonished. His "dark and blackening deeds are enough to make hell itself shudder, and to stand aghast and pale, and the hands of the very devil to tremble and palsy."[42]

THROWN INTO POLLUTION, WE WILL BECOME DIRTY
We swim in a sea of sin. It is simply impossible not to feel it wash over us. The tidal wave in our day has become a tsunami for our children.

---

41 See Matthew 24:24.
42 D&C 123:7–8, 10.

Why else would Mormon, who was writing only for our benefit, choose to include the rebellion and conversion stories of Alma the Younger and the sons of Mosiah?[43] Why would he make such a point about the heartbreaking epidemic of disbelieving children, the successors of righteous pioneer forefathers whose sacrifice had established the Church of God and the land of promise?[44] As a further witness, why would God inspire the compilers of the Bible to include the conversion story of the young, vile, and sinful Paul,[45] who, upon repenting, became one of the greatest Apostles and missionaries in history? Is there not a last-days' parallel in these accounts?

Clearly, we live in the prophesied generation whose decadences and perversions rival the generations of Enoch and Noah. But we must not collapse under the weight of latter-day realities. In every situation, the Lord prepares a way of escape. Nevertheless, when our children slip off the path of safety and appear to be spiraling into a free fall, we often panic and underestimate the far-reaching effects of the Atonement. Reminding us that "nothing shall be impossible"[46] with God and that nothing shall be impossible for us when we place our trust in God,[47] the Lord inspired prophets to fill the scriptures with purposely placed, extreme accounts of redemption that are often beyond the boundaries of our comprehension. Consider these examples:

Alma the Younger, who categorized the seriousness of his sins with near murder,[48] "became a very wicked and an idolatrous man . . . a man of many words, and did speak much flattery to the people . . . [and] he led many of the people to do after the manner of his iniquities."[49] Apparently he and the sons of Mosiah established a secret combination to "destroy the church" and "to lead astray the people of the Lord, contrary to the commandments of God, or even the king."[50]

---

43 See Mosiah 27–28.
44 See Mosiah 26:1–4.
45 See Acts 9.
46 Luke 1:37.
47 See Matthew 17:20.
48 See Alma 36:14.
49 Mosiah 27:8.
50 Mosiah 27:10.

They rebelled against God and stole away "the hearts of the people; causing much dissension among the people; giving a chance for the enemy of God to exercise his power over them."[51] Few of our wayward children will sink lower than did Alma, and yet within two days of his coming face-to-face with the truth, he repented and testified that he had been "born of God," "*snatched*"—grasped or seized hastily—from certain "everlasting burning" and "eternal torment."[52] Likewise, the sons of Mosiah, Alma's companions in rebellion, who were described as "the very vilest of sinners,"[53] repented and were promised eternal life.[54] Again, few of our children will fall this low, and yet God found a way to rescue them and make them "instruments in his hands."[55]

When Lamoni, a king so wicked that he murdered his servants merely for falling short in performing their duty, was presented with the truth, he embraced it so thoroughly that he was overwhelmed and his strength failed him so that he "fell unto the earth, as if he were dead."[56] Remaining in this condition for two days and two nights, he was "under the power of God" as "the dark veil of unbelief was . . . cast away from his mind." This occurred because "the light which did light up his mind . . . had infused such joy into his soul, the cloud of darkness having been dispelled, [that he was] . . . carried away in God."[57] When Lamoni awoke, he bore this testimony: "I have seen my Redeemer."[58] Again, few of our children will achieve the gross wickedness of Lamoni, but, nevertheless, the Lord was able to *snatch* him from an incalculable distance and draw him back.

Lamoni's father, the preeminent Lamanite king, also a documented murderer, experienced a mighty change of heart when he, too, was presented with the truth. Now realizing that no quantity of possessions or continued indulgence in sin could replace the loss of his soul, he

---

51 Mosiah 27:9.
52 Mosiah 27:28–29; emphasis added.
53 Mosiah 28:4.
54 See Mosiah 28:7.
55 Alma 26:15.
56 Alma 18:42.
57 Alma 19:6.
58 Alma 19:13.

cried out to Aaron, "What shall I do that I may have this eternal life of which thou hast spoken? Yea, what shall I do that I may be born of God, having this wicked spirit rooted out of my breast, and receive his Spirit, that I may be filled with joy, that I may not be cast off at the last day? Behold, said he, I will give up all that I possess, yea, I will forsake my kingdom, that I may receive this great joy."[59] Then praying mightily to God, he exclaimed, "I will give away all my sins to know thee, and that I may be raised from the dead, and be saved at the last day." Upon his cry for deliverance, the Spirit overcame him and "he [also] was struck as if he were dead,"[60] and when Aaron had raised him up, the old king became a missionary to his people, "minister[ing] unto them."[61] The unspoken lesson is repeated: few of our children will sink lower than the father of Lamoni, and yet the Lord had the power and the desire to rescue him.

Upon Lamoni's father's conversion, religious liberty was proclaimed throughout the land, and tens of thousands of Lamanites abandoned their sins, which had been perpetuated by the wicked traditions of their fathers. The strength of their conversion carries a comforting promise to latter-day parents: once these sinners were reclaimed by the power of the Atonement of Jesus Christ and had become "converted unto the Lord," they "never did fall away."[62] Mormon describes them with this language: "For they became a righteous people; they did lay down the weapons of their rebellion, that they did not fight against God any more, neither against any of their brethren."[63]

To distinguish themselves as people of God, they assumed the name Anti-Nephi-Lehi, "and the curse of God did no more follow them."[64] They had been "the most lost of all mankind" and had committed "many murders,"[65] and yet once they were presented with the truth and embraced it with all their hearts, they exclaimed, "the great God has had mercy on us, and made these things known

---

59 Alma 22:15.
60 Alma 22:18.
61 Alma 22:23.
62 Alma 23:6.
63 Alma 23:7.
64 Alma 23:18.
65 Alma 24:11.

unto us that we might not perish; yea, and he has made these things known unto us beforehand, because he loveth our souls *as well as he loveth our children.* . . . Oh, how merciful is our God!"[66]

Imagine, no more sin by false tradition; no more sin by choice; no more curse; no more weapons of rebellion; no more distance from God. Even the "most lost of all mankind," who had committed "many murders," can be "snatched" by the power of Jesus Christ from "everlasting burning and eternal torment."

Other scriptural accounts could be cited, but these examples should signal the universality of the Savior's redemptive power and message. Again, few of our children will approach the abysmal level of sin these people achieved, and yet the Lord fully forgave them and was able to use them as instruments for great good. With some degree of confidence, then, we might speculate that Mormon did not choose these stories randomly; rather, he likely chose them to demonstrate that even the vilest of sinners can be redeemed at a moment's notice. His tight grouping of these stories, which comprise chapters 27 and 28 of Mosiah and chapters 17 through 23 of Alma, seems to indicate that Mormon was trying to add evidence in support of at least two gospel messages:

> 1. No one, absolutely no one, is beyond the redemptive reach of the Savior. (This principle obviously excludes the sons of perdition.[67])
> 2. Every son and daughter of God will be presented with the full truth and given a clear choice. (This may not happen during mortality, but it will happen in the next life for certain.[68])

Clearly, the conversion experiences of Alma, the sons of Mosiah, Lamoni and his father, and the Anti-Nephi-Lehies are to be understood as universal experiences. Heavenly Father, who is both just and merciful, would not condemn His children with an immutable, eternal judgment without first laying out the truth and extending to them a choice. For beyond the issue of our sins, which by repentance

66 Alma 24:14–15; emphasis added.
67 Bruce R. McConkie, *Mormon Doctrine*, "Sons of Perdition," 746.
68 Joseph Fielding Smith, ed., *Teachings of the Prophet Joseph Smith*, 356–357.

can be covered by the Atonement, we will be judged by the desires of our hearts.[69] Heavenly Father will accomplish this miracle of redemption in His own time, and if there is one thing that He has lots of, it is time—all of this life, including life in the spirit world, up until the moment of our resurrection. Therefore, time is on His side. He is always on time, despite our occasional accusation that He is late. He has promised that He will not "[delay] his coming."[70] Rather, in His own wisdom and timing, He will employ all the resources of heaven to reclaim and redeem His wayward children.

CONVERSION CYCLE

We are all guilty of sin. "Repentant" sinners seem to fall into one of two categories: "those who pretend to be obedient [or think they will change] but are actually rebels, and those who begin as rebels but repent."[71] The conversion of sinners is set on a predictable cycle. It begins with facing temptation and adversity, both of which are designed to cause us to be humble, which humility invites the Lord to feel after us, which brings us to the crossroads of decision, which, if we accept, brings healing of the soul. "And after their temptations, and much tribulation, behold, I, the Lord, will feel after them, and if they harden not their hearts, and stiffen not their necks against me, they shall be converted, and I will heal them."[72]

1. Temptation and consequences/adversity
2. Humility
3. Lord feels after you
4. Conversion/healing

Most of our children are stationed somewhere along the pathway to conversion. Humility is the key to their completing the cycle successfully. They can choose to become humble or, as Alma said, they can be *compelled* to become humble.[73] One way or another,

---

69 See D&C 137:9.
70 3 Nephi 29:2.
71 MacArthur, quoted in Robert L. Millet's *When a Child Wanders*, 129.
72 D&C 112:13.
73 See Alma 32:12–16.

they must become humble for the Lord to feel after and heal them. If, as Mormon wrote to Moroni, they harden their hearts when the Lord feels after them, they run the risk of the Spirit's withdrawing, causing them to become "past feeling." When Mormon's people reached that point, he could no longer "recommend them unto God."[74] Nevertheless, a careful reading of the Book of Mormon reveals that this condition is the exception and only occurs after the Lord has expended extensive time and repeated efforts, and even then, He states that He will reach out to them in the spirit world.[75] An indication of the continuing conversion effort is found in Doctrine and Covenants 138, where we read of the Savior establishing a missionary effort to reach those in prison who "sometime were disobedient."[76]

Where, then, are our wayward children in the conversion cycle? Perhaps they are struggling with temptation and suffering the consequences of their actions. This is an agonizing stage for everyone involved. We parents might take comfort that the next step in the cycle—if we do not become impatient and interrupt the cycle by taking away the consequences—is humility. Until that happens, our job is to love wayward children unconditionally and, without stepping in front of God, do all that is prudent and within our power. Our faith is that one day our children will sense the Lord's feeling after them. This will bring them to a crossroads of choice. At the crossroads, the Lord will present them with a clear invitation to cease pursuing the pathway to destruction and to begin following the road to healing. Although we might imagine otherwise, most people will not reject the Lord's repeated invitations to follow Him. But even if that should happen, the Lord will continue to move them along the conversion cycle until they have completed it. We must remember that this is the Lord who "stretches forth his hands unto them all the day long"[77] and always seeks to gather them to Him as a nurturing, protective hen would gather her chicks.[78]

---

74 Moroni 9:20–21.
75 Alma 9:11.
76 D&C 138:9.
77 Jacob 6:4.
78 See 3 Nephi 10:4–6.

SUNDAY WILL COME

We were sent to earth because it is to become our eternal home. We have come here to stay; we are promised an inheritance here. The meek shall inherit the earth.[79] If the destiny of this earth is to become one of the greatest celestial bodies in the heavens, then that is *our* destiny too. Brigham Young noted this process, defining something I call the "universal law of opposites." To the extent that the righteous are abased, they will eventually be exalted. The same could be said of this earth. "In proportion as [the earth] has been reduced [,] so it will be exalted[—] with that portion of its inhabitants who in their humiliation have cleaved to righteousness and acknowledged God in all things. In proportion to our fall through sin, so shall we be exalted in the presence of our Father and God . . . through Jesus Christ and by living the righteousness of his Gospel. All this the people will understand in due time through their faithfulness, and learn to rejoice even in the midst of afflictions."[80]

We must cling to that hope, and we have every reason to expect that our hope is not in vain. As an illustration of this point, Elder Joseph B. Wirthlin shared the following insight in a conference address:

> On that Friday the Apostles were devastated. Jesus, their Savior—the man who had walked on water and raised the dead—was Himself at the mercy of wicked men. . . .
>
> On that Friday the Savior of mankind was humiliated and bruised, abused and reviled.
>
> It was a Friday filled with devastating, consuming sorrow that gnawed at the souls of those who loved and honored the Son of God.
>
> I think that of all the days since the beginning of this world's history, that Friday was the darkest.
>
> But the doom of that day did not endure.
>
> The despair did not linger, because on Sunday, the resurrected Lord burst the bonds of death. . . . The proof that death is merely the beginning of a new and wondrous existence.

---

79 See Matthew 5:5.

80 George D. Watt, ed., *Journal of Discourses,* Volume 10, 175.

Each of us will have our own Fridays—those days when the universe itself seems shattered and the shards of our world lie littered about us in pieces, [and] it seems we can never be put together again.

But I testify to you in the name of the One who conquered death—Sunday will come. In the darkness of our sorrow, Sunday will come.

No matter our desperation, no matter our grief, Sunday will come. In this life or the next, Sunday will come.[81]

---

81 Joseph B. Wirthlin, "Sunday Will Come," *Ensign,* November 2006, 29–30.

Chapter 2

WHO ARE THESE CHILDREN?

I do not believe that you are here upon the earth at this time by accident. I believe you qualified in the premortal life.

—*Elder Dean L. Larsen*[82]

ELDER NEAL A. MAXWELL DECLARED that the youth of Zion are living here and now by assignment. "These are your days!" he said. "You are in this time and circumstance by *Divine appointment*. God knows you and he knows what you have the capacity to achieve."[83]

Evelyn in Michigan wrote the following of her daughter:

> My husband and I knew that the child I was carrying was a special soul. Early in my pregnancy we began to have experiences with this child. Soon we perceived that a little girl was coming to us. And what a powerful person she was! When we would gather our children together for family prayer, our "little girl" would come and join us too. Sometimes, we could actually point to the place where she was kneeling. On a few occasions, when we had Monday night activities for family home evening, we perceived that she had come along. Although we had enjoyed special experiences with each of our children before they were born, we had never experienced anything like this.

---

82 Dean L. Larsen, "A Royal Generation," *Ensign,* May 1983.

83 Neal A. Maxwell, "These Are Your Days," *New Era,* January 1985; emphasis added.

When our daughter was born she was the joy of our life, and she lived up to the powerful personality that we had previously experienced. Then, when she entered high school, she hit a crisis point. In a class she was introduced to another element of friends who had a profound effect on her. Without our knowing, she began to experiment with alcohol, then marijuana. One thing led to another—sloppy appearance, sexual dalliance, more alcohol and drug experimentation—and soon she was spending less and less time with our family. . . . She abandoned the Church altogether. Our hearts were shattered one night when we received a call from the police station that she had been picked up for driving under the influence.

We do not know when this trial will end for us. We continue to love and encourage her, but we are settling in for what may be a long siege. Our peace lies in the fact that the Lord allowed us to experience early the power and importance of this child who was coming to our family. We know she is ours for a reason, and our responsibility for her is long-term. Our prayer is that our daughter might someday remember who she really is.

Divine Appointment and Positioning

Heavenly Father's children were not placed on this earth at this time and in their familial relationships by a cosmic roll of the dice. Heavenly Father's house is a house of order.[84] And especially children who are born or adopted into the lineage of Israel are placed there because of the role they will play in serving others. They were faithful and strong before this life, "marked" for greatness here because of their former greatness. Even the difficulties they would experience here could serve to save and exalt them and others.[85] Our children's divine positioning is intended to allow them to fulfill the roles their choices in the premortal realm prepared them for—the work of redemption, which comprises

---

84   See D&C 132:8.
85   See 1 Corinthians 10:13; Romans 8:28; Ether 12:27.

the gathering of the living and the dead to Christ and disseminating the gospel blessings to them, much in the same way "the faithful . . . of this dispensation, when they depart from mortal life, continue their labors . . . in the great world of the spirits of the dead."[86]

Additionally, because our children were assigned to come forth in the last days, they were given the singular assignment to prepare the world for the Savior's Second Coming. President Ezra Taft Benson said,

> In all ages prophets have looked down through the corridors of time to our day. Billions of the deceased and those yet to be born have their eyes on us. Make no mistake about it—this is a marked generation. There has never been more expected of the faithful in such a short period of time than there is of us. Never before on the face of this earth have the forces of evil and the forces of good been so well organized. Now is the great day of the devil's power. But now is also the great day of the Lord's power.[87]

At another time, he added: "God has saved for the final inning some of His stronger and most valiant children, who will help bear off the kingdom triumphantly. . . . You are the generation that must be prepared to meet your God. . . . The final outcome is certain—the forces of righteousness will finally win."[88]

Clearly, to be purposely and divinely positioned at this crucial time and place, each of our children had to have been proven premortally. Joseph Smith revealed, "There is a time appointed for every man, according as his works shall be."[89] Paul explained that this "time appointed" would be especially true of the latter-day children of Israel; they would be specifically singled out and strategically placed because premortally they had "conformed to the image of [God's] Son."[90] Therefore, God has taken careful note of their potential to

---

86 D&C 138:57.
87 Ezra Taft Benson, "In His Steps," *Ensign*, September 1988.
88 Ezra Taft Benson, "You Are a Marked Generation," *Ensign*, April 1987.
89 D&C 121:25.
90 Romans 8:29.

do good and deigned to position them in an era and circumstance that is best suited to their abilities. Elder Erastus Snow explained that the premortal ministry of God's "peculiar people" destined them to assume important mortal callings:

> He has had his eye upon the chosen spirits that have come upon the earth in the various ages from the beginning of the world up to this time. . . . The Lord has sent those noble spirits into the world to perform a special work, and appointed their times *. . . and their future glory and exaltation is secured unto them*; and that is what I understand by the doctrine of election spoken of by the Apostle Paul and other sacred writers: "For whom he did foreknow, he also did predestinate to be conformed to the image of His Son, that he might be the first-born among many brethren." Such were called and chosen and elected of God to perform a certain work at a certain time of the world's history[,] and in due time he fitted them for that work.[91]

This is an amazing statement that should give parents of "elect" albeit wayward children cause to patiently persevere and hope that their children will yet remember who they are and rise to the stature of their premortal greatness.

THE NOBLE AND GREAT ONES
Pursuant to the perfect foreknowledge of God, our children were likely assigned family placement, birth time, location, and mortal opportunities according to their strengths and weaknesses. They were among the noble and great ones who were shown to their forefather Abraham.

> Now the Lord had shown unto me, Abraham, the intelligences that were organized before the world was;

---

91 George D. Watt, ed., *Journal of Discourses*, Volume 23, 186–187; emphasis added.

and among all these there were many of the noble and great ones;

And God saw these souls that they were good, and he stood in the midst of them, and he said: These I will make my rulers; for he stood among those that were spirits, and he saw that they were good.[92]

Speaking of our children's premortal nobleness and greatness, President Spencer W. Kimball said, "The prophets in this dispensation have taught us that special spirits were reserved to come forth at this time in this last dispensation."[93] If you have a wayward child, this may be hard to believe. You might ask, "Was my troubled child included in the prophet's declaration?" Yes! Speaking to the youth of the Church, Elder H. Burke Peterson said, "My dear friends, you are a royal generation. You were preserved to come to the earth in this time for a special purpose. *Not just a few of you, but all of you.*"[94]

The Noble and Great Ones Do the Work of Redemption

What was the premortal work that our children did so well?

Redemption.

Redemption is not *a* work of God, it is *the* work of God, and therefore it is the preeminent work of all celestial beings—those who are or would be gods. Brigham Young University professor M. Catherine Thomas wrote the following:

> Out of all of Heavenly Father's spirit children, a smaller group distinguished itself by its exceeding faith in the Lord Jesus Christ during the conflicts that occurred incident to the war in heaven. Those who were valiant in these conflicts, and in other ways also, demonstrated both their abilities and their desires

---

92 Abraham 3:22–23.

93 Spencer W. Kimball, "In Love and Power and without Fear," *New Era*, July 1981.

94 H. Burke Peterson, "Your Special Purpose," *New Era*, October 2001; emphasis added.

to become actively involved in the cosmic work of redemption through the great Atonement of the Lord Jesus Christ. The thing that characterizes the Gods and those who aspire to godhood is the love of the work of redemption; that is, nurturing spirit children through the first estate of premortality, then leading them through a mortal probation, and finally raising them to the level of their parent Gods. . . . The great work of the Gods is family work. . . . You and I, as members of the literal house of Israel and of the Church of Jesus Christ, were called in the premortal world to participate in that work, everything else being trivial in comparison. Redemption is not just one of the things going on in the universe; it is *the* thing.[95]

If latter-day numbers are indicators—members of the Church in proportion to world population—our children were in the minority in the premortal world, and thus they were highly influential and important. Consider Nephi's vision of the last days: "And it came to pass that I beheld the church of the Lamb of God, and its numbers were few."[96] Weighing the present world population of about 6.6 billion against the current Church membership—approximately 13 million—our latter-day generations represent approximately one in 508; then comparing Church membership against the estimated 100 billion people who have ever lived (understanding that the Latter-day Saints in the dispensation of the fullness of times are responsible to gather and redeem all of God's children since the world began[97]), we are only 1 in 7,692. Clearly, God's divine positioning of righteous spirits is crucial for their ability to continue the work of redemption for the living and the dead.

Although proportionally few in number, today's Latter-day Saint youth comprise an unparalleled army in the earth's history. Elder Gene R. Cook said, "I salute a royal generation, the greatest generation of

95 M. Catherine Thomas, "Alma the Younger, Part 1," Neal A. Maxwell Institute for Religious Scholarship.

96 1 Nephi 14:12.

97 See D&C 128:22–24.

youth in number and quality to ever live on the face of the earth. The amount of good that is being done by you is immeasurable. Your influence will be felt worldwide before you have finished your stay on earth."[98]

Because the work of redemption is so essential, God designated a group of saviors, whom he called "Israel."[99] According to gospel scholar Wayne Brickey, in an *Education Week* address, *Israel* means "Men becoming like God": "*Is* [men] *ra* [becoming like] *el* [God]," or sometimes "men who prevail with God." Clearly, each of our children is one in the midst of many. If the Lord's intention is the redemption of all his children, no child's birth into a Latter-day Saint home is a mistake or a roll of the dice.

The Work of Redemption within Families

Let us consider that the organization of nations may be as it is so that the weak might be nurtured by the strong. If that is true, it is likely also true of families. God's divine positioning often calls for weak children to be placed with strong parents, strong children to be placed with weak parents, or strong individuals to marry into weak families. Why? To do the work of redemption.

Professor Catherine Thomas once suggested, "God may place spiritually challenging children in homes of spiritual and conscientious parents for their mutual benefit."[100] Elder Neal A. Maxwell spoke to the deliberate organization of families by quoting William Law, an English clergyman of the eighteenth century:

> If it is said the very hairs of your head are all numbered, is it not to teach us that nothing, not the smallest things imaginable, happen to us by chance? But if the smallest things we can conceive are declared to be under the divine direction, need we, or can we, be more plainly taught that the greatest things of life, such as the manner of our coming

---

98 Gene R. Cook, "The Seat Next to You," *New Era,* October 1983.

99 See Bruce R. McConkie, *A New Witness for the Articles of Faith,* 510.

100 M. Catherine Thomas, "Alma the Younger, Part 1," Neal A. Maxwell Institute for Religious Scholarship.

into the world, our parents, the time, and other circumstances of our birth and condition, are all according to the eternal purposes, direction, and appointment of Divine Providence?[101]

Carlfred Broderick, an LDS marriage and family therapist, wrote,

> My experience in various Church callings and in my profession as a family therapist has convinced me that God actively intervenes in some destructive lineages, assigning a valiant spirit to break the chain of destructiveness in such families. Although these children may suffer innocently as victims of violence, neglect, and exploitation, through the grace of God some find the strength to "metabolize" the poison within themselves, refusing to pass it on to future generations. Before them were generations of destructive pain; after them the line flows clear and pure. Their children and children's children will call them blessed.
>
> In suffering innocently that others might not suffer, such persons, in some degree, become as "saviors on Mount Zion" by helping to bring salvation to a lineage.[102]

THE COSMIC WAR

In our fear and impatience regarding troubled children, do we simultaneously disregard the volume of Restoration literature that pertains to redemptive work in the spirit world, the foreknowledge and mercy of God, and the far-reaching effects of the Atonement of Jesus Christ? If so, we do both God and Christ a disservice by imagining limits to Their ability to save. To gain perspective, let us review some truths.

Our children are ancient souls who practiced righteousness and did the work of redemption over vast periods of time. For how long

---

101 William Law, quoted in Neal A. Maxwell's *Wherefore, Ye Must Press Forward,* 67.

102 Carlfred Broderick, "I Have a Question," *Ensign,* August 1986, 38–39.

we do not know. The scriptures indicate that we existed as spirits before the world was created.[103] If the current estimate of the earth's age—about 4.55 billion years[104]—is accurate, we have existed for a very long time. During that enormous duration, the focus of our attention was to become like our heavenly parents by coming to earth, gaining a body, achieving a glorious resurrection, and earning exaltation. Our children bring with them mature gospel knowledge. It may be buried deep in their souls, but it is there just the same. The Fall may have caused them temporary amnesia, but God has not forgotten who they are or what they did. He said, "I will not forget thee. Behold, I have graven thee upon the palms of my hands."[105] Of course, neither has Satan forgotten our children. He remembers it was they who helped Michael cast out the devil and his angels from heaven, causing Satan to swear in his wrath that he would destroy them in the flesh. And for good reason. Satan knew that if our children were allowed to continue their premortal work, they would conquer him again and cast him into outer darkness forever. Therefore the war in heaven goes on, and this earth is its frontline. Hence, while the world is merely tempted,[106] Israel's children are viciously attacked.[107] Why are our children so ruthlessly confronted? Brigham Young had the answer:

> God never bestows upon his people, or upon an individual, superior blessings without a severe trial to prove them, to prove that individual, or that people, to see whether they will keep their covenants with him, and keep in remembrance what he has shown them. Then the greater the . . . [blessings], the greater the display of the power of the enemy.
>
> So when individuals are blessed with [temporal or spiritual success, with] visions, revelations, and great manifestations, look out, then the Devil is nigh you,

---

103 See Alma 13:3.
104 See G. Brent Dalrymple, *The Age of the Earth*, 1.
105 Isaiah 49:15–16.
106 D&C 29:39.
107 D&C 76:28–29.

and you will be tempted in proportion to [what] you
have received.[108]

Our children's premortal nobility, righteousness, and exceedingly
good works warranted extraordinary blessings and opportunities in
this life—royal birth, often immediate access to gospel blessings,
frequent temporal comforts, and so forth. But these blessings carried
a price. The adversary would attack in proportion to our children's
potential, would take opportunities to destroy them with their trials,
and would try to manipulate their views of their blessings. Thus, these
once seemingly invincible souls, weakened by the Fall, would now be
more susceptible to being cut down and wounded.

The Book of Mormon contains a possible latter-day parallel and a
promise. Imagine our children like the ancient stripling warriors, who,
like their Nephite counterparts, have been called upon to defend and
save the kingdom. Premortally, our children were "exceedingly valiant
for courage, and also for strength and activity; but behold, this was not
all—they were men [and women] who were true at all times in whatsoever thing they were entrusted. Yea, they were men [and women] of
truth and soberness, for they had been taught to keep the commandments of God and to walk uprightly before him."[109] Now, having
forgotten all, our children have come to earth to be born of goodly
mothers and fathers,[110] who try to teach them the gospel of Jesus
Christ and prepare them to face the battle for the kingdom. Here, then,
is an important lesson: although every one of the stripling warriors was
wounded in the battle with "many wounds," "not one soul of them . . .
did perish."[111] Although the comparison between the stripling warriors
and latter-day youth has its limitations, it nevertheless gives parents
reason to hope and persevere knowing that *perishing* is not in the Lord's
design. President J. Reuben Clark confirmed, "Our Heavenly Father
wants to save every one of his children."[112]

---

108 Brigham Young, *Discourses of Brigham Young,* 338.
109 Alma 53:20–21.
110 See Alma 56:47–48.
111 Alma 57:25.
112 J. Reuben Clark, Jr., *Conference Report,* October 1953, 84.

Divine Positioning at Work

One thing is certain: parents are not cursed with wayward children; parents are called by God to rear and redeem these precious souls in partnership with Jesus Christ. Therefore, we become to them "saviors on Mount Zion."[113] That they have been sent to our family is evidence of God's divine positioning at work, and the purpose of that divine positioning is to redeem those for whom we have a responsibility. Because God called us to this work, He will make us equal to the challenge. President Hugh B. Brown's promise to youth leaders may be applied to latter-day parents:

> God help us all that we may do our part to prepare for that future, ominous though it may be. I leave a blessing with you. . . . From my heart I pray God to bless and guide you as you undertake to help to guide the youth of the Church, the reserves of the army of the Lord. I pray that God will bless you in your homes, in your work, in your play, and that He will give you faith and courage and fortitude *to make you equal to your tasks.* I pronounce this blessing upon you and promise that these things will be yours.[114]

113 Mark E. Petersen, *Conference Report,* October 1959, 14.
114 Hugh B. Brown, *The Abundant Life,* 188–189; emphasis added.

Chapter 3

A NEW RESIDENCE: THE LONE AND DREARY WORLD

The still small voice whispers yet a deeper meaning.
Home is heaven. We are strangers here on earth.
My real home is not here, but there.

—*Elder Gene R. Cook*[115]

LIKE US, OUR CHILDREN ARE strangers here—not strangers on earth, necessarily, for it was created to be their eternal home,[116] but strangers in this remote sector of space in a telestial setting far from their Heavenly Father. To say that they fell is an understatement; they fell enormously. They, like the earth, once enjoyed celestial associations in a celestial environment in the celestial presence of God. President Brigham Young explained,

> When the earth was framed and brought into exis-
> tence and man was placed upon it, it was near the throne
> of our Father in heaven. And when man fell—though
> that was designed in the economy . . . the earth fell into
> space, and took up its abode in this planetary system, and
> the sun became our light. This is the glory the earth came
> from, and when it is glorified it will return again unto the
> presence of the Father, and it will dwell there.[117]

---

115 Gene R. Cook, "Home and Family: A Divine Eternal Pattern," *Ensign*, May 1984.
116 See Abraham 3:24.
117 Brigham Young, quoted in Joseph Fielding McConkie and Robert L. Millet's *The Man Adam*, 15.

The Fall was necessary. As we have learned, the universal law of opposites[118] states that to ascend up on high we must descend below all things, so that we might comprehend all things, and thereby gain the ability to become as the gods—above, and in all, and through all things.[119] For reasons that we do not completely understand, this process is the only way to become exalted.

OUR CHILDREN'S DESCENT

We cannot comprehend the distance and depth of the Fall. We fell physically, spiritually, and emotionally into a condition described by President Joseph F. Smith as "below all things."[120] A couple from Winnipeg, Manitoba, Canada described their son's mortal fall:

> Evan came to us as all babies do: innocent, pure, full of promise and fresh from Heavenly Father. But by the time Evan was a toddler, we knew that we were in for a rough ride. It was just a matter of time. The downslide began when he entered middle school and discovered the electric guitar. Soon some friends invited him to join a band. We were concerned about his friends and the influence they seemed to be exerting on him, but we also wanted him to have the freedom to develop his talent. We were so naïve. The band played hard rock, and soon Evan embraced everything that goes along with that culture. He began to dress sloppily . . . and experiment with alcohol. Six months ago, he began to smoke, and now he goes through a pack a day and cannot stop. He has tattooed his body, pierced his ears, nose and tongue, and has begun to wear eye makeup. He has dyed his hair strange colors, and most recently he has shaved his head except for a clump that he braids into a

118 See 2 Nephi 2:11.
119 See D&C 88:6.
120 Joseph Fielding Smith, *Gospel Doctrine: Selections from the Sermons and Writings of Joseph F. Smith*, 13.

ponytail that falls to the middle of his back. We don't know how to stop the hemorrhaging. We have tried calmly talking to him, screaming at him, and limiting his privileges; we have even threatened to send him away to a disciplinary school program—but nothing has worked. He has a girlfriend with whom he has frequent sexual encounters. He invites his friends to our home and they leave upon it a dark and terrible feeling. Our oldest son moved out after high school because he couldn't stand the atmosphere; our younger children are always tense, as if they are afraid. Four weeks ago, Evan nearly lost his life when he overdosed on drugs, slid into unconscious oblivion, and had to be rushed to the emergency room. Where, we ask ourselves, is the sweet, innocent spirit that came to us seventeen years ago? Evan is so far removed from the clean, angelic son of God whom we once welcomed into our family that now he is almost unrecognizable.

Our children's descent might be compared to the earth's descent. Between premortality and achieving God's presence loomed the experience of mortality. In effect, our children stood upon the safe ledge of the brilliant celestial kingdom and looked downward into the dark, knowing that once they stepped off, they would forfeit their memory and power and become helpless, completely incapable of making it on their own. Worse, they would have no immediate comprehension that they had descended into a fallen world. Unless they are taught differently and gain a testimony of their real identity and heritage, they will grow up believing that this mortal life is all there is, and worse, that this life is *normal*. Tragically, for a time, they might even embrace the dangers that permeate earth life.

In her Alma the Younger series, Catherine Thomas proposes that our children "would begin to make choices before [they] had much knowledge or judgment or ability to choose right over wrong consistently and would inevitably make mistakes and sin . . . . As [they] grew in a fallen environment, [they] would form wrong opinions and make false assumptions, by which [they] would then govern [their] lives, and would unwittingly be programmed by many precepts of men. [They] would make many choices before [they] had grasped the significance of even the Light that [they] had."[121]

We cannot fathom the range of emotions our children must have experienced as they contemplated their descent into this lone and dreary world. To have this mortal experience was what they had fought for. They had vigorously defended the Father's plan in the great war in heaven; they had shouted for joy at the prospect;[122] they had dedicated their lives to Christ, who was to become their Savior and the central figure of the plan; they had prepared in every way for this moment; and yet, they must have had some idea of the sobering reality that some might come here and succumb to sin. In Catherine Thomas's words, "The period of descent was surely seen by the righteous premortal spirits as a great sacrifice. The most righteous did not want to sin. They knew the truth about sin. A veil was necessary so that they would make the descent . . . into spiritual darkness." Only profound faith in Christ could have given them the strength to descend.

Therefore, armed only with the Light of Christ, they stepped off the celestial ledge and plummeted toward this dark telestial world. Imagine their courage, for we must assume that, because of agency, no one was compelled to come; imagine their hope, for the transcendent possibilities of eternity lay before them. But they knew that those possibilities were dependent upon their keeping their second estate.[123] Therefore they willingly left the arms of seasoned, perfect, Celestial Parents for the arms of novices—we, imperfect telestial parents. What we parents had going for us was love, but otherwise we would be learning through trial and error. President Howard W. Hunter said,

> Conscientious parents try their best, yet nearly all have made mistakes. One does not launch into such a project as parenthood without soon realizing that there will be many errors along the way. Surely our Heavenly

---

121 M. Catherine Thomas, "Alma the Younger, Part 2," Neal A. Maxwell Institute for Religious Scholarship.

122 See Job 38:7.

123 See Abraham 3:26.

Father knows, when he entrusts his spirit children into the care of young and inexperienced parents, that there will be mistakes and errors in judgment. . . . Especially at these first-time milestones when experience and understanding are somewhat lacking. Even after the parent has gained experience, the second-time and third-time occurrences of these milestones are sometimes not much easier to handle, nor do they come with much less chance of error.[124]

What amazing confidence God places in us new parents, and what profound power and grace He wields to undo our clumsy parenting and all that mortality can heap upon a child. Nevertheless, "trailing clouds of glory"[125] and for a divine purpose, our children descended into this benighted orb, dimly lit by the sun, to finally, after untold eons of waiting, claim an eternal tabernacle for their immortal spirits in which they might work out their salvation with "fear and trembling."[126]

THE BODY—THE ULTIMATE VEHICLE FOR MORAL AGENCY

What our children would gain here was the matchless gift of a physical body. Now they would become a *soul*—"The spirit and the body are the soul of man."[127] To achieve exaltation the soul needs experience in the two major spheres of which the universe is constituted: spirit and physical matter. The physical body is made of physical matter and becomes the palette the spirit uses to act upon things.[128] The physical body is the spirit's great tool of expression and feeling, and the physical world is its canvas.

Suddenly, with a body, our children could choose from and enjoy infinite possibilities. A spirit without a body is much like a mind without hands, arms, legs, and feet—a being who can think but not

---

124 Howard W. Hunter, "Parents' Concern for Children," *Ensign,* November 1983.

125 William Wordsworth, "Ode on Intimations of Immortality," www.bartleby.com.

126 Mormon 9:27.

127 D&C 88:15.

128 See 2 Nephi 2:13.

act.[129] President John Taylor said, "The body was formed as an agent for the spirit."[130] With a body, then, our children would have both the intellect and the vehicle to *think* and to *act out* their thoughts. They could give expression to their dreams, desires, and hungers. Therein were both amazing and frightening realities: with a body they would now have the potential to reach stratospheric, godlike heights, yet they would also have the potential to plunge to the hellish depths of the devil. With a body, they, as children of God with infinite potential, would be capable of literally anything—"nothing shall be impossible."[131] But to become as God, they would have to control the body and learn to point it toward exalted purposes.

And that would be no small feat.

By descending to this planet and taking up a fallen, telestial body made of fallen telestial material, our children would become "carnal, sensual, and devilish . . . by nature"[132] and consequently become subject to the devil.[133] This fallen condition, known as the "natural man," makes us an "enemy to God." Therefore, during their mortal sojourn, in order to progress toward exaltation, our children would need to experience a spiritual awakening and allow themselves to be enticed by "the Holy Spirit and [put] off the natural man and [become] a saint through the Atonement of Christ the Lord." To qualify for eternal life, they would need to learn to suppress their innate carnal, sensual, and devilish nature and learn to become childlike—"submissive, meek, humble, patient, full of love, willing to submit to all things which the Lord seeth fit to inflict upon [them]."[134] Moral agency would become a device that could accommodate this spiritual awakening. Thus, earth life was designed to be a test of wills between the physical and spiritual and between Satan and God. Our children's mortal test would involve learning to act as independent beings; they were to learn to be faithful even if their circumstances would be "darker than 10,000 midnights."[135]

---

129 See D&C 93:33–34.

130 John Taylor, *The Government of God*, 78.

131 Luke 1:37.

132 Alma 42:10.

133 See Mosiah 16:3.

134 Mosiah 3:19.

135 George D. Watt, ed., *Journal of Discourses*, Volume 3, 207.

Now, with a body, their every experience is heightened—they can fall lower or rise higher than they ever could without it. They feel more fully, hurt more completely, love more deeply, and, because they are now a *soul* composed of spirit and physical matter, they have the potential to "receive a fulness of joy."[136] Clearly, our children's destiny lies within the potential of their bodies. With a body they suddenly have the power to multiply and replenish the earth by procreating other carnate children of God—a powerful yet dangerous idea. Satan knows this, of course, and thus he tries to persuade our children to misuse their bodies and to experiment with the sacred powers of procreation. As his primary tool, he uses ignorance—ignorance about who they are, where they came from, why they are here, and what their glorious future will be. By keeping them ignorant, Satan can more easily tempt them to disobey their parents and God. He knows that disobedience can cut a wide gash in the soul, a gash that hemorrhages light and truth,[137] and that once this happens, our children become weakened and disempowered—so that Satan can gain control over them.[138]

The Influence of the Adversary

A mother of seven from Oregon spoke of this disempowering spiritual hemorrhaging that renders a person ignorant of God and of the simple truths of the gospel of Jesus Christ:

> Two of my seven children left the Church, leaving me hurt and confused. For a while, I beat myself up over my apparent failure as a mother, but that did little good. Despite all my suffering and soul-searching, I could not discover where my husband and I had gone wrong. Not that we are perfect parents—we are not—but why had we lost these two children? They were brought up alongside our other children who had remained true. When I decided to give myself a break and look for another reason, I took my question

136 D&C 93:34.
137 See D&C 93:39.
138 See Mosiah 16:3–5.

to the Lord. My conversation went something like this: "These children have not only left the Church and are critical of it, they seem absolutely ignorant of the most basic gospel principles. That is the most confusing part to me. It is as though they had never heard of gospel concepts before—like everything is foreign to them. How could this be? They grew up in our home where we had family prayers, family home evenings, and gospel discussions. Weren't they listening? They went to church with us and had equal opportunities in the gospel with our other children, and yet they seem to be as clueless as new investigators. They seem to have forgotten everything that we taught them. How did this happen?"

As I pondered, a scripture was impressed upon my mind: "That wicked one cometh and taketh away light and truth, through disobedience." I couldn't remember the location of the scripture, but I soon found it in Doctrine and Covenants 93:39. The adjoining verses read, "I have commanded you to bring up your children in light and truth," and "Light and truth forsake that evil one." Suddenly, I realized what had happened. My husband and I had tried to bring up our children in light and truth, but these two children had chosen to commit sin in their youth. Worse, they had failed to repent. Their disobedience and disregard for repentance had opened the door for Satan to come and take away their light and truth. Now they were rendered ignorant, as though they had no gospel literacy at all.

When they lost their light and truth, they filled the void by adopting bizarre philosophies to explain life and spiritual things. Now I knew why this had happened, and now I gained a greater appreciation for the prophets' counsel to repent quickly and sincerely. Procrastination, I learned, causes gospel stagnation at best and gospel illiteracy and captivity by the devil at worst. Armed with this understanding, I center my prayers on asking for opportunities to reintroduce basic gospel concepts to these children with the hope that they will one day remember and respond.

Because Satan knows that the body is highly susceptible to suggestion and can be acted upon by outside influences as well as its internal spirit, he tempts a person to sin. Then, once Satan has succeeded, he attempts to hold the sin in place by persuading the person to wink at the transgression, disregard it, or experience so much guilt that the person is paralyzed against repentance. The problem with unrepentant sin is that it is the seed of spiritual cancer, which grows inside the soul until it has consumed it. The seed of unrepentant sin is never dormant; its cells divide like cancer until the system is overwhelmed by and dying from it. When Satan succeeds in getting a person to sin and persuading him to procrastinate repentance, he has free rein to dull the person's conscience, steal away his light and truth, and render his soul spiritually illiterate. The cumulative effect weakens the soul so that Satan can lead it captive down to hell.[139] Only repentance made possible by the Atonement of Jesus Christ can once again infuse power into the soul and free it from Satan's grasp, reopening the door to light and truth. We parents must watch for the warning signs of unrepentant sin and help our children to confess their sins and fully repent. Otherwise, the consequences are dire. Elder Boyd K. Packer said,

> In the battle of life, the adversary takes enormous numbers of prisoners, and many know of no way to escape and are pressed into his service. Every soul confined to a concentration camp of sin and guilt has a key to the gate. The adversary cannot hold them if they know how to use it. The key is labeled *Repentance*. The twin principles of repentance and forgiveness exceed in strength the awesome power of the adversary.[140]

139 See 2 Nephi 2:29.
140 Boyd K. Packer, "Our Moral Environment," *Ensign*, May 1992.

The body, according to Joseph Smith, when properly used and understood, can put us beyond the power of Satan and all our enemies.[141] "All beings who have bodies have power over those who have not. The devil has no power over us only as we permit him. The moment we revolt at anything which comes from God, the devil takes power."[142] Therefore, "Satan's power over us *always* hinges upon our obedience or disobedience—our willingness or unwillingness to submit to the mind and will of the Father."[143] Moreover, the body is designed to be the "tabernacle of God,"[144] a holy, walled fortress to protect the spirit.[145] And we must not forget that the spirit—the actual offspring of God that animates the body—is a powerful being. Our spirit is made of the substance called *truth,* which is also referred to as spirit, light, light of truth, intelligence, glory, power, and law.[146]

Because the body is carnal, sensual, and devilish by nature, it may not perceive the entity of light and truth that resides within it, but the spirit knows who it is. By nature, the spirit is truth-discerning, constructed and instructed so that it can perceive both truth and error.[147] Beyond our limited five senses, an ocean of truth exists, and although we might try to stubbornly deny it, we are nevertheless surrounded by it. Within our children exists the potential—if it is allowed to develop—for the spirit to exercise dominion over that natural man and to embrace truth. The spirit is constantly seeking for ways to emerge and take control.

REDEMPTION FROM DECEPTION AND OFFENSE

To the Prophet Joseph Smith, the Lord revealed an astonishing doctrine that speaks to the far-reaching effects of the Atonement. This doctrine seems to make allowance for those who have been deceived

---

141 Andrew F. Ehat and Lyndon W. Cook, eds., *The Words of Joseph Smith: the contemporary accounts of the Nauvoo discourses of the Prophet Joseph,* 208.
142 Joseph Fielding Smith, ed., *Teachings of the Prophet Joseph Smith,* 181.
143 Blaine Yorgason, *I Need Thee Every Hour,* 348.
144 D&C 93:35.
145 See George D. Watt, ed., *Journal of Discourses,* Volume 9, 139–140.
146 See D&C 93:23–29, 36; 88:6–13.
147 See 2 Nephi 2:5.

by the doctrines of man or who have been misled by hypocritical members of the Church. "Behold, verily I say unto you, there are hypocrites among you, who have deceived some, which has given the adversary power; *but behold such shall be reclaimed.*"[148]

We can infer an important truth here: eternal judgments are *not* issued on the basis of deception. Not one of Satan's followers was cast out because they were deceived. Judgments are based on full light, knowledge, and choice. Without making excuses for our children's present behavior, we nevertheless might ask ourselves, *Have our children gone astray because they have been deceived or offended? Do they have full light and knowledge so that they can accurately choose between God and Satan?* According to the Lord's promise, if they are laboring under any degree of deception or offense, He will reach out to reclaim them.

But to the self-righteous and mean-spirited, the Lord pronounces a wo: "But wo unto them that are deceivers and hypocrites, for, thus saith the Lord, I will bring them to judgment. . . . But the hypocrites shall be detected and shall be cut off, either in life or in death, even as I will; and wo unto them who are cut off from my church, for the same are overcome of the world."[149] The Lord ends with a final caution: "Wherefore, let every man beware lest he do that which is not in truth and righteousness before me."[150]

Regarding our children's premortal righteousness, which we have learned was very great, eternal judgment—from the lines below—seems to take into account the sum of their existence. In the same revelation as quoted above, the Lord says, "Behold, ye are little children and ye cannot bear all things now; ye must grow in grace and in the knowledge of the truth. Fear not, little children, for you are mine, and I have overcome the world, *and you are of them that my Father hath given me; and none of them that my Father hath given me shall be lost.*"[151] Imagine! None that the Father has given the Savior shall be lost! But we ask ourselves, *Is our child one of those whom the Father has given to the Son?* The answer may lie in the fact that this revelation was

---

148 D&C 50:7; emphasis added.
149 D&C 50:6, 8.
150 D&C 50:9.
151 D&C 50:40–42; emphasis added.

given to weak members of the Church, whom the Lord was calling to repentance and yet was offering mercy. He knew them better than they knew themselves, and therefore was offering to take pity on them and methodically work with them until He had brought them home.

For further evidence, we turn to Jesus' words to His Apostles concerning His sheep: "And I give unto them eternal life; and they shall never perish, neither shall any man pluck them out of my hand. My Father, which gave them me, is greater than all; and no man is able to pluck them out of my Father's hand."[152]

No one can take our children from Jesus, and our children simply cannot break free from the Savior's embrace. The Father gave them to Him, and Jesus holds them in His hands as pearls of great price. Despite their present choices, they have a past that will be taken into account at the time of judgment. In the meantime, Jesus will carefully draw them to Him until the deceptions are stripped away, the offenses are healed, and until our children finally have enough light and knowledge to choose between God and Satan. If their premortal choices are any indication, we have every hope that they will choose right, which is more in their character than their present actions.

At least two important eternal truths are evident in these verses: nothing of an eternal nature can ever be lost because of the actions of someone else, and every great sinner has an infinitely greater Savior.

Physical "Hungers"

As our children contemplated mortality, they likely viewed the experience as both potentially difficult and rewarding—light years different from the environment they had known. Here on earth—thrust into a place where things hurt; where time is measured as if it matters; where lack rather than abundance is common; where competition instead of cooperation rules men's hearts and causes untold pain and disparity; where our best efforts can be neutralized by another person's bad behavior; where God is often known as a distant, vague, seldom-referred-to figure, invisible rather than ever-present, blasphemed rather than reverenced as the sovereign of the universe and central figure in all existence—our children would be like fish out of water.

---

152 John 10:28–29.

From the moment of our children's birth, they would be bombarded with foreign stimuli exclusive to this mortal, physical environment. Physical hunger, not the Spirit's presence, would become their new learning mechanism and motivator. They would begin to define their new environment in terms of feeling and responding to their hungers and sensory experiences. Unchecked, these hungers could compel them to sin, which, in turn, could cause them to die spiritually.

Of course, our children's primeval instinct to satisfy these mortal hungers would drive them to nourish, protect, and satisfy their bodies. But this would be risky. They could take satisfying their hungers to extremes; they might even respond to hungers recklessly and selfishly to the exclusion of everything healthy and good. Recognizing the danger of seeking to satisfy hungers without constraint, we parents must attempt to create boundaries with discipline and set rules. We must teach our children that God's commandments are patterns for safe and happy living.

As our children mature, we hope that their motivation for obeying the laws of family and of God will migrate from *duty* to *understanding* and finally to *love*. We hope they will raise their sights and take control of their hungers. We hope they will come to realize, as we do, that they exist in two very real dimensions: "that physical dimension, which our puny five senses perceive, and that spiritual dimension, which flourishes beyond our physical senses and is perceived only by an internal spiritual faculty, a sense that [they] only barely understand."[153] What we parents want our children to discover for themselves is that everything has spiritual underpinnings;[154] therefore, all physical hungers can be traced to a corresponding spiritual need. If they can grasp and embrace that concept, they will experience one of the greatest discoveries of life: To be hungry and thirsty is ultimately designed to lead them to Christ, the Bread of Life, and the Living Water.[155]

As physical hunger motivates the need for food, so spiritual hunger motivates the need for redemption. That is what we want for

---

153 M. Catherine Thomas, "Alma the Younger, Part 2," Neal A. Maxwell Institute for Religious Scholarship.

154 See D&C 29:34.

155 See John 6:35; John 4:10.

our children: to get themselves to Christ to be redeemed. Their physical hungers are designed to take them there, but Satan can use those hungers to take them to hell. Their starving, parched, noble spirits hunger and thirst for the righteousness they once knew; they are pleading, as they are trapped within their telestial bodies, to be filled. Jesus provided the answer for satisfying a famished spirit: "Blessed are all they who do hunger and thirst after righteousness, for they shall be filled with the Holy Ghost."[156] The only thing that can satisfy a hungry and thirsty soul is the Holy Ghost, and the satisfaction that He provides results in true joy, which transforms a life and returns it from the natural back to the spiritual.

SPIRITUALLY ASLEEP

Because of their fallen nature, children often do not arrive at the testimony of Jesus Christ and His redeeming gospel easily. They may struggle with spiritual concepts and more readily adopt portions of the prevailing anti-Christ philosophy:

- To discount prophetic teachings and warnings as foolish, and to embrace vain traditions and false hopes that are enslaving
- To view religion as the effect of a frenzied, deranged, or unenlightened mind
- To embrace the idea that men, independently of God, succeed or fail according to individual management, prosper according to individual initiative and genius, and conquer according to individual strength

Our children might imagine that pursuing this philosophy is natural, and thus no crime against man or God.[157]

Whereas they were born pure and innocent, "whole . . . even from the foundation of the world,"[158] sometime early in life, the Fall is fully in force in their lives. Gospel scholar Blaine Yorgason

---

156 3 Nephi 12:6.
157 See Alma 30:14–17.
158 Moroni 8:8, 12.

suggests that spiritual death can come more quickly than we might expect:

> I believe spiritual death is a prolonged process that begins early in our mortal lives, perhaps long before age eight. The Lord said, "Power is not given unto Satan to tempt little children, until they *begin to* become accountable before me" (D&C 29:47; italics mine). . . . These [pre–age-eight wrong] choices are not yet accounted to them as sins, of course, for they are not yet wholly accountable. . . . In a broader sense, they . . . have *begun* the process of submitting [themselves] to temptation. And from that moment, it seems to me, [they] *begin* the process of separation from God that is called spiritual death. [It amazes that] the hallways of our junior, middle, and high schools seem such . . . unholy places. . . . The thought of such newly spiritually dead children of God, who as yet have neither the experience nor the wisdom to see the damage of intentional, rampant sinning (which obviously seems to many of them as both fun and innocent) is sobering.[159]

Yorgason explains that the poor choices of youth "quickly develop into habits of disobedience," and cause or enhance the "veil of forgetfulness." This veil "thickens and expands until it is impenetrable, at least from [their] side, and [they] are cut off or shut out from the presence of God."[160]

Dr. David Dressler, in speaking to Brigham Young University students, offered a similar assessment of how quickly children can achieve spiritual death if not checked:

> It is no coincidence that . . . [of] all young people (and of some older people) who were getting into difficulties with the courts, fifty per cent showed marked

159 Blaine M. Yorgason, *I Need Thee Every Hour,* 66–67.
160 Ibid., 65.

behavior maladjustments before age eight and an additional forty per cent before age eleven. So ninety per
cent were showing behavior maladjustments indicating
emotional instability before the age of puberty.[161]

Those who are spiritually dead or asleep seldom believe it, and
that is the ignorant state in which Satan would like to keep them. To
be spiritually dead or asleep is to be "encircled about by the bands of
death, and the chains of hell, [with] an everlasting destruction . . .
await[ing] them."[162] Only God has the power to awaken them out
of that deep sleep and deliver them.[163] Until they gain a testimony
of their situation, they will either wallow in spiritual darkness with
absolutely no interest in or interaction with God, or they will fumble
about in a kind of spiritual twilight. Speaking of this spiritual twilight
and how Satan uses it to assuage our children's hungers, Catherine
Thomas wrote the following :

> This twilight zone is a transition state between
> having recognized one's fallenness [and] not yet
> reaching to the solution. . . . This is a state of hunger
> and bondage—not total darkness, but hunger for
> something indefinable. We can recognize it in
> ourselves when our souls cry out, "Is this all there is to
> the gospel? Can't I feel a richer inner experience?" We
> can get stuck in this twilight because we are . . . going
> through some motions . . . [or] we seem to be on the
> path; but still, there's that nagging hunger in the heart
> that doesn't know what it wants. People try lots of
> things to assuage the hunger. . . . But [these worldly
> pursuits are] counterproductive where happiness and
> being born again are concerned. . . .
> That half-and-half state is precisely the problem
> and the source of our hunger. The hunger comes

---

161 Dr. David Dressler, "Youth in a Troubled World," *Brigham Young University
     Speeches of the Year,* 1960, 5–6.
162 Alma 5:7.
163 See Alma 5:7–9.

> from the need for the most powerful nutrient a fallen
> human can receive: the Spirit of the Lord. . . . The Fall
> creates the hunger. Perhaps the most characteristic
> state of fallen man is the hunger and the feeling of
> darkness or spiritual twilight. Many people experience
> only the hunger for their entire lives.[164]

Many of our children are spiritually asleep, left to be driven by their hungers. Who can awaken them? Who can everlastingly, not temporarily, satisfy their hungers?

REDEMPTION—THE AWAKENING

Each child had their beginning with God,[165] and they are on the same continuum that is intended to lead them to eternal life. Each of them has a salvation timeline, their personal plan of salvation within *the* plan of salvation. Considering that truth, and remembering that our children enjoyed an exalted past, we realize that they comprise more assets than they may be presently demonstrating. For example, as we have discussed, they already proved valiant in the cause of truth (although presently they may be demonstrating weakness), and during premortality they developed a strong testimony (although it may be temporarily buried). Speaking to this point, Neal A. Maxwell, quoting Joseph F. Smith, said, "When . . . we 'catch a spark from the awakened memories of the immortal soul,' let us be quietly grateful. When of great truths we can say 'I know,' that powerful spiritual witness may also carry with it the sense of our having known before. With rediscovery, we are really saying 'I know—again!'"[166]

Jeffrey R. Holland calls these spiritual recollections "echoes of other earlier testimonies."[167] When properly stimulated, premortal testimonies like premortal talents will emerge and flourish. It simply remains for the *Awakener* to do the work of *awakening*.

---

164 M. Catherine Thomas, "Alma the Younger, Part 2," Neal A. Maxwell Institute for Religious Scholarship.

165 D&C 93:23, 29.

166 Neal A. Maxwell, "*But for a Small Moment,*" The Collected Works of Neal A. Maxwell, Volume 4, 103.

167 Jeffrey R. Holland, "Missionary Work and the Atonement," *Ensign,* March 2001.

So why must our innocent children be thrust into this harsh environment that seems to be programmed in every way to oppose them and to ensure that they will sin? A young father asked the same question:

> As I look at my boy, just learning to walk, curious about everything, three words to his vocabulary and determined to learn more, I wonder if life could get any better than this. But I also realize that life is hard and my boy will face his share of trials. I realize that someday he will sin. How inconceivable that seems to me right now. I don't mean to sound fatalistic, but it causes me to mourn. I wish I could shelter him from life and sin, but I cannot. I commit myself to partnering with the Lord and relying on His redemptive power to navigate my son through the pitfalls of life, deliver him, and successfully shepherd him home.

Life is a test, and the test will expose our children's weaknesses, force them to deal with those weaknesses, and thus qualify them for exaltation. President George Q. Cannon said,

> If any man or woman expects to enter into the celestial kingdom of our God without being tested to the very uttermost, they have not understood the Gospel. If there is a weak spot in our nature, or if there is a fibre that can be made to quiver or to shrink, we may rest assured that it will be tested. Our own weaknesses will be brought fully to light, and in seeking for help, the strength of our God will also be made manifest to us.[168]

There is another, deeper reason why our children must descend into this abysmal environment, where it is impossible not to sin. In a word: *redemption.*[169]

---

168 James R. Clark, comp., *Messages of the First Presidency of The Church of Jesus Christ of Latter-day Saints*, Volume 3, 27–28.

169 See D&C 109:34.

As we have learned, *the* work of God is redemption. Should we be surprised, then, that all aspects of this existence have redemption as their common denominator? This is not a sideline or hobby with God; neither should it be for us parents. If we will allow Him, God will actively teach and qualify us—we who once loved the work of redemption and wanted to be included in the redemptive order of Christ—to develop the power of redemption and become as He is. As we have learned, we cannot gain the power to redeem others without first having been redeemed. Likewise, our children are now given the opportunity to experience redemption. During their lives, they will sin and face seemingly insurmountable obstacles, and each time they do, if they will come to Christ, they will experience deliverance and redemption, which will increase their capacity and desire to save others. Once we grasp this concept, we begin to understand why substantially every encounter that we have with God has to do with redemption.

Trust in God is the ongoing theme of mortality. We can never escape it, although we may try to place our trust in someone or something we can see. Futilely, we sidle up to the influential and powerful, or we attempt to gather about us enough stuff to shelter us from life's risks. Our children often buy into this falsehood. But trust in Him, not in stuff, is the attitude Heavenly Father wants them to develop. Trust in God is redemptive trust—trust in His goodness; trust in His power; trust in His knowledge; trust in His love. To develop trust, which is essential to redemption, He will give them weakness as a gift.[170] Weakness will humble them and draw them to Christ, whom they can trust to strengthen, deliver, and redeem them.

Perhaps then, beyond every other reason, God places them in a situation where only He can deliver them.[171] They must learn to come to Him and trust Him. This is an important part of their earthly tutorial that is best learned in the blindness and harshness of mortality. Therefore, when we see our children bow under the weight of sin and ache with the agony of weakness, we are really observing the motions of redemption at work and the initiation of our children's personal plan of salvation. At such times, when we plead for divine intervention and do not perceive immediate response, we must not interpret

170 See Ether 12:27.
171 See Alma 36:2.

the silence to mean that we have not been heard or that the plan is not working. Adam and Eve also prayed and waited; they trusted in God's promise that He would hear their prayer; He had set in motion a process to answer it, but they did not know the details. They had no idea that their prayer had caused God to dispatch undetectable angels to assess the situation; they had no idea that these angels would become the agents of deliverance.[172] The implications of this revelation are sobering. Why else would the Lord explain this process to us in such detail if it were not a divine pattern that we could trust?

To trust God is to trust God's timing. Because He is perfect, His timing is perfect, and for us to urge Him to change His timing is to ask Him to cease to be perfect. Moreover, God's timing is an act of mercy: God might determine to snatch a wayward child from further harm because He knows that the child will now respond favorably; or God might wait while He patiently works with a wayward child because He knows that the child is not yet ready. Premature snatching, after all, carries with it the obligation of repentance and a full change of heart. Because "fullness of knowledge brings the fullness of accountability,"[173] a wayward child could rebel against God if he were not ready, and that would bring upon him condemnation—the last thing we would want to have happen.

"But our children are still rebelling and sinning!" we exclaim. "Are they lost?"

No.

"Even if they are rebelling and sinning grossly?"

Even then, they are not lost.

Elder Boyd K. Packer said, "I know of no sins connected with the moral standard for which we cannot be forgiven. I do not exempt abortion. The formula is stated in forty words: 'Behold, he who has repented of his sins, the same is forgiven, and I, the Lord, remember them no more. By this ye may know if a man repenteth of his sins—behold,

---

172 See James E. Faust, "A Royal Priesthood," *Ensign*, May 2006; Boyd K. Packer, *The Holy Temple*, 252, quoting John A. Widstoe, "Genealogical Activities in Europe," 104; Joseph F. Smith, *Gospel Doctrine: Selections from the Sermons and Writings of Joseph F. Smith*, 435.

173 Orson F. Whitney, *Conference Report*, April 1929, 110–11.

he will confess them and forsake them' (D&C 58:42–43)."[174] Clearly, except in the cases of shedding innocent blood (with *full* knowledge of light and truth) and sinning against the Holy Ghost, we must refrain from passing judgment, deciding a fate from our poor vantage point, imposing limitations on the Lord's saving ability, and believing that all is lost. As Mormon instructed Moroni, our obligation is to continue reaching out no matter how hopeless the situation may seem[175] and to leave all other issues, including timing, in God's hands.

We must remember that our children's waywardness was foreseen and planned for by the Father, and it was completely paid for and overcome by the Son. Therefore, there is divine opportunity waiting. From the scriptural accounts of Paul, Alma the Younger, the sons of Mosiah, Lamoni and his father, and the Anti-Nephi-Lehies, we should know that God can and will reach out to every wayward soul *when the time is right,* and if they respond when He offers to redeem them, they will become powerful in working redemption in others. Until then, we are told that the "eye of the Shepherd is upon them,"[176] and where there is much sin, the Lord offers, proportionately, much grace.

Nevertheless, once the Lord invites them out they must come out, stay out, and ascend. Catherine Thomas explains:

> Paul wrote: "Where sin abounded, grace did much more abound: That as sin hath reigned unto death, even so might grace reign through righteousness unto eternal life by Jesus Christ our Lord" (Rom. 5:20–21). *That is, the divine design made sin possible so that grace could abound . . . to deliver man from sin.* But in Paul's words, "Shall we continue in sin, that grace may abound? God forbid. How shall we, that are dead to sin, live any longer therein?" (Rom. 6:1–2). Once the Lord comes for us in the midst of our descent, we are accountable for the knowledge that he imparts. We must ascend. As Joseph Smith taught, "When God offers a blessing or knowledge to a man, and he refuses to receive it, he will

---

174 Boyd K. Packer, "Our Moral Environment," *Ensign,* May 1992.
175 See Moroni 9:6.
176 Orson F. Whitney, *Conference Report,* April 1929, 110.

be damned" [Joseph Fielding Smith, ed., *Teachings of the Prophet Joseph Smith*, 322].[177]

Redemption comes down to this one truth that we hope we can convey to our children: the Holy Spirit is the key to happiness, and to lack the Holy Spirit is the source of misery. The devil will attempt to keep our children in ignorance about this truth. When the Lord reaches out and blesses them with this knowledge, salvation is at hand. Joseph Smith defined salvation this way: "Salvation is nothing more nor less than to triumph over all our enemies and put them under our feet. And when we have power to put all enemies under our feet in this world, and a knowledge to triumph over all evil spirits in the world to come, then we are saved."[178]

Imagine the day when our children turn to Jesus Christ as Alma did. Then they will likewise experience the Lord's grace as He helps them triumph over all their enemies and "put them under their feet," never again to be afflicted by those evil spirits in this world or in the world to come. Then they will know as the gods know good and evil,[179] for engaging in a mortal experience and being redeemed was how the gods also became gods. First they experienced a fall wherein they encountered evil and sinned, whereby they were redeemed, whereby they gained the desire and power to redeem others, whereby they were exalted. It is a process that none of us can escape. It is the process of true happiness.

Like Paul and Alma, our children are experiencing an important part of the process of salvation, and, like Paul and Alma, once they have completed it, they will be presented with a merciful option—to forsake their sinful ways, experience redemption, ascend from their fallen state, and bring others up with them. This is the pattern, and this, we have good cause to hope, will be their destiny.

---

177 M. Catherine Thomas, "Alma the Younger, Part 2," Neal A. Maxwell Institute for Religious Scholarship.

178 Joseph Fielding Smith, ed., *Teachings of the Prophet Joseph Smith*, 297.

179 See Genesis 3–5.

Chapter 4

BECOMING SAVIORS ON MOUNT ZION: PARENTS' DIVINE APPOINTMENT

You are ministers of the Lord unto your children, and if
you will do your duty by your children, you will
be as saviors on Mount Zion to them.

—*Elder Mark E. Petersen*[180]

AFTER GOD CREATED ADAM AND Eve and united them in eternal marriage, He gave them a commandment, which He has renewed with every married couple, and which He has never rescinded: "And God blessed them, and God said unto them, Be fruitful, and multiply, and replenish the earth."[181] In "The Family: A Proclamation to the World," the prophet and Apostles made this statement: "The first commandment that God gave to Adam and Eve pertained to their potential for parenthood as husband and wife. We declare that God's commandment for His children to multiply and replenish the earth remains in force."

When Heavenly Father entrusts us parents with His children, we are under obligation to raise them unto God, to do all we can to return them to Him. President Howard W. Hunter said,

> Anyone who becomes a parent is under strict obligation to protect and love [God's] children and assist them to return to their Heavenly Father. All parents should understand that the Lord will not hold guiltless those who neglect these responsibilities.

---

180 Mark E. Petersen, *Conference Report*, October 1959, 14.
181 Genesis 1:28.

After the Exodus and while Israel was in the wilderness, Moses, in teaching his people, instructed them that the commandments of the Lord should be taught by parents to their children in the home. He said to them: "And these words, which I command thee this day, shall be in thine heart: And thou shalt teach them diligently unto thy children, and shalt talk of them when thou sittest in thine house, and when thou walkest by the way, and when thou liest down, and when thou risest up" (Deut. 6:6–7).[182]

Nevertheless, President Hunter added, "there are children who have come into the world that would challenge any set of parents under any set of circumstances." When we have taught our children correctly, he said, we can consider ourselves successful parents, a comforting reassurance from an Apostle. "A successful parent is one who has loved, one who has sacrificed, and one who has cared for, taught, and ministered to the needs of a child. If you have done all of these and your child is still wayward or troublesome or worldly, it could well be that you are, nevertheless, a successful parent."[183]

Mourning over her wayward children and struggling with her self-worth, a mother in Nevada wrote, "I always feel I could have done more, and I feel the guilt that comes when my parenting skills fall short. I always struggle when my children struggle, but I stand firm in my love for them and ask for help from my Heavenly Father. I try hard to forgive myself but always feel if I had been a better mom maybe they would have had a different life."

Like this suffering mother, too many parents take their children's problems personally. But, as noted above, our job is to love, sacrifice, care for, teach, and minister as much as our children will allow. These are comforting thoughts for parents whose children exercise their agency and refuse to respond to their parents' pleading, long-suffering, and sorrow.

Elder Hunter reminded us that "we should never let Satan fool us into thinking that all is lost. . . . Each child is unique. Just as each

---

182 Howard W. Hunter, "Parents' Concern for Children," *Ensign*, November 1983.
183 Ibid.

of us starts at a different point in the race of life, and just as each of us has different strengths and weaknesses and talents, so each child is blessed with his own special set of characteristics. We must not assume that the Lord will judge the success of one in precisely the same way as another. As parents we often assume that, if our child doesn't become an overachiever in every way, we have failed. We should be careful in our judgments."[184]

We are novices when it comes to parenting; we are like new missionaries arriving in their fields of labor. We, like missionaries, are called to do the work of salvation, but the Lord is patient with us as we strive to meet new challenges. The instructions that the Lord gives to missionaries might be applied to parents: "Now behold, a marvelous work is about to come forth among the children of men. [Something marvelous is about to occur in your family—a new baby!] Therefore, O ye [parents] that embark in the service of God, see that ye serve him with all your heart, might, mind and strength, that ye may stand blameless before God at the last day." According to the scripture, *desire* qualifies parents for the work, and they qualify for salvation by fulfilling parents' first commandment in righteousness. Continuing, what qualities do these scriptures state that parents should strive to develop? "Faith, hope, charity and love, with an eye single to the glory of God, qualify [them] for the work. Remember faith, virtue, knowledge, temperance, patience, brotherly kindness, godliness, charity, humility, diligence." And of course the promise is that God will not leave us alone in this monumental responsibility: "Ask, and ye shall receive; knock, and it shall be opened unto you."[185] Answers and support are just a prayer away.

The miracle of God's work is that weak things are divinely empowered to accomplish great things. "Wherefore, I call upon the weak things of the world, those who are unlearned and despised, to thrash the nations by the power of my Spirit."[186] The mighty are not necessarily chosen. The Lord is willing to call us *children* to rear His *children*. When it comes to parenting, we are mere babes; nevertheless, He allows us this privilege simply because we "desire" to do His

---

184 Howard W. Hunter, "Parents' Concern for Children," *Ensign*, November 1983.
185 D&C 4:1–7; emphasis added.
186 D&C 35:13.

work—to give physical life to His children and to teach them the principles of salvation. Because we desire, we are called to the work.

WE PARENTS WERE CALLED, PREPARED, AND WE HAVE COVENANTED TO SAVE
During the process of creation, God "came down in the beginning in the midst of all the intelligences,"[187] and there, as President J. Reuben Clark said, "he found many that were great and good . . . 'there were many of the noble and great ones.'"

President Clark continued:

> Following upon this general principle, the Prophet Joseph said: "Every man who has a calling," *every man,* "to minister to the inhabitants of the world was ordained to that very purpose in the grand council of heaven before this world was." . . .
>
> I do not know whether we have a right to interpret the Prophet's statement . . . but I like to think that it does include those of us of lesser calling and lesser stature. We have been told ever since I was old enough to remember that those who are coming forth among the Latter-day Saints were choice spirits, and I like to think that perhaps in that grand council something at least was said to us indicating what would be expected of us, and empowering us, subject to the reconfirmation here, to do certain things in building up the kingdom of God on earth.[188]

Our parental calling and preparation likely began in the premortal world—the "first place,"[189] as Alma calls it. There, a select group of people received a calling into the *holy order*[190] because they had "conformed to the image of [God's] Son."[191] The premortal holy order, of course, comprised those righteous men and women who

---

187 Abraham 3:21.
188 J. Reuben Clark, Jr., *Conference Report,* October 1950, 169–171; emphasis added.
189 Alma 13:5.
190 See Alma 13:1.
191 Romans 8:29.

were worthy of the blessings of the priesthood. We latter-day parents were included in that select group because we desired to help redeem God's children. Elder David B. Haight commented,

> John A. Widtsoe provides insight to an earth-life responsibility made in that premortal world which is of great importance. He highlights a contractual agreement we made concerning the eternal welfare of all of the sons and daughters of the Eternal Father:
>
> "Since the plan is intended for all men, we [the covenant people of the holy order] became parties to the salvation of every person under that plan. We agreed, right then and there, to be not only saviors for ourselves but . . . saviors for the whole human family. We went into a partnership with the Lord. . . . The least of us, the humblest, is in partnership with the Almighty in achieving the purpose of the eternal plan of salvation."[192]

The group of premortal noble and great ones that formed the holy order was called *Israel,* whose founding fathers would be Abraham, Isaac, and Jacob. Elder Bruce R. McConkie wrote: "Israel is an eternal people. She came into being as a chosen and separate congregation before the foundations of the earth were laid; she was a distinct and a peculiar people in preexistence, even as she is in this sphere."[193] As Israelites (or Israelites by adoption through baptism), we, like our father Abraham, wanted to come to earth to teach the gospel, administer the ordinances of salvation, and become a "father [or mother] of many nations, a prince [or princess] of peace."[194] Righteous men, who were premortally appointed "High Priests of God,"[195] having proved themselves by choosing good over evil in the conflict in heaven, had "undoubtedly labored among the spirits in the

---

192 John A. Widtsoe quoted in David B. Haight's "Temples and the Work Therein," *Ensign,* November 1990, 59.
193 Bruce R. McConkie, *A New Witness for the Articles of Faith,* 510.
194 Abraham 1:2.
195 Alma 13:10.

premortal world and were ordained and prepared to descend to earth and be leaders in the Lord's redeeming work here."[196] Additionally, as President Kimball noted, "faithful women were given certain assignments," which, like their male counterparts, they were accountable for, just as are the prophets and Apostles.[197]

By becoming part of the holy order in the premortal world, we entered into a covenant to become Saviors on Mount Zion to the whole human family, starting with our own families.

Catherine Thomas said the following:

> It is likely that many of the premortal house of Israel . . . entered into covenants with those who would be our ancestors as well as with those who would be our posterity. We did this for the express purpose of having a saving influence in both directions—on our ancestors through work for the dead and on our posterity through nurturing work for the living, all under the continuing direction of the great Redeemer.
>
> Likely our own labors with many spirits commenced in the spirit world, our hearts being bound together in love from our associations through eons. . . .
>
> We would, by our premortal covenants with loved ones and with the Lord, become extensions of God's power during our mortal probations and actually be able to exert a saving influence on an increasing number of people.[198]

Why would learning the process of redemption be so important?

Those who will persist in learning and perfecting that power will be exalted to the stature of their parent Gods. Is it any wonder, then, that God places so much weight on our learning the principles of redemption? And if that is the case, could we doubt for a

---

196 M. Catherine Thomas, "Alma the Younger, Part 1," Neal A. Maxwell Institute for Religious Scholarship.

197 Spencer W. Kimball, "The Role of Righteous Women," *Ensign,* November 1979.

198 M. Catherine Thomas, "Alma the Younger, Part 1," Neal A. Maxwell Institute for Religious Scholarship.

moment that covenant relationships are left to chance or that children enter families as randomly as a dealer distributing cards? Clearly, as prophets have said, there are few coincidences for covenant people,[199] and therefore no important person is in our lives by accident. That realization leaves us only one course to pursue: because we were called and prepared to do the work of redemption among our children, we must move forward in faith and labor diligently, even when no hope seems to be in sight. Mormon's exhortation to Moroni should become our mantra: "And now, my beloved son, notwithstanding their hardness, let us labor diligently; for if we should cease to labor, we should be brought under condemnation; for we have a labor to perform whilst in this tabernacle of clay, that we may conquer the enemy of all righteousness, and rest our souls in the kingdom of God."[200]

ECHOES OF EARLIER TESTIMONIES

Persisting with a wayward child includes, at the very least, patience, long-suffering, love, and bearing testimony in word and deed with the hope that it might spark a premortal remembrance in the child's soul. We might apply the counsel that Elder Jeffrey R. Holland gave to missionaries:

> There are several reasons for bearing testimony. One is that when you declare the truth, it will bring an echo, a memory, even if it is an unconscious memory to the [child], that they have heard this truth before—and of course they have. A [parent's] testimony invokes a great legacy of testimony dating back to the councils in heaven before this world was. There, in an earlier place, these same people heard this same plan outlined and heard there the role that Jesus Christ would play in their salvation. . . .
>
> The fact of the matter is [children] are not only hearing our testimony of Christ, but they are hearing echoes of other, earlier testimonies, including their own testimony

---

199 See Joseph B. Wirthlin, "Lessons Learned in the Journey of Life," *Liahona*, May 2001.

200 Moroni 9:6.

of Him. . . . We [should] bear frequent and powerful testimony of Christ as Savior, as Redeemer . . . because doing
so invites . . . the divine power of testimony borne by God
the Father and by the Holy Ghost, a testimony borne on
wings of fire to the very hearts of [children] [See 3 Ne.
11:35–36, 39].[201]

"HE THAT BELIEVETH IN ME, THOUGH HE WERE DEAD, YET SHALL HE LIVE"
Despite our best efforts, one of our children may pass away having
never abandoned his wayward ways. Is he lost? Have we failed? Not
necessarily. The Lord also anticipated this eventuality. To the grieving
Martha, Jesus explained that the power of redemption transcends this
life. The Lord's power of redemption can reach deep within the world
of spirits, offer the plan of salvation, and snatch a now-repentant,
believing soul from the jaws of hell. Consider the deeper meaning of
the Lord's words: "He that believeth in me, though he were dead, yet
shall he live."[202] Because we likely foreknew our children and their
problems, and because we were called and prepared to help redeem
them, it logically follows that we will be given power after death
to seek them out wherever they are and to continue our work with
them, even if that work requires our persistence up until the very last
moment before the Resurrection.

Prior to his death, President Joseph F. Smith received a vivid
vision of the spirit world, including its inhabitants, their condition,
Jesus' visit to them after His death, and the redeeming work that the
Lord organized, as found in Doctrine and Covenants 138:53–56.
Our stewardships extend into the spirit world. For example, former
prophets and righteous individuals—Adam, Eve, Abel, Seth, Noah,
Shem, Abraham, Isaac, Jacob, Moses, Isaiah, Ezekiel, Daniel, Elias,
Malachi, Elijah, "all these *and many more,* even the prophets who
dwelt among the Nephites"[203]—were taught by the Lord, and given
"power to come forth . . . *and continue thenceforth their labor as had*

---

201 Jeffrey R. Holland, "Missionary Work and the Atonement," *Ensign,* March
     2001, comments added.
202 John 11:25.
203 D&C 138:49; emphasis added.

been promised by the Lord."[204] That is, the righteous continue their work among those for whom they had stewardship upon the earth. As the revelation states, "The faithful elders [and women] of this dispensation, when they depart from mortal life, continue their labors in the preaching of the gospel of repentance and redemption, through the sacrifice of the Only Begotten Son of God, among those who are in darkness and under the bondage of sin in the great world of the spirits of the dead."[205] Inasmuch as prophets' stewardships continue among those for whom they had a responsibility, so it would make sense that righteous parents' stewardships continue among those for whom they have a responsibility. The Prophet Joseph Smith stated, "There is never a time when the spirit is too old to approach God. All are within the reach of pardoning mercy."[206] We can infer that the word *never* pertains to all of eternity.

President Lorenzo Snow assured us, "When the Gospel is preached to the spirits in prison, the success attending that preaching will be far greater than that attending the preaching of our Elders in this life. I believe there will be very few indeed of those spirits who will not gladly receive the Gospel when it is carried to them. The circumstances there will be a thousand times more favorable."[207] At another time President Snow stated,

> God has fulfilled His promises to us, and our prospects are grand and glorious. . . . In the next life we will have our wives, and our sons and daughters. If we do not get them all at once, we will have them [at] some time, for every knee shall bow and every tongue shall confess that Jesus is the Christ. You that are mourning about your children straying away will have your sons and your daughters. If you succeed in passing through these trials and afflictions and receive a resurrection, you will, by the power of the

---

204 D&C 138:51–52; emphasis added.
205 D&C 138:57.
206 Joseph Fielding Smith, ed., *Teachings of the Prophet Joseph Smith*, 191.
207 Lorenzo Snow, "Preaching the Gospel in the Spirit World," *Collected Discourses*, 363.

Priesthood, work and labor, as the Son of God has, until you get all your sons and daughters in the path of exaltation and glory. This is just as sure as that the sun rose this morning over yonder mountains. Therefore, mourn not because all your sons and daughters do not follow in the path that you have marked out to them, or give heed to your counsels. Inasmuch as we succeed in securing eternal glory, and stand as saviors, and as kings and priests to our God, we will save our posterity.[208]

Redemption, whenever and wherever it takes place, is our work and the work of Jesus Christ, and that work is not complete until our sons and daughters are fully taught, understand the gospel, repent with their own agency, embrace the truth, and experience redemption through the power of the Atonement. President Joseph F. Smith said,

Jesus had not finished his work when his body was slain, neither did he finish it after his resurrection from the dead; although he had accomplished the purpose for which he then came to the earth, he had not fulfilled all his work. And when will he? Not until he has redeemed and saved every son and daughter of our father Adam that have been or ever will be born upon this earth to the end of time, except the sons of perdition. That is his mission. *We will not finish our work until we have saved ourselves, and then not until we shall have saved all depending upon us;* for we are to become saviors upon Mount Zion, as well as Christ. We are called to this mission.[209]

And President Gordon B. Hinckley confirmed the apostolic promise made by Elder Orson F. Whitney, quoting,

---

208 Lorenzo Snow, *The Teachings of Lorenzo Snow*, 195.
209 Joseph F. Smith, *Gospel Doctrine: Selections from the Sermons and Writings of Joseph F. Smith*, 442; emphasis added.

The Prophet Joseph Smith declared—and he never taught more comforting doctrine—that the eternal sealings of faithful parents and the divine promises made to them for valiant service in the Cause of Truth, would save not only themselves, but likewise their posterity. Though some of the sheep may wander, the eye of the Shepherd is upon them, and sooner or later they will feel the tentacles of Divine Providence reaching out after them and drawing them back to the fold. *Either in this life or the life to come, they will return.* They will have to pay their debt to justice; they will suffer for their sins; and may tread a thorny path; but if it leads them at last, like the penitent Prodigal, to a loving and forgiving father's heart and home, the painful experience will not have been in vain. Pray for your careless and disobedient children; hold on to them with your faith. Hope on, trust on, till you see the salvation of God.[210]

THE SHEPHERD WILL FIND HIS SHEEP

Children who have received baptism and then abandon the gospel are tethered to Christ by a cord that cannot be broken. Teaching this point in the form of a question, Elder Whitney asked, "Who are these straying sheep—these wayward sons and daughters? They are children of the Covenant, heirs to the promises, and have received, if baptized, the gift of the Holy Ghost, which makes manifest the things of God. Could all that go for naught?"[211]

Then, encouraging parents to consider the eternal nature of the redemptive process and to persevere, he said, "You parents of the wilful and the wayward! Don't give them up. Don't cast them off. They are not utterly lost. The Shepherd will find his sheep. They were his before they were yours—long before he entrusted them to your care; and you cannot begin to love them as he loves them."[212]

---

210 Orson F. Whitney, quoted in Gordon B. Hinckley's *Teachings of Gordon B. Hinckley,* 54; emphasis added.

211 Orson F. Whitney, *Conference Report,* April 1929, 110–111.

212 Orson F. Whitney, *Conference Report,* April 1929, 110.

When wayward children break our hearts by their foolish and destructive choices, we often mourn that the only option within our control is prayer, and we sometimes imagine that prayer is a weak solution for what is really needed. But to our knees is exactly where we should go. The Lord hears and answers prayers—that is an oft-repeated promise and should be our confidence. Both the Father and the Son will help us work with our wayward children. As Elder Jeffrey R. Holland said, it is inherent in the very nature of the Father and the Son to help and bless us:

> Consider, for example, the Savior's benediction upon his disciples even as he moved toward the pain and agony of Gethsemane and Calvary. On that very night, the night of the greatest suffering that has ever taken place in the world or that ever will take place, the Savior said, "Peace I leave with you, my peace I give unto you. . . . Let not your heart be troubled, neither let it be afraid" (John 14:27).
>
> *I submit to you, that may be one of the Savior's commandments that is, even in the hearts of otherwise faithful Latter-day Saints, almost universally disobeyed;* and yet I wonder whether our resistance to this invitation could be any more grievous to the Lord's merciful heart. . . . I am convinced that none of us can appreciate how deeply it wounds the loving heart of the Savior of the world when he finds that his people do not feel confident in his care or secure in his hands or trust in his commandments.
>
> Just because God is God, just because Christ is Christ, they cannot do other than care for us and bless us and help us if we will but come unto them, approaching their throne of grace in meekness and lowliness of heart. They can't help but bless us. . . . It is their nature.[213]

---

213 Jeffrey R. Holland, "Come Unto Me," *Ensign,* April 1998; emphasis added.

Then Elder Holland extended this apostolic promise:

> Listen to this wonderful passage from President George Q. Cannon teaching precisely this very doctrine: "No matter how serious the trial, how deep the distress, how great the affliction, [God] will never desert us. He never has, and He never will. He cannot do it. It is not His character [to do so]. He is an unchangeable being; the same yesterday, the same today, and He will be the same throughout the eternal ages to come. We have found that God. We have made Him our friend, by obeying His Gospel; and He will stand by us. We may pass through the fiery furnace; we may pass through deep waters; but we shall not be consumed nor overwhelmed. We shall emerge from all these trials and difficulties the better and purer for them, if we only trust in our God and keep His commandments."[214]

Does this promise, along with other prophetic promises, not give parents of wayward children reason to hope? Does knowing the extent of our preparation not give parents of wayward children cause to reach down inside themselves and summon the strength that resulted from that preparation? As President Lorenzo Snow said, "Our prospects are grand and glorious."[215]

---

214 Jeffrey R. Holland, "Come Follow Me," *Ensign,* April 1998; George Q. Cannon, "Freedom of the Saints," in *Collected Discourses,* vol. 2, 185; emphasis added.
215 Lorenzo Snow, *The Teachings of Lorenzo Snow,* 195.

Section 2
SPIRITUAL TOOLS

Chapter 5
THIS IS MY WORK AND MY GLORY: THE PARABLES

No greater work has the Lord God of heaven ever undertaken than to save the souls of his children. It is the grandest, the greatest undertaking that ever has been inaugurated.

—*Elder Rulon S. Wells* [216]

ZENOS'S ALLEGORY OF THE TAME olive tree gone wild in the Book of Mormon is clearly symbolic of God's nourishing and reclaiming the house of Israel. But Israel is also a metaphor for the redemption of the individual. This allegory can thus be applied to God's dealings with His individual wayward children. Therefore, as we explore this allegory and the other related parables of salvation, insert the name of your wayward loved one in the place of the central characters.

When we are first introduced to the tree in Jacob 5, we are led to understand that this tree (a child or people) was a favorite of the Lord of the vineyard, who represents God the Father. Evidently, this was a tree He had lovingly nourished for a very long time. Then, as the tree grew, a crisis occurred—the tree "started to wither." Alarmed, the Lord attempted to save it. This was the first of His many attempts and His many extended periods of waiting. As each redemptive episode is described, the Lord's character is revealed.

The Lord's first attempt to save the tree spanned "many days" while He diligently pruned, dug about, and nourished the tree to prevent its demise. Interestingly, as a strategy to save the tame tree,

---

216 Rulon S. Wells, *Conference Report*, April 1927, 72–73.

the Lord grafted it to a wild olive tree to preserve the tame tree's roots, the only part that had not yet decayed. In allowing the tame tree to mix with the wild tree, He was attempting to save the undecayed part using any means available, even if that meant temporarily allowing otherwise unthinkable comingling. Although the Lord knew that the tame tree would bring forth wild fruit for a time, nevertheless, He was in control of the eventual outcome. In the meantime, He was willing to do whatever He had to do with present resources to save the tree. Equally disconcerting is the Lord's willingness to cut away the corrupted parts of the tame olive tree and cast them into the fire. This seems like an indication that sometimes almost every part of a life can be corrupted, and may need to be drastically pruned to reach a soul's potential.

Zenos is careful to describe not only the Lord's strategy but also His character as the prophet unfolds this allegory. For example, at every step the Lord is grieved that he should lose the tree, indicating the Lord's deep affection for and commitment to preserving His creation. Zenos lists the Lord's multiple efforts to save the tree and also emphasizes that each of the Lord's efforts is followed by long periods of the Lord's waiting to assess the tree's progress. Although each effort results in a failure or a complication, the Lord does not give up. Rather, He starts over with more digging about, pruning, and nourishing; He is always working to preserve the good parts of the tree.

Over time, the Lord guides the tree (or segments of it) on an extensive and agonizing journey. The tree ends up all over the vineyard; some segments end up in the "nethermost parts"(Jacob 5:13) of the vineyard and in "the poorest spot in all the land" (v. 21). The parable of the prodigal son calls this the "far country."[217] But even in these remote areas, the Lord knows where the tree is and how to bring it back. Periodically the Lord performs extreme surgery to save the tree. Finally, with its grafted-in wild branches, the tree appears so broken, fragmented, and disfigured that it no longer resembles its original self. At one point, when we finally allow ourselves to feel the tiniest hope that progress is being made, we discover that the tree's

---

217 Luke 15:13.

roots and top are out of balance and threaten its survival. Worse, the tame branches that the Lord had tried preserve in another part of the vineyard have now become corrupt and overrun with wild branches. Yet more surgery is needed. We wonder, who could ever put this tree back together and cause it to bring forth good fruit again?

An amazing thing happens here: "And it came to pass that the Lord of the vineyard wept, and said unto the servant: What could I have done more?"[218] In tears, the Lord reviews all that He has tried over long periods of time to save the tree, and now He mourns that the tree not only continues to bring forth "evil fruit" but it has corrupted the trees near it. Contemplating such a dire situation, God weeps! Who would not? After all His efforts and endurance, the perfect, long-suffering Father laments that He seemed to have no other option except to hew down the tree, along with those that it had corrupted, and cast them all into the fire. In the Doctrine and Covenants, the Lord speaks of this condition of exasperation as relating to dealing with unrepentant children. He states that these children try even the patience of the angels of heaven, who finally are compelled to cry out *enough is enough!* "Behold, verily I say unto you, the angels are crying unto the Lord day and night, who are ready and waiting to be sent forth to reap down the fields."[219]

Then, when the Lord fully intends to cast the corrupt tree and its companions "into the fire that they not cumber the ground of the vineyard,"[220] the mediating servant (Jesus Christ) steps forward and pleads, "Spare it a little longer."[221] The character and mission of the Savior are here revealed.

The Savior has suffered for these wicked ones and does not want His sacrifice to have been for naught. He suffered for their misdeeds and *overcame* everything that stood between these wayward ones and exaltation—if they would repent and come back to Him. Therefore, the Savior, pleading with the Lord of the vineyard for more patience and clemency for the corrupt tree, eventually, convinces the Lord of the vineyard, who is still grieved to lose His tree, to try yet one more

---

218 Jacob 5:41.
219 D&C 86:5.
220 Jacob 5:66.
221 Jacob 5:50.

time. Then the Lord of the vineyard comes up with a final, elaborate plan. (Notice that He is the one who devises the plan and is in charge of its execution). The plan involves yet another major surgery on the tree. The plan would also encompass the width and breadth of the vineyard.

Together, the Lord and His servant set out again to graft and pluck and work with every segment of the tree from its roots to its branches. Their combined effort is beyond anything that had previously been attempted. It requires segregating the tame tree from the wild ones, which now have fulfilled their purpose and are destined for the fire. The plan calls for the Lord's enlisting other servants: "Wherefore, let us go to and labor with our might this last time,"[222] the Lord tells his servants. "Prune . . . graft in the branches . . . dig about . . . dung them once more, for the last time."[223] The Lord instructs His servants to pay close attention that the tree would achieve balanced growth—its roots proportionate to its top. As the servants help to nurse the tree back to health, they are to carefully clear away any bad branches and nourish the good ones.

The Lord's enormous effort, which spans His kingdom and involves vast amounts of time and resources, ends with the full restoration and redemption of His *one* beloved olive tree, "which was most precious unto him from the beginning."[224] Now and forever, this saved *one* would produce good and natural fruit.

The lesson here is that God is who He is because He is the best at what He does, and what He does is the work of redemption. It is His work and His glory. His complete reason for being and His greatest source of joy are wrapped up in this single work. He has been doing it for a long time, and He doesn't fail.[225] The following parables teach of His commitment to this work.

LUKE 15—THE HEART OF THE GOSPEL MESSAGE
In compiling his gospel, Luke intentionally grouped a set of parables that attest to God's priority on redemption and His infinite power

---

222 Jacob 5:62.
223 Jacob 5:63–64.
224 Jacob 5:74.
225 See D&C 76:3.

to save. As much as Alma's redemption story is at the heart of the Book of Mormon, Luke's fifteenth chapter, which also deals with the redemption of the outcast, is at the heart of Luke's Gospel. In Luke 15, Jesus helps His listeners, and later readers of the cannon, to understand how God views the sinner.

Luke prefaces this chapter by stating that publicans and sinners had come to hear the Savior and that the Pharisees were incensed because Jesus was eating with known sinners.[226] The only thing that disturbed them more than the sinners' attendance was the Lord's subsequent willingness to go to the sinners' homes to dine with them. We might speculate that if the Lord were to suddenly appear, we would have to seek Him where He would be spending most of His time—with sinners. Should we doubt, then, in light of Luke's introduction to this chapter, that the Savior is with our wayward children even now? Where else would He be?

The Lord's response to the Pharisees' criticism was His proffering three parables that simultaneously reveal His character and describe His work and glory. The parable of the lost sheep concerns those who wander from the fold, after which searching occurs; the parable of the lost coin concerns those who are lost from view by someone's carelessness, after which seeking happens; the story of the prodigal son concerns those who rebel and follow a destructive path, after which patient waiting ensues. The central themes of these parables are the love of God and the value He places on a wayward soul. In the case of each parable, we should ask ourselves, *If a human being would exert such a profound effort to recover a sheep or a coin that is lost, how much more effort would God put forth to recover a lost soul?* Notice that every time the lost is found, a celebration follows—one that has a simultaneous counterpart in heaven.

The Lost Sheep

When Matthew recorded his version of the parable of the lost sheep, he added two important statements by the Savior that are not found in Luke: "For the Son of man is come to save that which was lost," and "Even so it is not the will of your Father which is in heaven, that

---

226 See Luke 15:1–2.

one of these little ones should perish."[227] Can we harbor any doubt about the intended meaning of the parable?

In the first parable recorded by Luke,[228] a shepherd loses one of his hundred sheep that has strayed. Leaving behind the ninety-nine, we assume with other able shepherds, the shepherd begins a diligent search. When he finds the lost sheep, he carries it back on his shoulders (possibly implying the weakened condition of the animal), then joyously celebrates its return with loved ones. The Savior pointedly notes the connection between earth and heaven, an indication that signals celestial participation in the search: "likewise joy shall be in heaven over one sinner that repenteth."[229]

President David O. McKay suggested that the lost sheep is like many who stray innocently with no rebellious intent. Rebelliousness is not always the issue, he said. In the parable, the sheep was seeking its livelihood legitimately, albeit ignorant of the consequences, and wandered into unknown and dangerous territory seeking better grass. Suddenly, it is lost. The sheep is no different from some children in the Church who wander unwittingly; seeking success in education, career, or other pursuits, they one day look up and find themselves far from the Church and disconnected from gospel principles. Their wandering has misled them in defining truth and what constitutes true success, and they are now too lost to find their way back without a good shepherd to guide them.[230]

For whatever reason, the straying sheep finds itself lost and in need of a savior—one who knows and loves him intimately and who will search the wilderness, valleys, and mountains to find him. Once he is found, and exhausted from wandering in sin, the lost sheep needs someone strong to carry him home—to that safe place where there is acceptance and where there will be rejoicing at his return.

The Lost Coin
To find lost souls, God sometimes *searches,* which means "to make a thorough examination of; look over carefully in order to find

---

227 Matthew 18:11, 14.
228 See Luke 15:3–7.
229 Luke 15:7.
230 See David O. Mckay, *Conference Report,* April 1945, 120.

something"[231] In the case of the lost sheep, the Lord *searched.* But at other times, He *seeks,* which means "to try to locate or discover."[232] In the parable of the lost coin,[233] a woman seeks for something valuable she has lost due to neglect. She is frantic to find it. Interestingly, she lights a candle and sweeps the house as she diligently seeks, suggesting that she needs not only more light in her life, but also a thorough cleaning. Eventually, her effort results in her ability to recover the coin, which she has carelessly lost in the clutter of her life.

The message may be stinging, but it is true nonetheless: personal repentance and subsequent sanctification are essential tools in petitioning for power from heaven in order to reclaim others. Alma taught, "God has said that the inward vessel shall be cleansed first, and then shall the outer vessel be cleansed also."[234] That is, if we will first concentrate on personal sanctification, we will then be in a better position to petition sanctifying blessings for others. This principle is stated consistently by the Savior in a variety of settings: "Therefore if thou bring thy gift to the altar, and there rememberest that thy brother hath ought against thee; Leave there thy gift before the altar, and go thy way; first be reconciled to thy brother, and then come and offer thy gift."[235] And, "First cast out the beam out of thine own eye; and then shalt thou see clearly to cast out the mote out of thy brother's eye."[236] To successfully seek out that which we may have neglected and carelessly lost, we need to shine an honest light on our own house and begin sweeping.

Elder J. Kent Jolley wrote that an Enos-like experience usually precedes our ability to perform the work of recovering lost coins. We must persist in following the Lord's prophets and in studying His word, and we must hunger and petition the Lord to ease our personal spiritual weaknesses and burdens. Then, like Enos, we will be in a position to effectively continue in prayer for the welfare of others who are spiritually "misplaced." The experience of Enos can happen to us if we seek for it as did Enos. When our hearts have been changed and

---

231 *American Heritage Dictionary,* "Search."
232 *American Heritage Dictionary,* "Seek."
233 See Luke 15:8–10.
234 Alma 60:23.
235 Matthew 5:23–24.
236 Matthew 7:5.

are right, we will be in a much better position to assume the great work of redemption.[237]

Although the woman in the parable could represent someone who is careless, neglectful, and in need of repentance, she also could represent our perfectly attentive Heavenly Father, who seeks diligently for those that are lost. When the woman finds the coin (as with the lost sheep), a celebration is in order, indicating how much value she places on the coin. The parable ends with Jesus repeating that heaven has participated in the seeking-and-finding process and therefore has a legitimate right to join in the rejoicing.

The Prodigal Son

The parable of the prodigal son[238] is about the Lord's waiting process. Brian M. Hauglid wrote, "With both the lost sheep and the lost coin, it is interesting that neither of the two can fully represent repentance because repentance is a human act. However . . . if the first two parables demonstrate God's initiative to search out those who are lost and then hold subsequent celebrations, the Parable of the Prodigal Son shows that sometimes God will wait for the lost to choose to repent and return and still hold a celebration."[239]

Prodigal is an adjective that means "rashly or wastefully extravagant."[240] In this parable, Jesus used the extreme situation of a wickedly rash and wasteful boy to illustrate abysmal sin that is eventually covered by infinite atoning love. The parable introduces a father who had two sons. Both boys, we will discover, had need of repentance, and in both cases the father becomes the reconciling and unifying agent. We learn at least two disconcerting things about the younger son: he sought his own terms, and he clearly rejected family and tradition.

Turning his property into quick cash, the prodigal now had all the resources he needed to lose himself. That he "took his journey

---

237 See J. Kent Jolley, "Parables of Jesus: The Lost Coin," *Ensign*, June 2003.

238 See Luke 15:11–32.

239 *The God of Old* quoted in Brian M. Hauglid's "Luke's Three Parables of the Lost and Found: A Textual Study," *The Life and Teachings of Jesus Christ,* Volume 2, 247.

240 *American Heritage Dictionary*, "Prodigal."

into a far country"[241] strikes a familiar chord in the heart of any parent of a wayward child. Jesus' description of this far country and its conditions suggests that the boy had departed the land of his inheritance to live with and like Gentiles—shedding himself of his covenants and trampling into the ground the teachings of his father. Worse, the boy brought shame to his father and the family's name by wasting "his substance with riotous living . . . and with harlots" until "he had spent all."[242] How many parents of wayward children have watched their children abandon their heritage and covenants, openly reject their family, and, finally, squander all their resources—and often the family's fortune—to live a perverse, gentile life?

Then came the "mighty famine";[243] it always does. No one can escape the law of the harvest—it holds everyone and every action in its grasp. Now no "friend" would help him; friends like that never will. Satan, the father of such "friends," won't allow support: "the devil will not support his children at the last day, but doth speedily drag them down to hell."[244] The plus side to this, as Ted Gibbons wrote, is that "This famine in the *far country* is as much a messenger of the love of God as was the angel who visited Alma."[245] Its purpose was to call the prodigal son home.

Now the boy was starving, but he had not yet hit rock bottom. In a frantic attempt to retain his residence in the far country and cling to his rebellious lifestyle, he "joined himself to a citizen of that country [who] sent him into his fields to feed swine."[246] Once again we see the depths to which the young man had fallen. Brian Hauglid wrote,

> Of course, the occupation of feeding pigs (as with the eating of them) is absolutely forbidden in Jewish law, so this act underscores the desperate and despicable state the young man had brought upon himself.

---

241 Luke 15:13.
242 Luke 15:13–14, 30.
243 Luke 15:14.
244 Alma 30:60.
245 Ted Gibbons, *Nowhere Else to Go* (unpublished manuscript in author's possession).
246 Luke 15:15.

As a feeder of pigs, "he was forced to be in contact
with unclean animals (Lev. 11:7) and could not have
observed the Sabbath; he must have been reduced to
the lowest depths of degradation and practically forced
to renounce the regular practice of his religion."[247]

Apparently, he finally hit rock bottom when "no man gave unto
him," and "he would fain [gladly] have filled his belly with the husks
that the swine did eat,"[248] suggesting that he had now arrived at the
point where he gladly would have eaten the food of the swine. Maybe
the boy's revulsion at eating with the pigs was the last thing tethering
him to his roots. Perhaps his disgust with being reduced to this level
finally called him back. Maybe in his heart he finally cried, "What
am I doing? Have I really fallen this far?" For whatever reason, as
the scripture says, "he came to himself."[249] Perhaps no phrase in all
scripture summons more relief than this. Every parent of a wayward
child weeps and prays and longs for the day that their child will come
to himself. As Ted Gibbons noted, "Like Alma, he reached out for
mercy. 'I will arise and go to my father' (Luke 15:18). Like Alma,
when there seemed to be nowhere else he could go, he remembered
that there was a place."[250]

We can almost hear the boy say, "I am ready to go home. I may
have to go home in shame and accept the lowliest place in my father's
home, but nonetheless I am going home. Even the lowliest place
there is loftier than the highest place in this far country."

President Gordon B. Hinckley said:

I know of no more beautiful story in all literature
than that found in the fifteenth chapter of Luke. It
is the story of a repentant son and a forgiving father.

---

247 Joachim Jeremias, quoted in Brian M. Hauglid's "Luke's Three Parables of
the Lost and Found: A Textual Study," *The Life and Teachings of Jesus Christ,*
Volume 2, 251–252.

248 Luke 15:16.

249 Luke 15:17.

250 Ted Gibbons, *Nowhere Else to Go* (unpublished manuscript in author's
possession).

It is the story of a son who wasted his inheritance in riotous living, rejecting his father's counsel, spurning those who loved him. When he had spent all, he was hungry and friendless, and "when he came to himself" (Luke 15:17), he turned back to his father, who, on seeing him afar off, 'ran, and fell on his neck, and kissed him' (Luke 15:20).

I ask you to read that story. Every parent ought to read it again and again. It is large enough to encompass every household, and enough larger than that to encompass all mankind, for are we not all prodigal sons and daughters who need to repent and partake of the forgiving mercy of our Heavenly Father and then follow His example?[251]

When the boy "came to himself," he *turned* toward home and his father. Elder Richard G. Hinckley said, "The Hebrew root of the word [*repentance*] means, simply, 'to turn,' or 'to *re*turn to God.'"[252] Now that the boy had turned, "he arose, and came to his father. But when he was yet a great way off, his father saw him, and had compassion, and ran, and fell on his neck, and kissed him."[253] No poet has ever captured the character of the Father better than these simple words spoken by His Beloved Son. The Father, who "stretches forth his hands unto them all the day long,"[254] has always had His arms outstretched, waiting for this embrace. The father and son's embrace is followed by the boy's confession and admission that his actions are worthy of the forfeiture of his name and status as son; but the father reacts only with the same forgiveness and compassion he displayed *even before the confession.*

Significantly, the prodigal's father saw his boy "a great way off" and ran to him. Gibbons says, "The Greek words for 'a great way off' and for 'far country' are from the same root. *The implication is that*

---

251 Gordon B. Hinckley, "Of You It Is Required to Forgive," *Ensign*, June 1991.
252 Richard G. Hinckley, "Repentance, a Blessing of Membership," *Ensign*, May 2006, 48.
253 Luke 15:20.
254 Jacob 6:4.

the father may have seen the son the moment he started for home."[255]
The father's compassionate and forgiving nature may have been what
brought the boy home. Once the boy had turned for home, perhaps
the father had even walked the distance home with him.

In this parable, the father waits. He does not search for the young
man, as if the boy had strayed like the lost sheep; he does not seek the
young man, as if the boy, like the coin, had been lost due to careless
neglect; rather, the father waits for the boy to hit rock bottom. Often,
the kindest thing a parent can do is to allow a wayward child to
reach rock bottom as soon as possible, because that is the place where
reconsideration and change begin.

A parent's test of waiting is often much harder than the tests of
searching and seeking—at least we feel that we are in control when we
are actively working with the child. But to wait for pain to do its work on
a child can be excruciating for the parent; consequently, waiting requires
godlike discipline, maturity, and, most of all, faith that God is guiding the
situation. Nevertheless, we parents must learn this discipline if we expect
to become like God. He understands perfectly how to exhibit unconditional love while temporarily withholding unconditional support. If rock
bottom is where repentance is likely to take place, then He wants to get
the wayward child there as soon as possible. And He will do so unless we
impatient, albeit loving, parents get in His way.

Keep in mind that the father in this parable had the resources
to find and bail out his son at any time, but he did not. This is a
powerful lesson for parents who have exhausted searching and seeking
efforts and must make the agonizing decision to wait. Sometimes "all
we can do" is defined as choosing to do nothing except to love and to
wait for God to do the work that He has promised: "Therefore, dearly
beloved brethren, let us cheerfully do all things that lie in our power;
and then may we stand still, with the utmost assurance, to see the
salvation of God, and for his arm to be revealed."[256]

Another important point in the parable of the prodigal son relates
to the level of the boy's redemption. In the parable of the prodigal
son, after the son makes his confession, his father reacts only with

---

255 Ted Gibbons, *Nowhere Else to Go* (unpublished manuscript in author's
     possession); emphasis added.
256 D&C 123:17.

reconciliation and immediate restitution: "But the father said to his servants, Bring forth the best robe, and put it on him; and put a ring on his hand, and shoes on his feet: And bring hither the fatted calf, and kill it; and let us eat, and be merry: For this my son was dead, and is alive again; he was lost, and is found."[257]

This illustrates a principle I call "from prisoner to prince," which I believe can broaden our view of how similar exaltation might await every soul that has lingered in the captivity of sin. Joachim Jeremias observed the return of the prodigal son in light of this principle:

> (1) First comes the ceremonial robe, which in the East is a mark of high distinction. . . . The returning son is treated as a guest of honour. (2) The ring and shoes. Excavations have shown that the ring is to be regarded as a signet ring; the gift of a ring signified the bestowal of authority (cf. 1 Maccabees 6.15). Shoes are a luxury, worn by free men; here they mean that the son must no longer go about barefoot like a slave. (3) As a rule meat is rarely eaten. For special occasions a fatted calf is prepared. Its killing means a feast for the family and the servants, and the festal reception of the returning son to the family table.[258]

There is one last important point this parable makes; sometimes, in the battle for the soul of the prodigal, the other son may feel neglected and angry. Siblings of a prodigal may feel less important to parents and become jealous, or they may become misguided simply because we don't notice their struggles due to the smoke and clamor of the louder and more blinding battle before us. In the instance where our fear and guilt is aroused over such casualties of the fray, may we remember what we can do and what the Savior can do for us where our efforts and best intentions have fallen short. For instance, in the parable, the older son, upon observing the attention being

---

257 Luke 15:22–24.

258 Joachim Jeremias, quoted in Brian M. Hauglid's "Luke's Three Parables of the Lost and Found: A Textual Study," *The Life and Teachings of Jesus Christ*, Volume 2, 253.

lavished upon his brother, becomes "angry, and would not go in."[259]
To take offense and refuse to go into the Father's house is at the heart
of many gospel abandonments. Taking offense, we have been taught,
is a personal choice that is symptomatic of a deeper spiritual sickness, which, unchecked, can lead to apostasy and misery. We cannot
hide behind the falsehood that the offense was inflicted or imposed
upon us, no matter how rude or crass the offender may have been.
Nonetheless, our children are often "offended" in one way or another
before they are spiritually mature enough to reason through their
"wounding" and resulting spiritual "infection."

In an effort to catch his older son before he, too, departs for a far
country, the father comes out "and entreat[s] him."[260] Reassuringly,
the father confirms the boy's standing in the family if he will only
remain faithful and not be consumed by offense: "Son, thou art ever
with me, and all that I have is thine."[261] What a terrible forfeiture of
blessings for the sake of an offense, and yet how many of our faithful
children have been offended by the attention their parents heap upon
their prodigal brothers and sisters? The example of the father in this
parable is one that could benefit every parent of wayward and faithful
children: *We should be sensitive to our faithful children who are ever
with us.* We should watch for their taking offense when, of necessity, we must pay inordinate attention to a prodigal child. We should
be willing to entreat our faithful children, pleading with them not
to take offense, specifically assuring them of our love and their solid
position in the family, lest they be "driven away."

In instances where we simply do not have the time and emotional
means to be perfect stewards over all our children's needs, the Lord
can make up for our shortcomings when we are trying our best and
sanctifying ourselves. He employs all the resources in heaven and on
earth to rescue all our wayward children. To imagine that we parents
are carrying the burden of any child's waywardness alone or that we
are somehow excluded from the Father's grace is to deny the scriptures, which state, "Behold I, even I, will both search my sheep and
seek them out. As a shepherd seeketh out his flock in the day that he

---

259 Luke 15:28.
260 Luke 15:28.
261 Luke 15:31.

is among his sheep that are scattered; so will I seek out my sheep, and will deliver them out of all places [and ways] they have been scattered in the cloudy and dark day. . . . I will seek that which was *lost,* and bring again that which was *driven away.*"[262]

Some children are lost, and others have been driven away, but the Father will find every one. As with the olive tree, He will work with the wayward child for long periods of time and make repeated efforts to save him. As with the lost sheep that strayed, He will search until He finds the child, then carry him home. As with the lost coin, He will shine a light on our lives, assist us in cleaning up our personal clutter, then help us seek that which is most valuable but was lost due to our careless neglect. As with the prodigal son, He will patiently wait until the child comes to himself, tires of living like a Gentile and eating with pigs, and desires to return to the safety and abundance of home and compassionate, forgiving parents. In every case, the Father and the Son will throw a banquet to rejoice over the returning wayward one.

The Work of Angels

Redemption is *the* work of celestial people; thus it is the work of angels, as the Father employs them. This is another way in which we are not alone in our quest to save our children. As both Hezekiah and Elisha testified, there are many more which stand to help us than the powers that oppose our children and us.[263] Joseph Smith taught, "The spirits of the just are exalted to a greater and more glorious work; hence they are blessed in their departure to the world of spirits. Enveloped in flaming fire, they are not far from us, and know and understand our thoughts, feelings, and motions, and are often pained therewith."[264]

Angels are agents of the Holy Ghost and speak and act by His power.[265] That the keys of the ministering of angels have been restored should fill us with hope and faith.[266] By virtue of the powers attendant

---

262 Ezekiel 34:11–12, 16; emphasis added.
263 See 2 Chronicles 32:7–8.
264 Alma P. Burton, ed., *Discourses of the Prophet Joseph Smith,* 128.
265 See 2 Nephi 32:3.
266 See D&C 13:1.

to the Aaronic Priesthood, parents have the right to ask for angelic help in behalf of their children. We all know that sometimes angels are those who now live on this earth, but often, angelic help comes in the form of our ancestors, they who perhaps understand better than we the power of the "welding link"[267] that binds us together through temple ordinances. They enjoy a clearer view of the importance of the children's and their fathers' hearts being turned to each other, and the sealing that must be set in place and not allowed to be broken lest "the earth will be smitten with a curse."[268] The Prophet Joseph revealed,

> And now, my dearly beloved brethren and sisters, let me assure you that these are principles in relation to the dead and the living that cannot be lightly passed over, as pertaining to our salvation. For their salvation is necessary and essential to our salvation, as Paul said concerning the fathers—that they without us cannot be made perfect—neither can we without our dead be made perfect.[269]

Heaven and earth are partners in the cosmic work of salvation. Likewise, neither can we be made perfect without our fathers (we need their help) nor can they be made perfect without us (we provide them the saving ordinances). When we bless them with saving ordinances, they are suddenly endowed with power to help save our/their children. Elder Boyd K. Packer wrote, "Brother Widtsoe reaffirmed that 'those who give themselves with all their might and main to this work [genealogical and temple work] receive help from the other side. Whoever seeks to help those on the other side receives help in return in all the affairs of life.'"[270]

In this mutual redemptive effort, the hearts of the children and their fathers are *turned* to each other, or welded together, and the "promises made to the fathers" are planted "in the hearts of the

---

267 D&C 128:18.
268 D&C 128:18.
269 D&C 128:15.
270 John A. Widstoe, quoted in Boyd K. Packer's *The Holy Temple*, 252.

children."[271] What promises? The promises of the Abrahamic covenant, which include the promise of salvation and eventual godhood.
That is, as the fathers have covenanted to save us, their children, so we
have covenanted to save them.

Our deceased ancestors, therefore, become ministering servants—
angels of God—and their redemptive work continues. President Joseph
F. Smith said, "When messengers are sent to minister to the inhabitants
of this earth, they are not strangers, but from the ranks of our kindred,
friends, and fellow-beings and fellow-servants."[272] Additionally, in his
vision of the spirit world, he declared, "I beheld that the faithful elders
[including sisters] of this dispensation, when they depart from mortal
life, continue their labors in the preaching of the gospel of repentance
and redemption, through the sacrifice of the Only Begotten Son of God,
among those who are in darkness and under the bondage of sin in the
great world of the spirits of the dead."[273]

Of the reality of ministering ancestral angels, a mother from Utah
wrote,

> One of my most precious experiences occurred
> when my wayward son had visited me and left me
> in tears once again. This child is like trying to hug a
> porcupine! He believes he is doing himself and everyone
> else a favor when he tells things "the way they are."
> That evening, I had been alone at home. Everyone in
> my support system was unavailable: my husband was
> away serving in a Church calling, my youngest son
> was at work, and my parents were out of town. I was
> completely defenseless when my son began to hurl
> unkind accusations and angry words. I remember the
> searing pain and agony I felt in the wake of his tirade.
> When he stomped out the door, I sank to the floor and
> sobbed. I felt myself spiraling into despair and loneli-
> ness. I thought that I had nowhere to run and nobody

271 D&C 2:2.

272 Joseph F. Smith, *Gospel Doctrine: Selections from the Sermons and Writings of
Joseph F. Smith*, 435.

273 D&C 138:57.

to turn to. As I wept uncontrollably, I realized that I wasn't alone; all I needed to do was talk to my Heavenly Father and ask for comfort.

What occurred then was unexpectedly beautiful and priceless. As I poured out my agony and begged not to be alone, I asked for someone to come be with me and help me through this horrible time. Soon, I began to feel a warmth creep across my body. Immediately to my right, I sensed the presence of a grandfather to whom I had been particularly close in my youth. Then, to my left, I sensed the presence of my husband's grandmother, whom I had met only twice in our early marriage. She was sympathetic to my plight; she had lived her life without seeing any of her sons active in the Church. As these two family members stayed with me, I felt surrounded by love, peace, and the knowledge that families are connected in this life and the next.

My husband and I have had many experiences with ancestors helping us, but this experience was especially sweet because it came to me in such a difficult moment. It was a vivid reminder that we are never alone. When we need help we will be ministered to by spirits who love us, know us, and want to help us succeed.

To discount the reality of the ministering of angels is to deny one of the supernal blessings of the restored gospel. As Moroni was closing the Book of Mormon, he exhorted us to believe in miracles and in the ministering of angels: "Wherefore, if these things have ceased wo be unto the children of men, for it is because of unbelief, and all is vain."[274]

At the April 2006 general conference, President James E. Faust, quoting Joseph F. Smith, confirmed,

In ancient and modern times angels have appeared and given instruction, warnings, and direction,

---

274 Moroni 7:37.

which benefited the people they visited. We do not consciously realize the extent to which ministering angels affect our lives. President Joseph F. Smith said, "In like manner *our fathers and mothers, brothers, sisters and friends who have passed away from this earth, having been faithful, and worthy to enjoy these rights and privileges, may have a mission given them to visit their relatives and friends upon the earth again, bringing from the divine Presence messages of love, of warning, or reproof and instruction, to those whom they had learned to love in the flesh.*" Many of us feel that we have had this experience. Their ministry has been and is an important part of the gospel.[275]

We must not despair. In working with our wayward children, God will assemble all the powers of heaven and earth to achieve His glorious work. Whether our children have strayed from the path of truth, become lost by following a forbidden path, or consciously rebelled and run away to a far county, their Heavenly Father can find and rescue them. Even when they are so broken that they are no longer recognizable, He will patiently put them back together until they can bring forth good fruit. No matter their choices and situations, God loves them and is constantly working to save and redeem them. And so are their family and friends that have gone before. We are never alone in the work of redemption.

---

275 James E. Faust, "A Royal Priesthood," *Ensign*, May 2006, 50; emphasis added.

Chapter 6

PERSONAL SANCTIFICATION:
THE KEY TO RESCUING WAYWARD CHILDREN

Holiness is the strength of the soul. It comes by faith
and through obedience to God's laws and ordinances. God then
purifies the heart by faith, and the heart becomes purged from
that which is profane and unworthy.

—President James E. Faust[276]

GAINING THE SPIRITUAL CAPACITY TO rescue a wayward child comes down to this: Sanctifying ourselves. When we ourselves are sanctified, we are in a better position to ask for and receive redeeming blessings for others. When you read the previous promises of the prophets (see also those in chapter 11), did you notice that the prophets often emphasize parents' personal sanctification—through keeping temple covenants and remaining faithful and Christlike through the trials— as *the* criteria to seek the blessings of heaven for their children?

Quoting Catherine Thomas,

> Parents' personal sanctification exerts a saving influence on [their children]. With the promise of eternal life, Alma the Elder's power to draw down appropriate grace from his Heavenly Father became very great. . . . When we face similar situations, consolation may come when we remember that life does not end with physical death. When our efforts in this life do not yield the

---

276 James E. Faust "Standing in Holy Places," *Ensign*, May 2005, 62.

> redemption of a loved one, *often the only labor that a person can engage in on behalf of his or her loved one is to persist in the personal sanctifying process. Sometimes the most miraculous things happen in relationships as that personal sanctification process goes forward.*[277]

Naturally, the more sanctified a parent is, the more qualified he or she is to ask. As an example, Heavenly Father honors Christ's requests.[278] Therefore, if we qualify ourselves, asking in Christ's name, we will receive every needful, righteous request, which, of course, we've been promised.[279] Thus, he who is the most Christlike is in the best position to ask and to receive. Parents have an obligation to love each other and their children with a love that is worthy of the "welding link"[280] that binds a family together when sealed in the temple, or to live worthy of that sealing when the opportunity comes. Thereafter, they are under obligation to sanctify themselves so that their "confidence [shall] wax strong in the presence of God"[281] so that they might gain power to ask for blessings upon their children.

The opposite is also true—parents who will not sanctify themselves often withhold blessings from their children. The following account, retold by Fredrick Babbel, occurred in the aftermath of World War II:

> [I was next asked to bless] a three-year-old from Scotland. He had been a deaf mute since birth. Now his parents had brought him to London for a special blessing. One of the brethren anointed his head with oil, and as I placed my hands upon his head to seal the anointing and to give him a blessing, I felt that the Lord's power was present in such abundance that there was no question about his being healed instantly.

---

277 M. Catherine Thomas, "Alma the Younger, Part 1," Neal A. Maxwell Institute for Religious Scholarship; emphasis added.

278 See Matthew 26:53.

279 See 3 Nephi 18:19–20.

280 D&C 128:18.

281 D&C 121:45.

Before I could say a word, I was told by the Spirit, "This young boy could be healed this very night if his parents would lose the hatred which they have in their hearts." I was decidedly shocked and troubled, because I had never before met his family and did not want to question their attitude. But I was restrained from sealing the anointing.

After a moment's pause, I removed by hands from the boy's head and said to his parents, "What is it that you hate so deeply?"

They looked startled. Then the husband said, "We can't tell you."

"I don't need to know," I replied, "but as I placed my hands upon your son's head, I was assured that he might be healed this very night and be restored to you whole if you will only lose the hatred which you have in your hearts."

After some troubled glances back and forth between the couple, the husband again spoke. "Well, if that is the case," he said, "our son will have to go through life as he is, because we won't give up our hating!"[282]

A similar situation occurred with a bishop from southeastern Idaho, who counseled four sets of parents concerning their wayward sons. Before he did so, he fasted, prayed, and took his question to the temple. Soon, an answer formed in his mind. "The account of Alma the Elder pressed upon me," he said, "and I knew what had to be done." He remembered that Elder Packer had said that asking God opens the door to answers and blessings. If a person cannot or will not ask for help, then the obligation to ask falls to someone else.[283] The bishop knew that the boys would not ask for themselves, so their parents and others must ask for them.

When the bishop called the individual couples into his office, he discussed their boys' situations and explained the feelings that he had.

---

282 Fredrick W. Babbel, *On Wings of Faith,* 160–161.
283 See Boyd K. Packer, "Personal Revelation: The Gift, the Test, and the Promise," *Ensign,* November 1994.

By virtue of his office, he promised them that if they would follow his counsel, which was for their particular situation, they could pray their boys to a crossroads of decision. Like Alma the Younger, the boys would be presented with a "conversion opportunity" in the Lord's time. At the crossroads, the boys, like Alma, would then have a choice: they could choose to continue on their destructive path and accept the consequences, or they could choose to change and enjoy the rewards. The parents were only to pray to get their boy to the crossroads where the conversion opportunity would be presented; they were not to dictate a method or a timetable, and they were not to bargain with the Lord. In the meantime, they were to recommit to their covenants, relationships, and callings, and they were to attend the temple at least every two weeks to personally place their child's name on the prayer roll. The bishop promised the parents that the deceased people for whom they did proxy work would return the blessing by helping with their boys.

The parents reacted differently to the challenge. Two embraced it, one was lukewarm, and one discarded it. In that case, the child never changed but grew worse. Today, over twenty years later, the boy—now a man—continues along the same destructive path he entered as a youth. However, in this chapter, in addition to other accounts, we will retell the three success stories.

WHAT IS SANCTIFICATION?

Blaine M. Yorgason wrote, "Sanctification is the process of becoming pure and spotless before God through the power of the sanctifier, who is the Holy Ghost, through true and constant repentance and a love of that which is good."[284]

And the *Encyclopedia of Mormonism* states,

> "Sanctification is the process of becoming a saint, holy and spiritually clean and pure, by purging all sin from the soul." At the heart of sanctification is the Atonement of Jesus Christ, which makes possible baptism, which washes us "clean in a way that extends beyond remission of sins at baptism." Then comes

---

284 Blaine M. Yorgason, *Spiritual Progression in the Last Days,* 103.

the *Sanctifier* or the Holy Ghost. "The Holy Ghost . . . [is] the agent that purifies the heart and gives abhorrence of sin." We persist in the sanctification process "through personal righteousness. Faithful men and women fast; pray; repent of their sins; grow in humility, faith, joy, and consolation; and yield their hearts to God. . . . They also receive essential ordinances such as baptism . . . and, if necessary, endure chastening. . . . Thus, Latter-day Saints are exhorted to 'sanctify yourselves' (D&C 43:11) by purging all their iniquity (*Mormon Doctrine*, 675–76).

"I Sanctify Myself, That They Also Might Be Sanctified"

In His great intercessory prayer, the Savior taught that personal sanctification is *the* principle by which one person might save another. Just moments before Gethsemane, Jesus made the following statement: "For their sakes I sanctify myself, that they also might be sanctified."[285] In other words, the first action, *personal sanctification,* makes possible the second action, *the sanctification or saving of another.* We often think of sanctification in the context of being cleansed from sin—and it is certainly that—but here we see Jesus, who had no sin, sanctifying Himself. Obviously, there are greater reasons to persist in the process of sanctification beyond repentance. So how did Jesus sanctify Himself? We see the answer in the context of John 17. He sanctified himself through strict obedience, partaking of the sacrament, fasting, making a sacrifice, and offering mighty prayer.

In Jesus' example we find keys to the sanctification process. In the last hours of His life, what did He do? After having lived a life of perfect *obedience,* he partook of the *sacrament;* then entered into a *fast,* in which he did not eat or drink through the end of His life; then He offered an infinite vicarious *sacrifice* coupled with *mighty prayer.* Clearly, in addition to other sanctifying principles, obedience, partaking of the sacrament, fasting, offering sacrifice, and mighty prayer are some essential keys to personal sanctification.

---

285 John 17:19.

Ellen, a mother in San Diego, California, learned an extraordinary lesson in the power of personal sanctification.

My patience was wearing thin. First, I lost patience with my daughter, Angela, whom I could not reach no matter what tactic I used; and second, I lost patience with the Lord for not stepping in to help. My husband and I counseled with our bishop, after which I felt even more hopeless. All he did was run down the checklist: Were we praying as a couple, individually, and as a family? Were we fasting for our daughter? Were we holding family home evening, diligent in our callings, reading the scriptures, attending the temple—you get the idea. I felt as though I was in a temple recommend interview. *That is not what is needed!* I screamed inside. *Give me something concrete that I can do to change Angela!* My husband and I left the bishop's office with his parting counsel, "Take everything up a notch. When *you* shine more brightly, you'll be able to shine a brighter beam on your daughter."

I was so disappointed, and I told my husband as much. It was Angela who needed changing, not us. I felt as though the Church had let me down; the gospel was merely theory and void of practical application—a set of pat Sunday School answers with no substance.

My patient husband listened to me rant, then presented another view. He had actually felt something when the bishop had talked to us about light. Quoting D&C 93:37, my husband said, "The scriptures say 'light and truth forsake that evil one.' If light is what is needed then we should do as the bishop counseled and try to bring more light into our lives."

After that, I repented of my tantrum and followed my husband's lead. Over the next few months, we examined every spiritual aspect of our lives and tried to bring our spirituality up a notch: better prayers, more consistent scripture study, more frequent family home evening and temple attendance—anything to infuse more spiritual light into our lives. Although I felt a decided improvement in me, I noticed no improvement in my daughter. Nevertheless, I persevered in increasing the *light*.

One day when I was reading the scriptures, two visual images came into my mind. First, I imagined that I was holding a spotlight with the beam fixed on my daughter. Every time I prayed, fasted, studied the scriptures, attended the temple, etc., the beam grew more intense. Despite Angela's ongoing attempts to seek the darkness, she could not escape the light that I was shining on her. Then I saw Angela under a magnifying glass that the Lord was holding. She was also under its light, although the glass was far away from her now. Nevertheless, I realized that the Lord was slowly moving the glass toward her, and in the process, the light was growing more and more concentrated. In time, the light would form a focused beam and become very intense. When that happened, the concentrated light—depending upon her choice— would either burn out all her impurities or burn her up. Clearly, someone skilled and someone who knew Angela very well needed to be in charge of the magnifying glass. I understood that I was not that person. If I were holding the magnifying glass, I might incinerate Angela due to my impatience; but gratefully, the Lord held the glass, and He knew how to focus the light through the lens to purify her. His intention was to save and not to destroy her.

I gained an appreciation for the bishop's counsel. The gospel was truly a practical remedy for spiritual problems. If I simply focused on filling myself with light—Jesus said we are the light of the world—then I would gain the ability to cast a continual, bright beam on my daughter, which would illuminate her while the Lord worked the magnifying glass to concentrate the light. The Lord and I were partners in the light!

Angela has not totally forsaken her wayward ways, but my husband and I have noticed marked improvement. Recently she was involved in a serious accident that could have taken her life. Miraculously, she walked away unscathed, knowing that God had saved her and given her a second chance. There was no other explanation. She has given up alcohol and has begun to pray. Spiritual ideas nag at her constantly, as though she is under a persistent beam of light. She can't get those thoughts out of her mind. Now, when she brings them up of her own free will, we have opportunities to talk about the gospel. My husband I and know that Angela will return; it is just a matter of time. But in the meantime, we continue to try and bring more light into our lives.[286]

Sanctification makes us more in tune with the Lord's will. Being thus in tune allows us to pray with greater faith, which results in our requests being more frequently granted since we are already praying for that which we know to be the Lord's will. Our power to redeem is increased as we become more like Christ—more in tune with the will of our Father.

Consider Enos's example. He sanctified himself by first repenting. Yearning for the promise of eternal life and knowing that no unclean thing can dwell in God's presence,[287] he wrestled before God to receive a remission of sins. "And my soul hungered; and I kneeled down before my Maker, and I cried unto him in mighty prayer and supplication for mine own soul. . . . And there came a voice unto me, saying: Enos, thy sins are forgiven thee, and thou shalt be blessed."[288]

Notice that coupled with the Lord's assurance of forgiveness is His promise to Enos of future blessings—*The sanctified will be blessed.* Having achieved a higher level of sanctification, Enos immediately began to seek

---

286 See pp. 283–284
287 See 3 Nephi 27:19.
288 Enos 1:4–5.

for those promised blessings, which included the power to seek redemptive power for an increasing number of people. He had the confidence to seek these blessings because the Lord had promised, "Whatsoever thing ye shall ask in faith, believing that ye shall receive in the name of Christ, ye shall receive it."[289] First, Enos gained power to ask the Lord to bless his people [his family]: "I began to feel a desire for the welfare of my brethren, the Nephites; wherefore, I did pour out my whole soul unto God for them."[290] Then, having received the Lord's promise to bless his family, Enos's power to redeem increased, which is an important principle: the redeemed gain power to become the redeemers, and as they continue to sanctify themselves the power to redeem grows within them so that they might influence a greater number of people.

Now that Enos's faith "began to be unshaken in the Lord,"[291] he prayed for his enemies—those estranged family members who opposed him: "I prayed unto [God] with many long strugglings for my brethren, the Lamanites. And it came to pass that after I had prayed and labored with all diligence, the Lord said unto me: I will grant unto thee according to thy desires, because of thy faith."[292] The redemptive promise that Enos then received had eternal implications. It would transcend Enos's mortal life and extend to the coming forth of the Book of Mormon, which book would redeem his brethren and prepare the world for the Second Coming of Jesus Christ. Such was the redemptive power given to one man who persisted in the sanctification process, prayed blessings down upon his troubled family, and claimed the associated blessings.

Similarly, Joseph, who was sold into Egypt, sanctified himself during his fourteen-year ordeal in Pharaoh's prison. Catherine Thomas wrote, "Our ancestor and patriarch Joseph, who was sold into Egypt, was the model for us as he sanctified himself to have a sanctifying influence on his very troubled family and, like his Savior, exercised a saving power on his brethren."[293] We, who are Joseph's children

---

289 Enos 1:15.
290 Enos 1:9.
291 Enos 1:11.
292 Enos 1:11–12.
293 M. Catherine Thomas, "Alma the Younger, Part 1," Neal A. Maxwell Institute for Religious Scholarship.

(or otherwise born of or adopted into Israel), enjoy the blessings of Joseph's sanctification. Just so, parents who are willing to sanctify themselves obtain power to save their troubled children and bless their family for many generations.

Nancy, a mother of five from Idaho, recalled her response to her bishop's counsel regarding her wayward son:

> My husband and I were terribly worried about our son. We had been praying to know what course to take when the bishop invited us to his office to discuss the matter. None of the things he asked us to do were extraordinary, only things that we should have been doing anyway.
>
> We committed to reconsider our covenants and callings and try to do a little better. That included temple attendance. We had been going to the temple monthly, and now we increased our attendance to twice a month so we could do proxy work in combination with placing our son's name on the temple roll. I know that this formula might not be for everyone, but it was our bishop's counsel to us, and so we followed it.
>
> His promise, as the representative of Jesus Christ to us, was that our son would be presented with an Alma experience—a realization of his bad behavior with a clear choice to change. We prayed that he would not only have the experience but also choose the right "when the choice was placed before him."
>
> The result was beyond our comprehension. After several months, my husband and I knelt one morning and prayed again for a conversion opportunity for our boy. That same morning, he took off with a friend for what we were sure would be another wild weekend. But en route, they had a terrible accident. Our son was life-flighted to a hospital. Although he only sustained a broken leg and some minor injuries, the outcome could have been much worse. And he knew it. He realized that God had miraculously spared his life, and he knew he had to do something about it—right now!

He made an immediate change. When he was able, he asked for an interview with the bishop; he confessed his sins, and then he started down the long road of repentance. Over the next year, his change was so complete that he was able to serve a mission. Today, he has a wonderful temple marriage and two darling children. My husband and I believe that our recommitment to our covenants and following our bishop's counsel brought power to our prayers that opened the door for the Lord to offer our son a way out.

The Savior's example of personal sanctification teaches us that we can sanctify ourselves and thus sanctify others by focusing on fundamental gospel principles and commandments, such as increasing our *obedience,* worthily partaking of the *sacrament, fasting* with purpose, attending the *temple,* and offering *mighty prayer* coupled with *sacrifice.*

With regard to offering sacrifice, interestingly, the sacrifice that seems to be most Christlike—or Saviorlike—is vicarious sacrifice, or proxy sacrifice. Is it any wonder, then, that some of the most powerful prayers that we offer are in the temple *after* we have performed a vicarious sacrifice for someone who could not otherwise achieve salvation?

Understanding, therefore, that it is personal sanctification that empowers us to do the work of redemption, let us examine the example of Jesus in the areas of obedience, partaking of the sacrament, fasting, sacrifice, and mighty prayer.

OBEDIENCE

A man from Pennsylvania remembered his seminary teacher's extraordinary example of obedience:

I grew up in a little branch in Pennsylvania. I was the only LDS student in my high school, and our seminary teacher was a woman in the branch, who I will call "Sister Williams." She had joined the Church by herself several years earlier; neither her husband nor her five children joined. Her husband was supportive but otherwise uninterested. I knew the children, especially the boys, who were the definition of hooligans.

Sister Williams had volunteered to teach seminary and I was one her five students. We came to the branch building twice a month on Sundays from a radius of sixty miles. I remember very clearly that Sister Williams said that she held family home evening in her home each week. Knowing her kids, I wondered how she managed that feat. They despised the Church. I soon learned that she held it with only herself. She told us that even though her family would not join with her in family home evening, she was going to hold it faithfully because the prophet had promised that great blessings would follow: "If the [families] obey this counsel, we promise that great blessings will result. Love at home and obedience to parents will increase. Faith will be developed in the hearts of the youth of Israel, and they will gain power to combat the evil influences and temptations which beset them."[294] It was a principle with a promise, she would tell us, and she was going to be obedient to it. I remember thinking that this [promise] was going to be pretty tough for the Lord [to fulfill], given the condition of Sister Williams's family. Although I believed that the Lord could do anything, I was not optimistic in this case.

I was closest in age to two of her boys; one was a couple of grades ahead of me and one was a grade behind me. They were both hanging out with bad company and doing terrible things. The younger boy, who I will call "Jim," was the worst. Jim was the leader of a gang that terrorized the town and school. I always saw him smoking before, during, and after school, drinking and doing drugs. He openly flaunted his lifestyle, and he was the central figure in most of the school brawls. Jim knew that I was a Mormon, but he never

---

294 The First Presidency, *Improvement Era*, 1915, Volume 18, 734.

tried to hide his behavior from me. We never fought, thank goodness, but I remember feeling anger towards him because of how he was disgracing and openly disrespecting his mother by his actions. I truly felt embarrassed for Sister Williams, and at the same time, I was amazed that she could persevere in so faithfully holding family home evening year after year when her children seemed to be growing steadily worse.

After I graduated from high school, I received a mission call to the Utah Salt Lake City mission. When I had been out a year, I was laboring in Utah County. One Tuesday morning I received permission to take my district to a devotional where President Spencer W. Kimball was going to speak. As I was hustling to get a good seat in BYU's Marriott Center, I heard someone call out my name. I turned around and saw a nice-looking, clean-cut young man whom I did not recognize. We exchanged pleasantries for a few minutes, but I still could not place him. Then he smiled and said, "I am Jim Williams." My jaw dropped to the floor. The last time I saw Jim, his hair was hanging down to the middle of his back and it stuck out from his head about as far. I had always seen him wearing ratty clothes, he smelled like a smoke bomb most of the time, and his eyes always looked glazed. Finally, as I looked hard, I thought I could recognize his face.

He must have noticed my shock. He embraced me heartily and laughed again. That gave me the courage to ask him what had happened to him. He said he hadn't graduated from high school, which didn't surprise me. Instead, he had decided to hitchhike to California. On the way, he stopped in Utah and stayed for a few days, then a week, and then a month. He was so impressed with the people that he'd hooked up with that he decided to meet with the missionaries. Soon he got a job, cut his hair, cleaned up his life—cold turkey! Later, he was baptized, and now he had set his sights on serving a mission. Now I was completely floored. But he certainly looked like a missionary that day: white shirt and tie. It was great!

We exchanged phone numbers, and a couple of weeks later we did missionary splits together. We shared some very spiritual moments. Jim went on to straighten out his schooling and his life, and about a year later he was able to serve a mission. When he returned, he married a wonderful woman in the temple, and today they have four children. Eventually, his two brothers and two sisters joined the Church and married in the temple. Sister Williams's husband was also baptized and served faithfully in the branch for many years. He took Sister Williams and his children to the temple, where they were sealed together for eternity. When Brother Williams retired, he and his wife served two missions.

Prior to my meeting Jim that day in the Marriott Center, I really had thought he'd been one of Satan's hosts who had somehow slipped through the cracks. But I have since repented. What has always struck me is the amazing miracle that happened in the Williams family because of the faith and obedience of a mother who believed in the Lord enough to persist against all odds. When I miss family home evening in my own home, I am reminded of Sister Williams's example, and I regroup and set out to be more obedient.

God places enormous weight on obedience, this "first law of heaven."[295] In the beginning, God created a master law—obedience—on which all other *specific* laws are dependent: "There is a [master] law, irrevocably decreed in heaven before the foundations of this world, upon which all [specific] blessings are predicated—And when we obtain any [specific] blessing from God, it is by obedience to that [specific] law upon which . . . [that specific blessing] is predicated."[296]

---

295 George D. Watt, ed., *Journal of Discourses*, Volume 16, 248.
296 D&C 130:20–21; commentary added.

Also, "For all who will have a blessing at my hands shall abide the [specific] law which was appointed for that [specific] blessing, and the conditions thereof, as were instituted from before the foundation of the world."[297] Because God is a God of truth and cannot lie,[298] the promised blessings for obedience to any specific law are certain under the terms of the *master* law of obedience. "What I the Lord have spoken, I have spoken, and I excuse not myself; and though the heavens and the earth pass away, my word shall not pass away, but shall all be fulfilled, whether by mine own voice or by the voice of my servants, it is the same."[299] The Lord binds Himself to deliver the promised blessings associated with every obeyed law: "I, the Lord, am bound when ye do what I say; but when ye do not what I say, ye have no promise."[300]

Obedience is always accomplished by sacrifice; if nothing else, by the sacrifice of our wills or temporal priorities. "Verily I say unto you, all among them who know their hearts are honest, and are broken, and their spirits contrite, and are willing *to observe their covenants by sacrifice—yea, every sacrifice which I, the Lord, shall command*—they are accepted of me."[301] Two separate sets of parents I know had children who announced that they were gay. Clive and Jennifer objected to what they perceived as the Church's "unfair, harsh judgment" of their son and abandoned their membership altogether. They could not sacrifice their pride or allegiance with their son. Their attempt to *punish* the Church as a means of supporting their son did not change the Church or their son. But what they did succeed in accomplishing was risking their eternal salvation, marriage, and family. Though parents might find it difficult to determine exactly how to support and love their child without supporting the sin, we cannot make a problem better by abandoning our covenants. The Lord will help couples do this the right way. For instance, the other couple, Dan and Rita, dealt with the same issue by redoubling their efforts to live their covenants. They tried harder to sanctify themselves. While

297 D&C 132:5; commentary added.
298 See Ether 3:12.
299 D&C 1:38.
300 D&C 82:10.
301 D&C 97:8; emphasis added.

their daughter has not yet abandoned her gay lifestyle, Dan and Rita's marriage is solidly rooted in their obedience to their covenants, and their relationship with their daughter is healthy. These mutually inclusive commitments to covenants and relationships provide a foundation upon which the Lord can build a redeeming opportunity for their daughter, and their obedience gives Dan and Rita the assurance of eternal marriage and eternal family relationships. The disposition to be obedient by sacrificing has the power to sanctify a person. Clearly, as the scriptures dictate, parents who strive to sanctify themselves through obedience will gain greater power to rescue their wayward children.

Specific Blessings for Obedience

What blessings can parents of wayward children expect to claim by their obedience to God's laws? Adam's example is prime.[302] After Adam had obediently sacrificed for many days, an angel of the Lord appeared to him and proclaimed the Atonement of Jesus Christ. The angel's message was one of redemption and sanctification. Now that Adam had experienced personal redemption, he was empowered to help redeem others by bringing them to Christ. "And Adam and Eve blessed the name of God, and they made all things known unto their sons and their daughters."[303] Notice that Adam had observed the law of obedience by long years of sacrificing, and now he was rewarded with the blessings associated with the law of obedience, which blessings were his personal redemption and his increased capacity to help to redeem his children.

Our effort to obey is always worth the price. Adam discovered that obedience results in greater knowledge and understanding of God and His purposes, and we are told that those who are willing to live the law of obedience will "have glory added upon their heads for ever and ever."[304] Obedience results in "liberty and eternal life,"[305] the very blessings we seek for our children. The discipline of obedience requires "the heart and a willing mind," with this supernal

---

302 See Moses 5:5–8.
303 Moses 5:12.
304 Abraham 3:26.
305 2 Nephi 2:27.

blessing: "the willing and obedient shall eat the good of the land of Zion in these last days."[306] Clearly, increasing our level of obedience increases our level of sanctification, which empowers us to petition blessings for us and our children.

THE SACRAMENT

Worthily partaken of and understood, the sacrament, like obedience, sanctifies us. The sacrament serves to align our lives with Jesus Christ like a compass aligns us. When we are faced with a child who is off course, a most useful, redeeming tool for parents is to remain on course. The sacrament, Dan and Rita said, was the single gospel principle upon which they relied to weekly anchor them to their covenants and to infuse them with power to press forward in faith and hope.

The ordinances of the sacrament and baptism are interconnected. Baptism is the covenant of salvation;[307] Jesus Christ is the agent of salvation. When we renew our baptismal covenants by partaking of the sacrament, we should recommit to the terms of baptism that ensure our salvation, and we should recommit our lives to Jesus Christ. The major purpose of our gathering in sacrament meeting is to partake of the sacrament. "When ye come together therefore into one place, is it not to eat the Lord's supper?"[308] The Apostle Paul suggests three great purposes for the sacrament:

- The sacrament is a *memorial.* "This do ye . . . in remembrance of me."[309]
- The sacrament is a *testimonial.* When we partake, we "shew the Lord's death till he come."[310] (Note that the word *shew* means to "proclaim or announce.")
- The sacrament is an *examination.* "But let a man examine himself."[311]

---

306 D&C 64:34.
307 See Bruce R. McConkie, *Mormon Doctrine,* "Abrahamic Covenant," 13.
308 JST 1 Corinthians 11:20.
309 1 Corinthians 11:25.
310 1 Corinthians 11:26.
311 1 Corinthians 11:28.

When we partake of the sacrament, do we fulfill these three main purposes? Do we rejoice in our recollection of the wonder and majesty of the Atonement? Does our partaking of the sacrament testify of our faith in the Redeemer? Do we look closely at our lives to see if we are worthy and if we are conducting ourselves as disciples ought? Each parent who contributed stories to this book testified that the sacrament, because it focuses on our relationship with Jesus Christ, brought them comfort, purpose, hope, and the power to face their challenges and to obtain divine assistance for their children.

The Sacrament and the Holy Ghost

Nothing in the process of redeeming a wayward child is as essential as having the guidance of the Holy Ghost. The sacrament's sanctifying promise is the constant companionship of the Holy Ghost: "Those who partake of the sacrament place themselves under covenant with the Lord to take upon them the name of Christ, to always remember him, and to keep his commandments. The Lord in turn covenants that they may always have his Spirit to be with them."[312] This implication is often missed. When we are baptized and confirmed, we are commanded to "receive the Holy Ghost." Elder Bruce R. McConkie points out that this commandment is also a gift—a *right,* not a guarantee—"based on faithfulness, to the constant companionship of the member of the Godhead. It is the right to receive revelation, guidance, light, and truth."[313] Our ability to *retain* the companionship of the Holy Ghost is apparently dependent upon our honoring our baptismal covenants by means of the sacrament. That is, the sacrament is the ordinance that makes retention of the Holy Ghost possible. Elder Dallin H. Oaks said, "When we worthily partake of the sacrament, we are promised that we will 'always have his Spirit to be with [us].' To qualify for that promise we covenant that we will 'always remember him' (D&C 20:77)."[314] Because we enjoy the constant companionship of the Holy Ghost, we enjoy the constant sanctifying power of that gift, which sanctification, in addition to all other considerations, enables us to seek redeeming blessings for those whom we love.

---

312 *Encyclopedia of Mormonism,* "Sacrament," 1243–1244.

313 Bruce R. McConkie, "Gift of the Holy Ghost," *Mormon Doctrine,* 312.

314 Dallin H. Oaks, "Pornography," *Ensign,* May 2005, 88.

The Holy Ghost is the *Sanctifier.* Receipt of the Holy Ghost is called the baptism of fire, which follows the baptism by water. We are immersed both in water and in the Spirit. Remission of sins is not possible without the baptism of fire. Of the necessity of these two baptisms, the Prophet Joseph Smith said, "You might as well baptize a bag of sand as a man, if not done in view of the remission of sins and getting of the Holy Ghost. Baptism by water is but half a baptism, and is good for nothing without the other half—that is, the baptism of the Holy Ghost."[315] Because "no unclean thing can dwell in a divine presence," and because "people are saved to the extent that they are sanctified,"[316] we cherish and rely on the Holy Ghost, who burns out of us all impurities and creates of us a "new creature."[317]

As its name implies, baptism by fire is *hot.* Malachi described the work of the Lord and His agent, the Holy Ghost, as a refiner's fire.[318] Both the Savior and the Holy Ghost are engaged in the work of refining souls. This knowledge is important to parents of wayward children and speaks to the theme of this book: *the redeemed become the redeemers.* Our ability to rescue and redeem a wayward soul is directly linked to our level of sanctification. Therefore, we are told that before we attempt to pluck out the mote in another's eye we must first excise the beam from our own.[319] That process requires the Holy Ghost. As we pray for the Lord's help to rescue our children, we might be surprised that He focuses His attention on us first. The Lord might use the child's situation to sanctify us. If we will submit to the refiner's fire, once we emerge from it, we will be in a much better position to help our children when they experience it.

Elder Bruce R. McConkie wrote of the sacramental covenant and the Holy Ghost as paths to redemption:

> Those who partake of the sacrament worthily thereby put themselves under covenant with the Lord: 1. To

---

315 Robert, B. H., *History of The Church of Jesus Christ of Latter-day Saints,* Volume 5, 499.
316 *Encyclopedia of Mormonism,* "Holy Ghost," 649–650.
317 2 Corinthians 5:17.
318 See Malachi 3:2.
319 See Matthew 7:3–4.

always remember the broken body and spilled blood of Him who was crucified for the sins of the world; 2. To take upon themselves the name of Christ and always remember him; and 3. To keep the commandments of God, that is, to "live by every word that proceedeth forth from the mouth of God." (D&C 84:44.)

As his part of the contract, the Lord covenants: 1. That such worthy saints shall have his Spirit to be with them; and 2. That in due course they shall inherit eternal life. (D&C 20:75–79; Moro. 4; 5.) "Whoso eateth my flesh, and drinketh my blood, hath eternal life; and I will raise him up at the last day." (John 6:54.) In the light of these covenants, promises, and blessings, is it any wonder that the Lord commanded: "It is expedient that the church meet together often to partake of bread and wine in the remembrance of the Lord Jesus." (D&C 20:75; *Doctrines of Salvation*, Volume 2, 338–350.)"[320]

Coming to the Altar of Sacrifice

Each Sunday our attention should be focused on the sacramental table—the altar of sacrifice—where the priests of God prepare emblems of bread and water that remind us of the Lord's sacrifice. Jesus said that He is the Bread of Life[321] and the Living Water.[322] In the sacramental covenant, both parties sacrifice for and make promises to each other. The Lord's promise is the constant companionship of the Holy Ghost; our promises are those that we made at baptism, specifically, to take upon us the name of Christ, to always remember Him, and to keep His commandments. His sacrifice is His body and His blood; our sacrifice is a "broken heart and a contrite spirit."[323] The altar is where all of this takes place. The priests of God prepare and consecrate the sacrifice and set forth the terms of the covenant. (Interestingly, in Old Testament times, the sacrificing of a lamb, which foreshadowed the sacrifice of *the* Lamb, involved a person coming to

---

320 Bruce R. McConkie, "Sacrament," *Mormon Doctrine*, 660.
321 See John 6:35.
322 See John 4:10.
323 D&C 59:8.

the altar, laying his sacrifice upon it, symbolically transferring his sins to the sacrificial lamb by the laying on of hands, and then—after offering a prayer of atonement—the priests would *slay* the lamb and the person's sins would die with it.)[324]

Today, the sacrament, like the Passover, is the memorial of our salvation and deliverance. That single hope should sink deeply within our souls as we consider the Atonement's saving and liberating implications for our children. By living in a way that we always honor our baptismal covenants, we "retain a remission of our sins,"[325] "and the remission of sins bringeth meekness, and lowliness of heart; *and because of meekness and lowliness of heart cometh the visitation of the Holy Ghost,* which Comforter filleth with hope and perfect love, which love endureth by diligence unto prayer, until the end shall come, when all the saints shall dwell with God."[326] The promise of the Holy Ghost is unequalled: "The Holy Ghost shall be thy constant companion, and thy scepter an unchanging scepter of righteousness and truth; and thy dominion shall be an everlasting dominion, and without compulsory means it shall flow unto thee forever and ever."[327]

Therefore—and in no other way—by the simple, sanctifying act of worthily partaking of the sacrament, we renew our baptismal covenants and secure the promise that we received in our confirmation of the constant companionship of the Holy Ghost. And we know that it is the Holy Ghost who sanctifies us, which sanctification fills us with power to rescue our wayward children.

FASTING COUPLED WITH PRAYER

To fast is to go without food or drink for a dedicated period of time.[328] Fasting is a powerful principle of sanctification, which carries with it specific promises to repair family problems. Remember the bishop from Idaho mentioned earlier? He recounted one of his three success experiences that began with fasting:

---

324 See *Old Testament Student Manual 301,* 164.
325 Mosiah 4:12.
326 Moroni 8:26; emphasis added.
327 D&C 121:46.
328 See Joseph Fielding Smith, *Gospel Doctrine,* 243.

I received mixed responses when I approached the parents of four wayward boys in my ward and asked those parents to sanctify themselves and pray for a conversion opportunity to come to their sons. [In one case] because one mother was lukewarm about the idea, I took another approach. I called a meeting with some men who were influential in the boy's life: my counselors, the boy's Young Men leader, his Sunday School teacher, and even his coach at school. I explained the boy's situation and asked them to join with me in a fast. Then I asked them to pray and go to the temple to determine what the Lord would have them do to help the boy. A week later we met again and talked about our impressions. Each man had received specific instructions from the Spirit. We set about to do what the Lord had told us, and in a short period of time, the boy ceased his downward slide, repented, and made a full about-face to genuine activity in the Church. Within nine months, he was serving a mission.

Fasting and prayer are interconnected. President Benson said, "To make a fast most fruitful, it should be coupled with prayer and meditation . . . and it's a blessing if one can ponder on the scriptures and the reason for the fast."[329] Fasting and prayer are commandments of God;[330] therefore, as then Elder Spencer W. Kimball wrote, "Failing to fast is a sin."[331] Elder Delbert L. Stapley taught that fasting and prayer are principles of great spiritual power and strength, the opportunity of which summons the blessings of God. Then he made the sad observation that members of the Church are remiss in availing ourselves of this power, which can be employed to bless others.[332]

There is another principle here, a principle we will discuss later in more detail: the power of several people united in purpose and faith as they fast and pray. This principle of multiple voices united in prayer

---

329 Ezra Taft Benson, "Do Not Despair," *Ensign,* November 1974.
330 D&C 59:13–14.
331 Spencer W. Kimball, *The Miracle of Forgiveness,* 98.
332 See Delbert L. Stapley, *Conference Report,* October 1951, 122.

and fasting is the power that this wise bishop drew upon to rescue the wayward youths in his ward.

Great blessings flow from fasting and prayer. Elder Bruce R. McConkie said, "Fasting . . . gives a man a sense of his utter dependence upon the Lord so that he is in a better frame of mind to get in tune with the Spirit."[333] Moreover, he noted, fasting and prayer increase spirituality, foster devotion and love of God, increase faith, encourage humility and contrition of soul, and hasten us along the path to salvation.[334]

The prophet Isaiah listed some of the extraordinary blessings that flow from fasting and prayer. As you read these blessings, imagine how fasting and prayer could sanctify and empower you to rescue your children. Fasting and prayer:

- Loosen "the bands of wickedness."
- Undo "heavy burdens."
- Let "the oppressed go free."
- Break "every yoke that binds you."

Fasting also results in the following:

- "Thy light shall break forth as the morning." [The light of Christ will fill you.]
- "Thine health shall spring forth speedily." [Physical, spiritual, and emotional health will return to you quickly.]
- "Thy righteousness shall go before thee." [Your righteousness will precede you, prepare the way, and ensure your future.]
- "The glory of the Lord shall be thy rereward." [Spiritual protection.]
- "Then shalt thou call, and the Lord shall answer." [Your prayers will become more powerful.]
- "Thou shalt cry, and [God] shall say, Here I am." [Your prayers will become more intimate.]

---

333 Bruce R. McConkie, *The Mortal Messiah,* Volume 2, 152.
334 See Bruce R. McConkie, *Mormon Doctrine,* "Fasting," 276.

- "Thy light shall rise in obscurity, and thy darkness shall be as the noonday." [The darkness that has been in your life will dissipate.]
- "The Lord shall guide thee continually." [He will never leave you.]
- "The Lord shall satisfy thy soul in drought, and make fat thy bones: and thou shalt be like a watered garden, and like a spring of water, whose waters fail not." [Where you have experienced spiritual and emotional drought and starvation, the Lord will make you like the Garden of Eden. As you drink from the Living Waters, you will become the same: a spring capable of giving never-ending nourishment to those you love.][335]

Considering these blessings, who would not seek to observe the law of fasting and prayer? Furthermore, Isaiah taught that true fasting and prayer necessitate forgiving one another, neither assigning blame nor speaking ill nor clinging to pride to sooth our vanity.[336] Rather, true fasting and prayer draw out our souls in charity, "to [feed] the hungry . . . and satisfy the afflicted soul . . . [to] bring the poor that are cast out to thy house . . . [and] when thou seest the naked, that thou cover him."[337] Charity, of course, is the gift that we need to feed the spiritually hungry, minister to the afflicted, and rescue the poor and outcast. Isaiah can be interpreted as saying that fasting and prayer infuse us with power to draw our children back home, where we can lovingly clothe and cover them in the covenant. President Joseph F. Smith said, "The aim in fasting is to secure perfect purity of heart and simplicity of intention—a fasting unto God in the fullest and deepest sense—*for such a fast would be a cure for every practical and intellectual error.*"[338]

Fasting and Prayer Heal Families
As Isaiah and President Joseph F. Smith imply, fasting can heal our families.

---

335 Isaiah 58:6–12.
336 See Isaiah 58:9.
337 Isaiah 58:7, 10.
338 Joseph F. Smith, "Observance of Fast Day," *Improvement Era,* December 1902; emphasis added.

Gary, a father from northern Utah, recounted an experience with fasting that led to rescuing his daughter Pamela.

> After my divorce, my family splintered. Alternately, my children lived with my ex-wife or with me. My seventeen-year-old daughter, Pam, made a decision to permanently live with her mother, who had left the Church and was excommunicated for adultery. Pam bought into her mother's anti-LDS propaganda, especially the part about men controlling the Church, which filters down to men controlling their wives. Pam began to follow her mother's example of drinking, and she experimented with drugs. I remarried a wonderful woman, and together we began to pray and fast weekly for Pam. Often we would fast and attend the temple. We were in for a long exercise of endurance.
>
> After Pam received her college degree, she left for Europe and eventually hooked up with a man and moved in with him. During these heartbreaking years, we continued to fast, pray, and attend the temple in her behalf. We made the extra effort to stay in touch with Pam and keep her up-to-date on all the family news. At age twenty-six, she moved back to the United States, disillusioned with some of the [world views] that she had encountered [in Europe]. Pam had experienced enough of life to know that she wanted nothing to do with the kinds of lifestyles that she had seen, and she had decided that marriage and family were the best way to find happiness and individual fulfillment—the example that we had tried to set for her.
>
> An answer to our fasting and prayer came through our returned-missionary son, Devin, who realized that what his sister needed was fellowshipping. Thereafter, Devin and Pam were inseparable. He introduced her to his friends, took her to dances, and constantly hung out with her. He took her to institute and arranged for her to meet with the teacher and ask him questions. The

teacher kindly and intelligently fielded her questions about male/female relationships as they pertain to the gospel, and he gave her solid answers that satisfied her. One of our fasts resulted in a breakthrough—Pam began to read the Book of Mormon. That event gave her a testimony of the gospel, and finally we had our girl back. Today, Pam is thirty years old, active in the Church, dating within a choice group of LDS friends, and praying to find the right young man to take her to the temple. My wife and I believe that the price we paid to fast and pray often, coupled with attending the temple, directly rescued our daughter Pamela and brought her back to us.

Isaiah counseled, "Hide not thyself from thine own flesh [your own family]."[339] That is, love them, pray for them, and fast for them. We expect the Lord to stand by our children despite their waywardness. Would He not, therefore, expect the same of us? Our willingness to sanctify ourselves through fasting and prayer in behalf of our children and our continuing to love and reach out to them serve to repair relationships. Through fasting and prayer we sanctify ourselves to become, according to Isaiah, "the repairer of the breach."[340] That is, fasting and prayer empower us to repair anything that has torn the relationship apart.

Concerning our becoming repairers of the breach, Elder Bruce C. Hafen taught that we, through fasting and prayer and applying the Atonement of Jesus Christ, gain power to repair even generational family problems and to stop the "intergenerational flow of affliction," which plagues one generation of our family after another. These generational problems are often the reasons our children are presently suffering. Some damaging family traits reduce agency and continue to afflict several generations of a family. But by means of the sanctifying principles of faith, fasting, prayer, and diligence, these negative traits can be halted and severed. Repairers of the breach can seek heavenly power to ensure that those harmful traits will never again distress

339 Isaiah 58:8.
340 Isaiah 58:12.

subsequent generations. Elder Hafen said we can "fill the void left by a former generation and raise a new foundation for the next, thus repairing the breach in the intergenerational linkage: 'They that shall be of thee shall build the old waste places: thou shalt raise up the foundations of many generations; and thou shalt be called, The repairer of the breach; the restorer of paths to dwell in.' (Isa. 58:12)"[341]

Isaiah's doctrine is astonishing. Through focused fasting, our families, "they that shall be of thee," will "build the old waste places," that is, repair the injured souls or generations. What will be the result? "Thou shalt raise up the foundations of many generations [to follow]"; that is, you will help them lay a new foundation for their lives upon which salvation will come to them and to those of their subsequent generations. Therefore, you will be called, "The repairer of the breach"—the one who helps them overcome their weakness, repairs their broken lives, and brings them back to the correct path.[342]

Remarkably, Isaiah's language concerning generational healing might suggest that even our deceased loved ones could be healed and set free because of our becoming repairers of the breach to our families.

SACRIFICE AND PRAYER

The combination of sacrifice and prayer has always been part of the true gospel. Together, they summon unparalleled sanctifying blessings, which parents of wayward children must seek if they hope to develop redeeming power. Just as fasting (which is a sacrifice) is counted as nothing more than going hungry if it is not combined with prayer, so sacrifice is counted as nothing more than giving something up if it is not combined with prayer. Such a one-dimensional sacrifice can result in no compensating blessing. Speaking for the Lord, the prophet Isaiah directed us to sacrifice with a purpose. "To what purpose is the multitude of your sacrifices unto me? saith the LORD."[343] That is, sacrifice must have a defined purpose that we express in prayer; otherwise the sacrifice can achieve no sanctifying effect. On the other

---

341 Bruce C. Hafen and Marie K. Hafen, *The Belonging Heart: The Atonement and Relationships with God and Family Heart,* 119.

342 See also John H. Vandenberg, *Conference Report,* April 1963.

343 Isaiah 1:11.

hand, the combination of sacrifice and prayer constitutes a powerful form of worship that sanctifies us. Therefore, let us examine sacrifice and prayer individually and then the combination of the two.

Sacrifice

The dynamic principle of sacrifice propels personal sanctification, which we need in order to petition blessings for our children. As we practice this principle, we arrive at a point where we can ultimately make the sacrifice of all things. According to Joseph Smith, this sacrifice is *the* requirement for exalting salvation.[344] We make this sacrifice by continually recommitting to our covenants and by constantly sacrificing when opportunities are presented or when we seek them out. It stands to reason, then, that the greater our willingness and ability to sacrifice, the greater the blessings received. For parents of wayward children, the blessing that we seek is greater power to redeem, and so we must sacrifice.

The last couple that was counseled by the bishop from Idaho agreed to follow his instructions. They set out to sanctify themselves—sacrificing all previous priorities for the Lord—by recommitting themselves to their covenants; their church callings; the holding of family home evening; their temple attendance; and their personal, couple, and family prayers. In their prayers, they specifically asked the Lord to accept their sacrifice and present a "conversion opportunity" to their wayward son. The bishop's promise was that the boy would, in the Lord's time, come to a decision-making crossroads at which he would be presented with a clear choice and an invitation from the Lord. How the boy would respond to that opportunity would be according to his agency.

> We did everything that the bishop counseled. One day, our son's girlfriend broke up with him. He was so distraught that he felt he could no longer go on living, so he decided that taking his life was his only alternative. He climbed on his motorcycle, took off, and looked for a place to end it all. Soon he saw a wall. Closing his eyes, he headed for it at full speed.

344 Joseph Smith, *Lectures on Faith*, 6:7.

The next thing he knew, he was on the other side of the wall. Nothing had happened! He was so startled. He knew that the Lord had intervened and saved his life. Now the weight of his sins pressed upon him and he made his way to the bishop. When he entered the bishop's office one afternoon, he asked if the bishop would turn the lights off. He felt so dirty that he couldn't stand the light. For the next few hours, he confessed and wept bitterly.

Two days later, our son drove his bike to the bishop's house and invited him to go for a ride. The bishop hesitated, knowing this was the same bike that our son had been riding when he had tried to commit suicide. Nevertheless, he climbed aboard and they drove for a while. When they stopped, our son asked the bishop what it would take to serve a mission. "A long time," the bishop replied. Our son considered the bishop's answer then told him that he had been at work when a voice came into his mind and said, "You need to serve a mission."

To our utter amazement, our boy paid the full price required of him. When he finally had all the necessary interviews, he was cleared to serve. Today, he is married in the temple and is the father of three wonderful children. He received his education and is a very successful businessman. We attribute this miraculous change to our willingness to sanctify ourselves according to the bishop's counsel so that we could ask in faith as did Alma the Elder.

Sacrifice and Service

Jesus taught, "Inasmuch as ye have done it unto one of the least of these my brethren, ye have done it unto me."[345] Because we love the Lord, we seek to serve Him. But because He needs nothing, He instructs us to transfer our service or sacrifice to those who do need help—His children.

---

345 Matthew 25:40.

Jesus counts our service to His children as though we had done it unto Him.

Think of a time when someone blessed your life. Did you not feel indebted to that person and wish to repay her service with a greater service? What you felt was not really indebtedness or even—as some would presume—competition; it was simply a manifestation of the principle that like begets like.[346] In other words, good deeds beget good deeds. But for lack of a better term, we will describe this impulse as a symptom of *indebtedness*—we feel indebted when we are served, so we seek to repay the gift. Due to His infinite Atonement and the merciful plan of salvation, Jesus can be *in debt* to no one. But, when we serve His children, He rewards us beyond the value of our service, and thus we are always in debt to Him. King Benjamin said it this way: "He doth require that ye should do as he hath commanded you; for which if ye do, he doth immediately bless you; and therefore he hath paid you. And ye are still indebted unto him, and are, and will be, forever and ever."[347]

When we serve Christ's children, He repays us with blessings that sanctify us, which sanctification empowers us to bless more and serve more. And, of course, increased sanctification results in increased ability to ask for blessings to be poured out upon the heads of those we love—Christ's children.

As an example, it is upon this principle of *indebtedness and imbalance* that tithes and offerings work. Our meager payment of tithing's ten percent, along with fast offerings, is repaid magnanimously as the resources of heaven are poured out (not trickled) upon us until there is not enough room to hold them.[348] The ultimate example of this principle is the Atonement. Our meager agreement to enter into the new and everlasting covenant and to abide by its conditions is rewarded by the sacrifice of Jesus Christ, who *overpaid* the debt of our sins so much so that justice can never make a claim. In a like manner, when we sacrifice to serve one of Christ's children, He personally assumes the responsibility to recompense us; He pours out blessings far in excess of our effort. Thus we can never say that we give more

---

346 See D&C 88:38–40.
347 Mosiah 2:24.
348 See Malachi 3:10.

than He; we are always indebted to Him. Therefore, we should have no fear in the sacrifice of serving, blessing, and giving—even when our effort goes seemingly unappreciated. As a wise Indian proverb states, "All that is not given is lost."[349]

Vicarious Sacrifice Is Christlike Sacrifice

As mentioned at the beginning of this chapter, vicarious sacrifice is Christlike sacrifice, and thus it carries tremendous power. To use our body in serving someone who is disembodied, to act and speak in behalf of the deceased, to offer our time and effort to someone who has no power to function in a physical world where saving ordinances must be received and covenants must be consummated—all of these are acts of unselfish Christlike sacrifice and love. Elder John A. Widtsoe said that true love is evidenced and measured by sacrifice. This is the love that the Savior demonstrated when He gave His life for us. To sacrifice for someone who is powerless to help himself— that is, to stand in the stead of another—is the highest form of love because it is the most Christlike. This kind of love lifts us toward the likeness of God and Jesus Christ.[350]

We will speak more about this important principle later in this chapter as we note its value in relationship to prayer.

Prayer

Prayer is a commandment. Adam and Eve were commanded, "Thou shalt repent and call upon God in the name of the Son forevermore."[351] As with every law of God, the commandment to pray carries the promise of blessings: "And all things, whatsoever ye shall ask in prayer, believing, *ye shall receive*."[352] Other blessings attendant to prayer are gaining knowledge of the mysteries of God and receiving revelation that has never before been revealed to us *personally*, including line-upon-line guidance and instruction from God. "Yea, he that repenteth and exerciseth faith, and bringeth forth good works, and prayeth continually without ceasing—unto such it is given to know the mysteries of God;

---

349 CityofJoyAid.org.
350 See John A. Widtsoe, *Conference Report*, April 1943, 38.
351 Moses 5:8.
352 Matthew 21:22; emphasis added.

yea, unto such it shall be given to reveal things which never have been revealed."[353] Additionally, and of particular interest to parents of wayward children, is prayer's inherent power to bring souls to repentance: "Yea, and it shall be given unto such to bring thousands of souls to repentance, even as it has been given unto us to bring these our brethren to repentance."[354]

Emily from Georgia wrote,

> My brother, Sam, is now forty-nine years old. After he was ordained to the Aaronic Priesthood, he started going around with an undesirable crowd. Soon, he was doing most everything contrary to the way he was brought up. He was the black sheep of the family. No one wanted to deal with him. He was so obstinate that he would not listen to anyone. For years my mother would refer to him as "poor Sam." When I would ask her what we could do for him, her reply was simply, "Pray for him." For over thirty years, she prayed for him, and we children prayed for him, too. Every night I would ask Heavenly Father to watch over him, but inside I believed that there was no way that Sam would ever change. Then, two years ago, to our utter surprise, Sam called my brother out of the blue and told him that he wanted him to go with him through the temple. A year later, they both went through for Sam's endowments. He gave up smoking overnight. He stopped drinking completely. He gave up drugs and bad habits. He started going to church and now holds a calling. His testimony is one that no one can hear and forget. The power of persistent prayer *can* work miracles!

Prayer Is the Gateway to Revelation

Prayer opens the door to divine direction, inspiration, and instruction. If we truly desire to obtain God's perspective and His help regarding our children, we must pray. Moreover, we must prepare before we pray as Jesus prepared. Elder L. Lionel Kendrick taught that receiving

---

353 Alma 26:22.
354 Alma 26:22.

personal revelation requires our active involvement. Preparation is essential. According to President Kimball, God sends revelations to people who prepare themselves for sacred experiences. Such preparation includes faith, repentance, asking in prayer, obedience, scripture study, fasting, purity of thoughts, and a spirit of reverence.[355]

Prayer Accesses the Power to Give Life
We are taught that "the essential character of prayer" is "faith, sincerity, obedience and seeking."[356] When we pray with this attitude, we receive increased power to redeem others: "And this is the confidence that we have in him, that, if we ask any thing according to his will, he heareth us: And if we know that he hear us, whatsoever we ask, we know that we have the petitions that we desired of him. If any man see his brother sin a sin which is not unto death, he shall ask, *and he shall give him life*."[357]

Alma the Younger was *given life* by his sanctified father, who prayed for him. Therefore, when Alma the Younger was later faced with the daunting task of *giving life* to very wicked people and rescuing them from the chains of sin, he used the power of prayer to further sanctify himself so that he could obtain power from heaven to accomplish his mission. Through prayer he sought power to bear up under the weight of sorrow that he felt for the sins of his people, to gain strength to suffer with patience the afflictions that he would face as he worked with them, and to be given the Lord's assurance that he would eventually experience success. Parents of wayward children could easily personalize Alma's prayer:

> O Lord, my heart is exceedingly sorrowful; wilt thou comfort my soul in Christ. O Lord, wilt thou grant unto me that I may have strength, that I may suffer with patience these afflictions which shall come upon me, because of the iniquity of this people.
>
> O Lord, wilt thou comfort my soul, and give unto me success, and also my fellow laborers who are with me. . . .

---

355 See L. Lionel Kendrick, "Personal Revelation," *Ensign,* September 1999.
356 *Encyclopedia of Mormonism,* "Prayer," 1117–1118.
357 1 John 5:14–16; emphasis added.

Wilt thou grant unto them that they may have strength, that they may bear their afflictions which shall come upon them because of the iniquities of this people.

O Lord, wilt thou grant unto us that we may have success in bringing them again unto thee in Christ.

Behold, O Lord, their souls are precious . . . therefore, give unto us, O Lord, power and wisdom that we may bring these, our brethren, again unto thee.[358]

Our Hearts Must Be Right for Prayer

We cannot expect to receive answers to our prayers in behalf of our children without being *right* before God. *Rightness* brings forth prayer's promise—*to receive, to find, and to have doors opened.*[359] The following qualities make the heart right and prepare us for prayer:

And now I would that ye should be humble, and be submissive and gentle; easy to be entreated; full of patience and long-suffering; being temperate in all things; being diligent in keeping the commandments of God at all times; asking for whatsoever things ye stand in need, both spiritual and temporal; always returning thanks unto God for whatsoever things ye do receive.

And see that ye have faith, hope, and charity, and then ye will always abound in good works.[360]

Moreover, our relationships must be *right* for our prayers to be effective,[361] and our works must be worthy of a Saint: "I say unto you, do not suppose that this [prayer] is all; for after ye have done all these things, if ye turn away the needy, and the naked, and visit not the sick and afflicted, and impart of your substance, if ye have, to those who stand in need—I say unto you, *if ye do not any of these*

---

358 Alma 31:31–35; emphasis added.
359 See Matthew 7:7.
360 Alma 7:23–24.
361 See Matthew 6:14–15.

things, behold, your prayer is vain, and availeth you nothing, and ye are as hypocrites who do deny the faith."[362]

Praying for Our Enemies

We don't often think of our children as our enemies, but often wayward children are the enemies of our righteousness. Concerning our praying for our enemies, the prophet Zenos said, "Thou art merciful, O God, for thou hast heard my prayer . . . when I prayed concerning those who were mine enemies, and *thou didst turn them to me.*"[363] Jesus taught that our enemies are often "[those] of our [own] household,"[364] and gratefully, we see in Zenos's words a promise that prayer can turn them to us. The criterion for such a prayer is a pure heart. Those who seek to purify themselves, as did Alma the Elder, may likewise approach the Lord in behalf of their wayward children and receive this promise: "And if ye are purified and cleansed from all sin, ye shall ask whatsoever you will in the name of Jesus and it shall be done."[365] Clearly, we have scriptural evidence that this promise is and has been continually validated, even when we are facing the bitter opposition of those who can be defined as enemies in one sense or another.

Vicarious Sacrifice and Mighty Prayer in the Temple

Prayer does not necessarily qualify as mighty prayer simply because of its length or fervency. Prayer, I believe, also becomes mighty when it is *preceded* by sacrifice. As we have noted, Jesus sanctified Himself so that He could offer mighty prayer through His obedience, His partaking of the sacrament, fasting, and sacrifice.

In ancient times, such mighty prayers were offered at an altar in a temple setting. Imagine the level of faith exhibited by Adam, Noah, Abraham, Nephi, and others who built altars upon which they sacrificed and then prayed. The preparation time for such prayers would have been considerable. Typically, these righteous individuals had to gather and heft sufficient unhewn stones to a consecrated high

---

362 Alma 34:28; emphasis added.
363 Alma 33:4; emphasis added.
364 Matthew 10:36.
365 D&C 50:29.

place where they created a platform of adequate height, width, and depth. Once there, they sacrificed something very valuable. *After* they made their sacrifice, they knelt at the altar and offered mighty prayer. We note with interest that their effort was always rewarded with extraordinary blessings.

Perhaps today in a similar manner, the mightiest prayers that we can offer are at the altar of the holy temple *after* we have performed a sacrifice. There, at the altar, we place our prayers; then we add our faith to others', that our prayers might be answered. After having completed our sacrificial service, we are invited into the holy place that is symbolically nearest to God, where we continue to offer individual mighty prayer. Now, having sacrificed and prayed, as did Adam, Noah, Abraham, Nephi, and others, can we not expect the same blessings of the Lord?

Because proxy sacrifice is Christlike sacrifice, it is perhaps one of the greatest sacrifices of all. Jesus said, "Greater love hath no man than this, that a man lay down his life for his friends."[366] Taking Jesus as our example, whose proxy sacrifice exceeded all other sacrifices, we too can do for a helpless individual what he cannot do for himself. President Gordon B. Hinckley said, "Just as our Redeemer gave His life as a vicarious sacrifice for all men, and in so doing became our Savior, even so we, in a small measure, when we engage in proxy work in the temple, become as saviors to those on the other side who have no means of advancing unless something is done in their behalf by those on earth."[367] Thus, as we act as did the Savior, we become saviors on Mount Zion[368] and thereby place ourselves in a powerful position to receive answers to our prayers.

Having made our vicarious sacrifice, it is our turn to seek God on the other side of the veil. We then enter what is the holiest place on earth, and there we offer the prayers of our heart. These are mighty prayers. Would God not hear and honor such prayers after we make such a sacrifice? Many parents point to their sacrifice of attending the temple more regularly as *the* agent which attracted extraordinary help

---

366 John 15:13.

367 Gordon B. Hinckley, "Closing Remarks," *Ensign*, November 2004, 105.

368 See B. H. Roberts, *History of The Church of Jesus Christ of Latter-day Saints,* Volume 4, 359–360.

from heaven to rescue their children. Truly, vicarious sacrifice makes prayer mighty, and such a prayer offered in the temple seems to carry increased redeeming weight.

Many people have felt that the deceased people for whom they performed vicarious ordinances have subsequently aided them, as a gesture of thanks, with their wayward children. Might it be possible, then, to assemble a veritable army of family and friends among both the dead and the living to help you?

Furthermore, in the temple we are taught that multiple voices raised in prayer summon blessings from heaven. As we place the names of our children upon the prayer rolls of the temple, they are being prayed for at the altars of sacrifice in a most powerful priesthood manner and in a most sacred setting.

One man who had just learned that he had cancer sat in church one Sunday contemplating the many friends and family members who had placed his name on the prayer rolls of the temple and who were fasting and praying for him that day. Suddenly, he felt an overwhelming power settle upon him—something tangible, as though he were being enveloped in a strong yet loving embrace. In the midst of the experience he heard the Spirit whisper, "These are the prayers."

Every Prayer Counts

Because prayer opens the door through which blessings can flow from God,[369] someone, somewhere, must ask. Elder Boyd K. Packer taught that inspiration flows by asking, *or by someone asking for you.*[370] According to the LDS Bible Dictionary, God has determined that asking in prayer is the means whereby we may obtain the highest of all blessings.[371] In some way that we do not fully understand, the unity of multiple people praying multiple times carries *weight* that attracts the Lord's favor.

Evan, now in his fifties, recalled a time when his father called his family together to pray for a wayward daughter. Evan was six years old at the time. The daughter was hardened with her sins, which were

---

369 See LDS Bible Dictionary, "Prayer," 752–753.
370 See Boyd K. Packer, "Personal Revelation: The Gift, the Test and the Promise," *Ensign,* November 1994.
371 See LDS Bible Dictionary, "Prayer," 752–753.

many. Later, the father brought the girl into a family gathering that amounted to an intervention. But rather than being confrontational, the meeting was one of love. One by one, each family member expressed his or her love for the daughter and the desire that the girl would forsake her ways and return to the family. When it came to six-year-old Evan's turn, he wept uncontrollably as he told his sister how, over the last weeks, he had prayed for her night and day. Ten years later, when the girl finally started to show signs of softening, she pointed to that night and her little brother's declaration of love. She said, "I felt the walls of my rebellion begin to crumble when I realized how fervently little Evan was praying for me. Something began to work on me, and I could no longer maintain my sinful ways without putting forth an enormous effort."

If the scriptures teach us anything, it is that the most sinful person can be prayed for and reached, after all. Otherwise, why would we have the stories of Paul, Alma, the sons of Mosiah, the Ammonites, and many others? Why would Mormon make such a point concerning Alma's grandsons, Nephi and Lehi (whom we could liken to two parents),[372] who prayed and sanctified themselves and then gained the power to convert a gross and sinful nation? Wasn't Mormon trying to teach us something? Mighty prayer increases our level of sanctification, which increases our ability to redeem others. May we take advantage of such power.

---

372 See Helaman chapters 4–11.

Chapter 7
BLESSINGS FROM WORKING WITH A WAYWARD CHILD

The greatest force in all the world [is] to develop character, to bring righteousness into the lives of men and women.

—*Elder Matthew Cowley*[373]

WHAT'S IN THIS FOR ME? It is not necessarily a selfish question. Peter asked and was given an answer to this same query. Parents might apply the interchange between Peter and Jesus to themselves: "We have forsaken all, and followed thee; what shall we have therefore? And Jesus said unto them . . . Every one that hath forsaken houses, or brethren, or sisters, or father, or mother, or wife, or children, or lands, for my name's sake, shall receive an hundredfold, and shall inherit everlasting life."[374]

Sacrifices made for the sake of Christ's work are rewarded "an hundredfold" and with "everlasting life"! Persistently and righteously dealing with a wayward child is counted as a sacrifice in time and self-lessness, among other things.

When adversity strikes, we often focus on what it is doing *to* us rather than what it is doing *for* us. The process of experiencing adversity is designed to chip away at our rough edges and strengthen muscles of character and spirituality that are essential to becoming gods. Joseph Smith said, "I am like a huge, rough stone rolling down from a high mountain; and the only polishing I get is when some corner gets rubbed off by coming in contact with something

---

373 Matthew Cowley, *Matthew Cowley Speaks*, 47.
374 Matthew 19:27–29.

else . . . all hell knocking off a corner here and a corner there. Thus I will become a smooth and polished shaft in the quiver of the Almighty."[375]

Adversity is painful but necessary for spiritual fervency. As long as the brother of Jared was struggling in the wilderness, he offered consistent, urgent prayer, which not only guided him day by day but also opened the windows of heaven to the vast library of celestial truth. But when he experienced a season of calm, he, one of the greatest prophets, became spiritually lax, for which the Lord severely chastised him.[376] Likewise, because the Lord wants us to keep growing in spirituality and moving toward exaltation, He will give us pressing reasons to pray (praying for a wayward child is an example). The present adversity simply acts as a catalyst to bring us to the Lord. The brother of Jared prayed to overcome the adversity of darkness in his barges and he was brought into the presence of the Lord.[377] Joseph Smith prayed for deliverance from Liberty Jail and was blessed with astounding information about the functions and promises of the priesthood.[378] Abraham prayed for deliverance from the wicked priest of Elkenah and was given an amazing promise of priesthood ministry through which all of God's children would be blessed.[379] These prophets received answers to their individual prayers, but the Lord had even more to give them. Adversity got them there. Praying over anything, even wayward children, can unlock the treasury of heaven. Contemplated in this light, then, adversity can be a gift. Humans seem to be naturally incapable of maintaining mighty prayer without the motivator of adversity.

Remembering Lehi's exposition on the law of opposites, we learn that adversity is also essential for happiness to exist.[380] We wouldn't know joy for what it was without pain to compare it to. In addition, *happiness* is only one of the rewards for enduring adversity in faith; *gain* is another: God "shall consecrate thine afflictions for thy

---

375 Joseph Fielding Smith, ed., *Teachings of the Prophet Joseph Smith*, 304.
376 See Ether 1–2.
377 See Ether 2–3.
378 See D&C 121.
379 See Abraham 1:15–19.
380 See 2 Nephi 2:11.

gain."[381] Like the examples of the brother of Jared, Joseph Smith, and Abraham, compensation that goes beyond the price of our present adversity occurs when God consecrates our afflictions for our gain. Heavenly Father enjoys the perfection of this principle; He deals with the adversity of wayward children all the time and yet describes His life as having a "fulness of joy."[382] That fact should give us hope as we progress toward godhood; we should remember that our adversity will not always overwhelm us but will actually propel us into a life of complete joy.

Sometimes we may feel exhausted in trying to comprehend all that is required of us to reach this eternal goal. One exasperated father who was struggling with a rebellious son, joked, "The terrestrial kingdom is looking better and better all the time." We might feel the same way—*Is forever dealing with difficult children the definition of heaven?* Perhaps understanding the opportunity in adversity might help us set our sights higher.

But our residence is not yet the celestial kingdom. For now the scales are tipped in favor of adversity, not joy. To help us arrive where He is at, be like He is, and experience a fulness of joy, Heavenly Father is not timid about allowing us to confront adversity. Because we desired to become like Him and covenanted do His redeeming work, should we be surprised that He takes our desires and our covenants seriously and therefore hands us redeeming assignments? The work of redemption can be long-term, excruciating work, but, as missionaries can testify, no work is more satisfying to the soul than that of redemption. Or, as parents can testify, the only joy greater than giving physical life is giving spiritual life—that is, to see their children turn from error and discover the safety and joy of living righteous lives. Likewise, the only pain worse than physical pain is spiritual pain.

A mother in Arizona wrote,

> Nothing could have prepared me for the excruciating pain of my first delivery. I had thought that I wanted to have the *full experience,* so I turned down the epidural. I did fine for the first few hours, and

---

381 2 Nephi 2:2.
382 3 Nephi 28:10.

then my water broke. The sudden, blinding pain was more than I could bear, and I was only dilated to three—I had hours to go. When the nurse offered me the epidural, I gladly agreed. In fact, when the doctor was delayed because he was treating another patient, I began to panic. I couldn't get relief from the pain fast enough. At the time, I thought, *Who would knowingly go through pregnancy and delivery again?* But for as much pain as I experienced that day, it was nothing compared to the spiritual suffering I experienced when that same, sweet little boy abandoned the Church and broke my heart. And I have felt no [greater] joy and satisfaction than from lovingly and patiently working with him, and finally seeing him return to God and marry in the temple.

God knows something about the work of redemption that we are in the process of discovering. With His eternal perspective, He must find great satisfaction in rearing children through all the stages of their existence and patiently working them through their periodic bouts of waywardness until He finally brings them to the point that they embrace the truth and never again depart from it. To learn the satisfying and eternal work of redemption, we need training, and what better place and time than here and now, when the need for redemption is so great and the stakes are so high?

Speaking of the plan of happiness that we first must learn and then teach, Elder Bruce C. Hafen made the following statement:

> We are away at school, trying to master the lessons of "the great plan of happiness" so we can return home and *know what it means to be there.* Over and over the Lord tells us why the plan is worth our sacrifice—and His. Eve called it "the joy of our redemption" (Moses 5:11). Jacob called it "that happiness which is prepared for the saints" (2 Ne. 9:43). Of necessity, the plan is full of thorns and tears—His and ours. But because He and we are so totally in this together, our being "at

one" with Him in overcoming all opposition will itself bring us "incomprehensible joy."[383]

To increase our capacity to do the work of redemption, Heavenly Father gives us gifts that would be difficult to develop without the vehicle of adversity. In this and the following chapter, we will discuss a few of these gifts.

The Gift of Experience and Redemption

The Lord's words, "all these things shall give thee experience,"[384] are not always comforting. Of course, by *experience* we usually mean *adverse experience*. One father from Idaho said, "This is at once the most frightening and comforting phrase in the scriptures." Somehow we anticipate that our *experience* might include, as Joseph Smith was told in the bowels of Liberty Jail, our being "cast into the pit" where we helplessly stand by as our enemies decide our fate; or our being "cast into the deep" amidst the "billowing surge" and "fierce winds"; or our being enveloped by gathering "blackness," while "all the elements combine to hedge up the way"; or worse, our being threatened by "the very jaws of hell" that seek to devour us.[385] We feel the weight of *experience* when our children rebel and break our hearts and when there seems to be little we can do to stop them. At such times of difficulty, we may ask, *How can such harsh experience be for my good?*

Somewhere deep inside us, we know the answer: by means of harsh experience we will gain, not lose; and, beyond every other consideration, what we will gain is the power of redemption. In the process, we are being blessed with invaluable spiritual gifts, and we are developing the necessary qualities of character to do redeeming work.

Evidently, eternal law requires that the receipt of *power* be preceded and developed by *experience*. Lehi put it another way—that to gain anything desirable, we must experience its corresponding opposite: "it must needs be, that there is an opposition in all things."[386] Therefore, there is opportunity in experiencing the adversity of weakness, sickness,

---

383 Bruce C. Hafen, "The Atonement: All for All," *Ensign,* May 2004, 98.
384 D&C 122:7.
385 Ibid.
386 2 Nephi 2:11.

financial woes, relationship problems, disagreeable people, *wayward children,* or, as Lehi listed, wickedness, misery, death, corruption, and insensibility.[387] Opposition "must needs be," Lehi declared. We must experience the opposites or *opposition* in all things. Therefore, we are not sheltered from opposition here. Otherwise, there could be no righteousness, holiness, goodness, incorruption, happiness, sensation, or existence.[388] Thankfully, in the process of experiencing opposition, we secure power through the Atonement to overcome opposition. That is, our *opposition experience* leads to *power.* "Ye receive no witness [blessing] until after the trial [opposition] of your faith."[389] To become like God, we must experience what He has experienced, so that we, like Him, might gain the power to triumph.[390]

Here, then, as stated before, every effort we make to sanctify ourselves has a redeeming effect upon the person for whom we are praying. Sanctification infuses us with power to do the work of redemption; that is, the redeemed do the redeeming. We are sanctified by our experiences, our efforts to improve ourselves spiritually, and our encounters with the Holy Spirit. These things lead to wisdom, which leads to power. Thus, the cycle of redemption is one of divine rescue, repentance, sanctification, then duplicating that cycle in others.

Consider Enos, who went through the cycle of experiencing adversity then redemption by the teaching of his redeemed father, Jacob. Enos then desired to extend the blessings of redemption to his family, his countrymen, and even his enemies. Once he had been redeemed, he could not rest without trying to redeem someone else. Evidently his desire and consequent bestowed power to redeem others remained with him to the end of his life. When he was about to die, he declared that he had been "wrought upon by the power of God that I must preach and prophesy unto this people, and declare the word according to the truth which is in Christ. And I have declared it in all my days, and have rejoiced in it above that of the world."[391]

---

387 See 2 Nephi 2:11.
388 See 2 Nephi 2:11.
389 Ether 12:6.
390 See Joseph Fielding Smith, ed., *Teachings of the Prophet Joseph Smith,* 297.
391 Enos 1:26.

Consider Alma the Elder, who experienced adversity and then repented of his sins at the preaching of a redeemed Abinadi. When Alma experienced personal redemption, he "went about privately among the people, and began to teach the words of Abinadi—Yea, concerning that which was to come, and also concerning the resurrection of the dead, *and the redemption of the people,* which was to be brought to pass through the power, and sufferings, and death of Christ, and his resurrection and ascension into heaven."[392] The now-redeemed Alma the Elder had gained, through the cycle of experiencing adversity and being redeemed from it, the power of redemption by which he helped to redeem the entire Church and his own wayward son.

Consider Alma's son, Alma the Younger, who experienced adversity, then also repented of his sins after remembering the teachings of his redeemed father, who had developed the power of redemption to the extent that he could call down angelic help from heaven. When the now-redeemed younger Alma had experienced the adversity–redemption cycle, he declared that he had been "redeemed of the Lord . . . redeemed from the gall of bitterness and bonds of iniquity."[393] Thereafter, the redeemed Alma the Younger went about "from this time forward" to teach the unredeemed people, "preaching the word of God in much tribulation, being greatly persecuted by those who were unbelievers, being smitten by many of them"[394] in order that he, along with the sons of Mosiah, might become the redeeming "instruments in the hands of God in bringing many to the knowledge of the truth, yea, to the knowledge of their Redeemer."[395] Within eight years, the redeemed Alma the Younger developed the power of redemption to the point that he could succeed his father as president of the Church and thereby extend his redeeming influence to embrace many people.

Consider the sons of Mosiah, whom Mormon described as "the very vilest of sinners."[396] Nevertheless, by the teachings and prayers of their redeemed father, they were rescued by the same angelic experience as Alma the Younger. Now having experienced the

---

392 Mosiah 18:1–2; emphasis added.
393 Mosiah 27:24, 29.
394 Mosiah 27:32.
395 Mosiah 27:36.
396 Mosiah 28:4.

adversity-redemption cycle, they sought to become the redeemers: "Now they were desirous that salvation should be declared to every creature, for they could not bear that any human soul should perish; yea, even the very thought that any soul should endure endless torment did cause them to quake and tremble."[397] Through experiencing adversity and redemption, the sons of Mosiah gained the power of redemption and helped to save "many thousands of [their] brethren . . . from the pains of hell; and they are brought to sing redeeming love."[398]

And so it is with each of us who experiences adversity followed by redemption. Once we are redeemed we begin to gain the power to redeem others, and as we seek to sanctify ourselves through righteous living, that power to redeem increases.

One mother expressed how her personal cycle of redemption resulted in her helping to redeem others. This mother from Arizona, Joy, felt a desire to redeem others after having been redeemed from her own suffering during a difficult recovery after childbirth. One day, while she was bathing her child, she felt an overwhelming gratitude for Heavenly Father's mercy in helping her overcome that difficult period; she thus offered a prayer asking how she might extend that mercy to others. Suddenly, a beautiful woman appeared to her and told her that she was Joy's third great-grandmother. The woman said that she loved Joy as if there were no generational distance between them. She desired to be sealed to Joy and asked Joy to help her. Although Joy had never done family history work before, she began immediately and was filled with the testimony of that work. Over time, her capacity grew, and her joy eventually exceeded the suffering of the former difficult recovery that had brought her to this point. Having experienced the Lord's redeeming mercy in her life, she now received the desire, and likewise divine power, to become a redeemer. Through her efforts, Joy not only brought the blessings of salvation to her third great-grandmother but to thousands of her kindred dead.

Within every experience of adversity there is a waiting blessing that will transcend the experience, and that blessing will usually come in the form of greater ability to redeem others.

---

397 Mosiah 28:3.
398 Alma 26:13.

So here is the point: if the only way we can gain the power of redemption is through personally experiencing redemption, it stands to reason that we need something to be redeemed from. As we have discussed, Heavenly Father placed us in a fallen situation where weakness and adversity were certain and where sin was inevitable. The plan of salvation provided that once we were hurt or had slipped, He would be there to heal and redeem us. Then, having experienced redemption firsthand, we would gain the desire and power to become the redeemers. Over time, as we exercised the power of redemption, we would grow in our capacity to redeem until we became like God, who has infinite redemptive power. The Fall, therefore, was necessary and potentially a huge blessing. Nevertheless, experiencing its effects and watching it break those whom we love can be heart wrenching. During such times, we pray for perspective to see the opportunity in the present adverse experience, and we plead that God will increase our ability to redeem so that we might help to save wayward souls. Our ultimate hope, of course, is that the wayward will overcome the adversity and experience redemption, and when our children do that, they will gain the power of redemption and desire to redeem others.

The Gift of Joy

A strange gospel irony is that *affliction brings joy.* Affliction, if we allow it to, brings us to a state of humility where the Holy Ghost can more readily work within us. Former general Relief Society president Barbara W. Winder gave this explanation of joy:

> Joy, it seems, is not only happiness, *but the resultant feeling of the Holy Ghost manifest within us.*
>
> How can we provide a climate in our lives to foster the presence of the Holy Ghost, that our lives may be more joyful? Just as a reservoir stores water to bring relief and replenish the thirsty land, so we can store experiences, knowledge, and desires to replenish and fortify our spiritual needs. Four ways may be helpful in developing reservoirs of righteousness and spiritual self-reliance. We prepare by—

1. Developing a cheerful disposition wherein the Spirit can dwell.
2. Learning the Savior's will for us, that we may know our divine potential.
3. Understanding and accepting his atoning sacrifice and repenting of our sins.
4. Keeping his commandments and having a firm determination to serve him.[399]

Joy, like peace, is a gift of the Spirit. We cannot conjure it up, and Satan cannot duplicate it.[400] Only the Holy Ghost can produce joy, and He often produces it from the seedbed of affliction. A father from Idaho spoke of what he felt after having emerged from the hellish experience of his son's rebellion: "Oh what joy! The feeling was indescribable. Neither my wife nor I had felt anything so exquisite in our lives as when our son returned to us in sackcloth and ashes; the Spirit consumed us with overwhelming gratitude. We feel so very blessed, and we thank our Father in Heaven continually for blessing us with His revelation of joy. He saved our son's life, and we will be forever blessed because we had this experience."

Lehi taught his children that if Adam and Eve had not transgressed, they would have remained in the Garden of Eden. Had that happened, Adam and Eve "*would have had no children;* wherefore they would have remained in a state of innocence, having no joy, for they knew no misery; doing no good, for they knew no sin. . . . Adam fell that men might be; and men are, that they might have joy" (2 Ne. 2:23–25; emphasis added).

Astute parents will notice an interesting connection here: no children, no misery! There is actually some truth to that point. For without being expelled from the innocent comfort of Eden into the turbulence of mortality, Adam and Eve would not only have had no children and no misery, but they would never have found joy; *hence, the very meaning of life would have been lost on them.* There

---

399 Barbara W. Winder, "Finding Joy in Life," *Ensign,* November 1987, 95; emphasis added.
400 See Sheri L. Dew, "Living on the Lord's Side of the Line," Brigham Young University devotional, March 21, 2000.

really is a deep connection between the hard things of life and the best things of life.[401]

Amazingly, through the power of the Atonement, the Lord can "consecrate thine afflictions for thy gain"[402] and turn misery into joy. "Because they received the Atonement of Christ, Adam and Eve were able to learn from their experience without being condemned by it."[403]

Elder Hafen continues by stating that the mortal condition is not one of punishment but one of discovery and experience: "'They taste the bitter,' the Lord explained to Adam, 'that they might know to prize the good' (Moses 6:55). In fact, He said, 'If they [Adam and Eve] never should have bitter [experiences] they *could not know the sweet*' (D&C 29:39; italics added). In other words, sometimes the twists and turns of life *are* the straight and narrow path."[404]

Here, therefore, is the gospel irony of affliction and joy: God created man to have joy, which we all want, but joy can only be realized by experiencing its opposite, *affliction,* which we do not want. Moreover—and this is the harsh reality—*if joy is a gift, so is affliction.* Spiritually mature people have developed the capacity and perspective to express gratitude for their joys *and* their afflictions. They are not necessarily being noble; they obviously have learned something that the gods know: *no affliction, no joy.*

In this light, therefore, we can appreciate the Fall as an act of love, not as an act of condemnation. Heavenly Father provided the Fall, which introduces to each of us the means by which we can *learn from our experience.* Experience can be seen as the gateway to joy. Because God is a God of truth who cannot lie,[405] we are assured that His promise will be fulfilled: "After much tribulation come the blessings [joy]."[406] Ultimately, the affliction will result in joy and will help rather than injure us: "For God sent not his Son into the world to condemn the world; but that the world through him might be saved."[407]

---

401 Bruce C. Hafen, *Covenant Hearts,* 65–66; emphasis added.
402 2 Nephi 2:2.
403 Bruce C. Hafen, *Covenant Hearts,* 66.
404 Ibid.
405 See Ether 3:12.
406 D&C 58:4.
407 John 3:17.

Finally, while we are experiencing the invaluable connection between affliction and joy, the Savior, who will sanctify the effects of our affliction for our eternal gain, will sustain us in this difficult experience.[408]

THE GIFT OF WEAKNESS

A special gift that Heavenly Father gives to each one of us is the gift of *weakness*. Every specific weakness or *weakness* in general is designed to draw us quickly and urgently to the Lord for the purpose of experiencing redemption. Remember, to *obtain* the power of redemption, we must first *experience* redemption. Therefore God gives us weakness. "I give unto men weakness that they may be humble; and my grace is sufficient for all men that humble themselves before me; for if they humble themselves before me, and have faith in me, then will I make weak things become strong unto them."[409]

To deal with weakness, we need strength beyond our own. According to the preceding verse, humility is how we obtain strength, and weakness gets the ball rolling toward humility. Moreover, humility causes us to become keenly aware of God's interactions with us, and humility drives away pride. Elder James E. Talmage said, "Gratitude is twin sister to humility; pride is a foe to both."[410]

One couple in Missouri suffered through their daughter Shelly's overt rebellion, but, as the following account illustrates, they learned the above truth:

Shelly became so obstinate that she would curse and throw things. She was going to drink! She was going to smoke! She was going to have sexual relations, and that was all there was to it! We couldn't do anything about it. We threatened to send her away, but she beat us to the punch and ran away. When we found her harbored in her boyfriend's home [pregnant at age fifteen], we attempted to bring her home, and she threatened suicide. She had claimed we were

408 See 2 Nephi 2:2.
409 Ether 12:27.
410 James E. Talmage, *Sunday Night Talks*, 483.

abusing her. Only when we sat down with the boy and his father and explained her lies and the financial implications of a baby did they begin to cooperate. During that time, all our weaknesses surfaced and seemed so visible that they could have been under a spotlight. And then the miracle happened. Not with Shelly; that miracle is yet to come. Our miracle is what happened to us when we became humble. Realizing that our weaknesses were so acute and our ability so limited to deal with this situation, we went to the Lord in urgent, heartfelt prayer. Humbly, we acknowledged our great lack and His great strength. Then a calming peace settled upon us. It was as though a voice whispered to us, "Now I can help you, and I will be with you every step of the way."

Parents are keenly aware of their weakness when they are trying to deal with a wayward child. But it is their weakness that is their key to strength. If parents will recognize weakness for its intended purpose and allow the weakness to draw out of them humility, this act of faith will signal the beginning of the parents gaining redeeming power.

Great blessings flow from humility. Strength and knowledge are two of them. The Lord said, "And inasmuch as they were humble they might be made strong, and blessed from on high, and receive knowledge from time to time."[411]

When we acknowledge our weaknesses before the Lord in prayer, we nourish the powerful attribute of humility. President Spencer W. Kimball said, "How does one get humble? To me, one must constantly be reminded of his dependence. On whom dependent? On the Lord. How [to] remind one's self? By real, constant, worshipful, grateful prayer."[412]

Weakness, then, is a gift from God. Weakness is structured to spawn humility, which brings us to God, who turns our weakness into redeeming knowledge and redeeming strength.

---

411 D&C 1:28.
412 Spencer W. Kimball, quoted in Edward L. Kimball's *The Teachings of Spencer W. Kimball*, 233.

THE GIFT OF GRACE—BEING YOKED WITH CHRIST

Heavenly Father programmed the experience of mortality to be one of continual lacking. Our resources and abilities seldom equal what is required of us. Thus, to cope and progress, we find ourselves in a constant state of needing help from a higher, stronger source. We cannot change this reality of mortality. Once we admit that we will never have enough and that we will always need help, we are in a position to humbly come to the one abundant Source, praying that He will make up the difference.

We usually experience grace when we are at the end of our rope. One mother of three discovered grace this way:

> My husband and I made a decision to go back to church. Then our world fell apart. I've heard that this is normal. Suddenly, our marriage seemed under attack—critical remarks, misunderstandings. I spent a couple of weeks crying. Then our finances plummeted when we couldn't sell a second house in a timely manner. And the worst thing of all was our son's dropping out of school because of alcohol and drugs.
>
> I have dabbled with church activity for years, but I have never been too committed. Until recently, my husband has never been interested at all. But a friend had talked to me about the Savior's love and willingness to help. "Prayer and scripture study bring a power into your life," my friend said. It all sounded too simplistic, something that Mormons are taught to say in Primary. But I needed real help—and now! [So], as a last resort I decided one night to take my friend's advice [and] read a chapter in the Book of Mormon, then pray. What did I have to lose?
>
> Nothing, I was to find out; in fact, I had everything to gain. While I read the Book of Mormon, it was as though light was shining from the pages. That gave me confidence. I knelt in prayer and poured out my soul for help. I told the Lord that any one of my problems

was too great to handle, and I was dealing with three huge ones. Soon, I felt a quiet prompting to hand over my problems to God. I felt a little strange, as though I were in a meeting for Alcoholics Anonymous. Nevertheless, I followed the prompting and asked God to please help carry my problems and deal with them—I couldn't handle them anymore.

Then sweetly and tenderly, I felt something, like a hand, that had reached down and lifted my problems off my shoulders. I had the distinct feeling that I had a Partner now. Is this what grace was all about? Is this what I had been missing all these years? It was so simple that I had missed it. I had always thought that the definition of a responsible adult was being strong and independent—not asking anyone for anything. What a Satanic lie that is!

For the last two weeks, as the storm has raged around me, I have been at peace. I do what I can do and daily hand the rest to my *Partner*. And He always takes it. By the way, we received an offer on our house the morning after I prayed.

One of the great discoveries of mortality is that *God can take care of us.* When we humbly come to Him, expressing our weakness and our need for His help, He proffers us His *grace.* According to the LDS Bible Dictionary, grace is

> Divine means of help or strength, given through the bounteous mercy and love of Jesus Christ. . . .
>
> [To] receive strength and assistance to do good works that [we] otherwise would not be able to maintain if left to [our] own means. This grace is an enabling power that allows men and women to lay hold on eternal life and exaltation after they have expended their own best efforts.
>
> Divine grace is needed by every soul in consequence of the fall of Adam and also because of

man's weaknesses and shortcomings. However, grace cannot suffice without total effort on the part of the recipient.[413]

Here, then, is a formula for receiving grace: we come unto Christ in humility and faith, we do all we can do,[414] and He will make up the difference. And we will never be found lacking.

Rehearsing God's abundant grace to the wandering Israelites, the prophet Nehemiah taught,

> This is thy God that brought thee up out of Egypt, and had wrought great provocations;
>
> Yet thou [the Lord] in thy manifold mercies *forsookest them* [Israelites] *not* in the wilderness: the pillar of the *cloud departed not* from them by day, to lead them in the way; *neither the pillar of fire* by night, to shew them light, and the way wherein they should go.
>
> Thou gavest also thy good spirit to *instruct them,* and withheldest not thy *manna* from their mouth, and gavest them *water* for their thirst.
>
> *Yea, forty years didst thou sustain them* in the wilderness, so that they *lacked nothing;* their *clothes waxed not old, and their feet swelled not.*[415]

The Lord never forsook them. He was with them both day and night. He constantly instructed them. He provided manna and water to sustain them. For four decades of wandering, they lacked nothing. Amazingly, neither their clothing nor their shoes wore out. The Israelites experienced the Lord's grace.

At the end of Jesus' life, just before He entered Gethsemane, He reminded His Apostles of their early missions when He had purposely placed them in a condition of want by sending them out with neither purse nor scrip. Now He asked them, "When I sent you without purse, and scrip, and shoes, lacked ye any thing? And

---

413 LDS Bible Dictionary, "Grace," 697.

414 See 2 Nephi 25:23.

415 Nehemiah 9:18–21; emphasis added.

they said, Nothing."[416] If the Apostles needed firsthand experience with the Lord's grace to gain the necessary power to fulfill their callings, so do we. When we lack, we should go to the Lord; He will take care of us.

James, the Lord's brother, gave the solution for those of us who lack: "If any of you lack wisdom, let him ask of God, that giveth to all men liberally, and upbraideth not, and it shall be given him."[417] Personalized, this scripture could read: "If any person lacks *anything,* let him ask of God, that will give to that person *abundantly,* and will never chastise him for asking for the Lord's *grace,* and that *grace* shall be given him." *This is a promise!*

Grace allows our *lack* to be swallowed up in God's abundance: *we come unto Christ in humility and faith, we do all we can do, and He will make up the difference. And we will never be found lacking.* What do we parents lack when we deal with a wayward child? Our lack might include our inability to confront our weakness, such as our impatience, anger, embarrassment, depression, or lack of unconditional love. Our lack would certainly include our limited capacity to rescue and redeem our child. Until we become perfect in the principle of redemption, we must rely upon the Savior's power—His grace. Because we cannot become like God without divine help, because we can neither redeem ourselves nor anyone else without divine help; we are always in a condition of *lacking* and are totally and continually dependent upon the Lord's grace.

When we go to the Savior for grace, we will not find someone who is lacking in grace. He is *full* of grace.[418] John the Baptist revealed that Jesus developed a fullness of grace by giving grace away. That is, Jesus grew from grace *to* grace by giving grace *for* grace. In other words, as Jesus received grace from His Heavenly Father, He extended that grace to others, grace *for* grace, and His capacity to give grace increased [grace *to* grace]. Ultimately, He achieved a fullness of "grace and truth."[419] And so it is with us. We grow from one capacity of grace to another by extending the grace that we have received to someone in need.

---

416 Luke 22:35.
417 James 1:5.
418 See D&C 93:11.
419 See D&C 93:11–14.

When a child goes wayward and we try with all our souls to rescue him only to come up short, we must seek more grace from Jesus Christ that we might be able to give more grace. Hence, as John revealed, the answer for receiving grace is to give grace. It is a formula for all gospel principles: "Blessed are the merciful: for they shall obtain mercy."[420] We could say, "Blessed are those who extend grace, for they shall obtain more grace." This principle also applies to those to whom we give grace. Elder Mark E. Petersen said, "love and understanding—cooperation and brotherhood—will reproduce themselves in the hearts of others when given willingly and sincerely."[421]

If you plant a kernel of corn and nourish it, the kernel will grow into a stalk with several ears and many more kernels. Then, if you plant those kernels, you will eventually have a field of corn and a huge harvest—all from a single kernel. As we humbly seek and receive the Lord's grace, then extend that grace to others [our wayward children included], the Lord will give us more grace. Elder Boyd K. Packer said, "As you give what you have, there is a replacement, with increase!"[422]

What does this mean for parents of wayward children?

Just this: we grow in our ability to redeem by extending, to our children and to others, the grace that we have been given. As we seek to serve more, love better, live more as would the Savior, and redouble our efforts to hold true to the gospel, the Lord will move us from one grace to another until, like Him, we are full of grace.[423] Extending grace increases grace, and our capacity to redeem rises proportionately. What President Gordon B. Hinckley said of mercy might be said of grace: "One cannot be merciful to others without receiving a harvest of mercy in return."[424]

Grace provides us divine strength to *carry* a heavy burden. Because of grace, we do not have to carry our burden alone. Jesus extended this invitation: "Come unto me, all ye that labour and are heavy laden, and I will give you rest. Take my yoke upon you, and learn of

---

420 Matthew 5:7.
421 Mark E. Petersen, *Conference Report,* October 1967, 67.
422 Boyd K. Packer, "The Candle of the Lord," *Ensign,* January 1983, 54–55.
423 See D&C 93:11.
424 Gordon B. Hinckley, "Blessed Are the Merciful," *Ensign,* May 1990.

me; for I am meek and lowly in heart: and ye shall find rest unto your souls. For my yoke is easy, and my burden is light."[425] Four verbs and phrases describe the pattern of shifting a heavy burden to the Lord:

1. *Come* unto the Savior
2. *Take* His yoke upon you
3. *Learn* of the Savior
4. *Find* rest in the Savior

(1) Come to the Savior. That is, don't try to see how long you can tough it out. Don't drive yourself into spiritual and mental exhaustion by trying to carry the burden alone. Come to me—*all of you* "that labour and are heavy laden." The word *labour* summons the picture of a woman travailing in labor, descending into the valley of death to bring forth new life. To get through her labor, she needs comforting and coaching. When we labor, pouring out our souls, we also seek the Lord's comfort and coaching—His grace. We do not have the power to labor alone.

(2) Take His yoke upon you. President Howard W. Hunter describes a yoke:

> In biblical times, the yoke was a device of great assistance to those who tilled the field. It allowed the strength of a second animal to be linked and coupled with the strength of a single animal, sharing and reducing the heavy labor of the plow or wagon. A burden that was overwhelming or perhaps impossible for one to bear could be equitably and comfortably borne by two bound together with a common yoke. . . .
>
> Why face life's burdens alone, Christ asks, or why face them with temporal support that will quickly falter? To the heavy laden it is Christ's yoke, it is the power and peace of standing side by side with a God that will provide the support, balance, and the

425 Matthew 11:28–30.

strength to meet our challenges and endure our tasks
here in the hardpan field of mortality.[426]

When the Savior said, "Take my yoke upon you," notice whose
yoke it is—the Savior's yoke. Essentially He is saying, "Because I am
the Savior, I am already wearing a yoke. I see that you are laboring
under a heavy burden and could use some help. I am going your way
and have a place open in my yoke, if you want to pile your burden
on and take up the yoke with me." Then, as if to assuage our anxiety,
He adds, "My yoke is easy and my burden is light." In other words,
"When you take a place in my yoke, you are going to notice a marked
difference in the weight of your load."

Christ said that His yoke is *easy*. Compared to trying to carry our
heavy burden without him, being yoked to Christ makes our burden
much easier to manage. But we often dismiss how easy it is. Alma said,
"For behold, it is . . . *easy* to give heed to the word of Christ, which will
point to you a straight course to eternal bliss. . . . O my son, do not
let us be slothful because of the *easiness of the way;* for so was it with
our fathers; for so was it prepared for them, that if they would look
they might live; even so it is with us. The way is prepared, and if we
will look [unto Christ] we may live forever."[427] Alma was referring to a
critical incident where many Israelites declined the Lord's yoke because
it seemed too easy. "[The Lord] sent fiery flying serpents among them;
and after they were bitten he prepared a way that they might be healed;
and the labor which they had to perform was to look; and because of
the simpleness of the way, or the easiness of it, there were many who
perished."[428] They missed the point and opportunity entirely: *Christ's
yoke is inherently easy!* The ancient Israelites refused to *easily* come unto
Christ and take their place in His yoke. Consequently, their burden
crushed them; they perished under the weight of it.

How long will *we* stagger alone under the weight of dealing with
a wayward child before we accept a place in the Lord's yoke and allow
him to share or even assume the burden? Ted Gibbons offered these
examples of the lightness of Christ's yoke:

---

426 Howard W. Hunter, "Come Unto Me," *Ensign,* November 1990, 20.
427 Alma 37:44, 46; emphasis added.
428 1 Nephi 17:41.

The paralytic [man] lowered through the roof had a bed to carry home after his healing . . . but the bed cannot have weighed more than the infirmity the Savior removed from him. The peace that came to Alma following his repentance and conversion required a lifetime of sacrifice and service, but [such still] required less of him than the burden of pain he felt when [he'd come] face to face with his own rebellion. "Yea . . . and in fine so great had been my iniquities, that the very thought of coming into the presence of my God did rack my soul with inexpressible horror."[429]

When we accept a place in the Lord's yoke, taking advantage of His grace, He essentially says to us, "Now we are in this together." When the tax collectors asked Peter if Jesus paid tribute, Peter, who represented Christ, erroneously answered yes. Later, Jesus corrected him, and, because they were yoked together, Jesus provided a joint solution "lest *we* should offend them."[430] Notice that Jesus included Himself in the solution, although He had not falsely claimed to pay taxes. He required Peter to do all that he could do—a requirement of grace—to obtain the tribute money, and then by means of a miracle (grace), Jesus provided the money. When Peter paid the tribute money, Christ said it was to be "for me and thee." Why? Because they were in it together—yoked.

Later, Peter made another mistake that Jesus rectified. In Gethsemane, when Judas betrayed the Savior, Peter drew his sword and cut off the ear of the servant of the high priest. Because Peter represented the Savior as His Apostle, Peter's actions were Christ's actions—they were yoked together. Jesus told Peter to put away his sword, then He healed the servant's ear and repaired the mistake of his *partner*.[431] When we are yoked together with the Savior, His grace covers our mistakes and lightens our burdens. These are comforting thoughts for parents trying to do their best and coming up short.

---

429 Ted Gibbons, "Take My Yoke Upon You," Gospel Doctrine lesson at LDSLiving.com.

430 Matthew 17:27.

431 See Matthew 26:51.

(3) Learn of the Savior. Friends and loved ones learn of each other. Jesus' invitation, "learn of me," suggests a loving relationship that He wishes to improve upon. One could surmise that He is saying, "We are family and we are friends. As we travel along, yoked together, I invite you to get to know me better. "I am meek and lowly in heart."[432] I am "wise yet harmless,"[433] and I am always willing to help you." What we learn about Jesus helps us, and this is only made possible *after* we have taken His yoke upon us. If adversity drives us to Christ, who offers us His yoke, that adversity is a great blessing after all. Then, as we travel with Christ, what will we learn about Him? Joseph Smith taught that Jesus, like His Father, is everlasting, merciful, gracious, slow to anger, abundant in goodness, perfectly consistent, a God of truth who cannot lie, He plays no favorites, is all-knowing, all-powerful, completely just, has judgment that never fails, and is full of grace and truth and perfect love.[434]

Once we are yoked to Christ, shift our burden, and begin to journey toward godhood, we will enjoy lots of time learning of Him as He helps us carry our load. But we do not have to know everything about Him at once for His grace to be manifest in our lives. President Boyd K. Packer said, "You need not know everything before the power of the Atonement will work for you. Have faith in Christ; it begins to work the day you ask!"[435]

(4) Find rest in the Savior. "I will give you rest. . . . Ye shall find rest unto your souls."[436] Twice the Lord promises *rest* to the weary and heavy-laden who come to Him and take upon them His yoke. Essentially, He promises, "I will share your burden, or, if needs be, I will carry your burden. In either case, you can rest." This is one of the great promises of being yoked to the Savior: "Don't worry. I am carrying the burden. We're in this together. Rest."

---

432 Matthew 11:29.
433 Alma 18:21.
434 See Joseph Smith, *Lectures on Faith,* 4:1–30.
435 Boyd K. Packer, "Washed Clean," *Ensign,* May 1997, 10.
436 Matthew 11:28–29.

Inherent in being yoked to Jesus is the promise of His support in every circumstance. Alma understood the kind of *rest* that comes from being yoked to Christ. At the end of his ministry he testified, "And I have been supported under trials and troubles of every kind, yea, and in all manner of afflictions; yea, God has delivered me from prison, and from bonds, and from death; yea, and I do put my trust in him, and he will still deliver me."[437] We need not carry the burden of a wayward child alone; the invitation to take a place in Christ's yoke is ever before us. When we put our trust in Him, He will deliver us.

THE SOURCE OF POWER

In summary, the source of our power is Jesus Christ. When we need power, we must go to Him and rely upon that divine resource, His *grace*. To understand the meaning of this type of grace, we might insert "enabling and strengthening power" when we think of the word as we struggle with our trials.

Because of the Fall we are woefully powerless. We cannot make it alone. Jesus Christ is the single source of power in the universe. Only by entering into a covenant can we request His power to give us strength to do what otherwise would be impossible. When Nephi was bound by his brothers and rendered helpless (an interesting metaphor for mortality), he knew what to do and where to go to gain the power to change his circumstance. In 1 Nephi 7:17, we read, "O Lord, according to my faith which is in thee, wilt thou deliver me from the hands of my brethren; yea, even *give me strength that I may burst these bands* with which I am bound" (emphasis added).

Nephi did not pray for the Lord to eliminate his circumstances; rather, he prayed that the power of the Atonement would grant him strength to change his circumstances. Nephi knew that he had limited power, but he also knew that the Lord had infinite power. Because Nephi and the Lord were bound together by covenant, Nephi could tap into that higher power and change his situation.

Obviously, since Nephi asked for help, somewhere in the process, he must have done all he could to break the bands—remember, doing all you can do is what is required to obtain the Lord's grace

---

437 Alma 36:27.

and power. Then the Lord added His power to Nephi's effort, and the bands were broken. Nephi knew he could do all things "in the strength of the Lord."[438]

The application is clear: if we desire the Lord's power, we must pray for strength to *change* our situation rather than simply praying for our *situation to be changed.* There are times when the Lord will simply remove the burden, but most burdens are designed to strengthen our backs, as it were. Nonetheless, the Lord will add His power to ours after all we can do, and then we will have the power to act rather than be acted upon.[439]

When a child goes astray, and we watch helplessly as he spiritually hemorrhages right before our eyes, we are *not* helpless—we can do something, after all. With confidence, we can take a place in Christ's yoke, plead for His grace, and ultimately plead for the Atonement's divine enabling and strengthening power to "change the circumstance." Then, as we do all we can do, Christ will make up the difference. He may not completely remove the burden, for nothing trumps a child's agency, but the Lord will give us power to change our view or better manage the circumstance, just as He did for Nephi.

---

438 Mosiah 9:17.
439 See 2 Nephi 2:14.

Chapter 8
CHARITY NEVER FAILETH

Charity . . . is the greatest of all. . . . Charity is the
pure love of Christ, and it endureth forever.

—*Moroni 7:46–47*

TRUE LOVE IS CHARITY. It encompasses the two laws of love upon which hang all the law and the prophets: 1) "Thou shalt love the Lord thy God with all thy heart, with all thy might, mind, and strength," and 2) "Thou shalt love thy neighbor as thyself."[440] Charity, then, is the driving force of Jesus' higher law. Charity is saving love; charity lifts and rescues and forgives from enormous depths and distances. As we experience the giving and the receiving of charity, we eventually discover that we cannot escape its loving embrace, for "[charity] endureth forever."[441] Thus, this chapter will explore the various and enduring facets of charity as found in Moroni 7:45 and 1 Corinthians 13:4–8.

- Charity suffers long (patiently endures a hardship or endures with someone during his hardship)
- Charity is kind
- Charity does not envy
- Charity is not vaunted up (does not boast)
- Charity is not puffed up (is not proud)
- Charity does not behave unseemly (does not act rudely)
- Charity seeks not her own (is not selfish)

---

440 Matthew 22:39.
441 Moroni 7:47.

- Charity is not easily provoked (keeps anger under control)
- Charity thinks no evil (focuses on the good)
- Charity does not rejoice in iniquity but rejoices in the truth (is not glad when other people finally get their due; rather, it rejoices at the smallest positive movement forward)
- Charity bears all things (bears up under the weight of problems)
- Charity believes all things (recognizes and follows truth)
- Charity hopes all things (trusts that God is in charge)
- Charity endures all things (is willing to make the sacrifices required because the price will be worth the prize).[442]

Charity is exemplified by Christ. If we are to save our children through charity, we must emulate Christ.

Emulating Christ through Charity

We do not choose heroes from those who have never been through something hard. We admire and try to emulate those who have faced and overcome extreme adversity then emerged with their integrity intact. When we consider the life of the Savior, we find our ultimate Hero—He who faced and overcame *every* affliction, He who is worthy of our emulation. "Surely the best evidence of our adoration of Jesus is our emulation of Him," said Elder Russell M. Nelson.[443]

A study of the scriptures reveals an interesting point: the Savior's image is reflected in the countenances of righteous people[444]—mortal heroes. Because a hero's Christlike example is so inspiring, we who are weak seek to follow them as we would the Savior. God designed the plan of salvation this way. One could surmise that heroes, like great suns in the heavens, draw lesser planets (weaker souls) into their

---

442 See Moroni 7:45.
443 Russell M. Nelson, "The Message: His Mission and Ministry," *New Era*, December 1999.
444 See Alma 5:14.

orbits to give them light and life. That is, God makes *suns* of strong, Christlike people who exemplify or illuminate his Beloved *Son* to the weaker orbs/people. These *suns,* or heroes, draw attention to Christ so that "the people might know in what manner to look forward to his Son for redemption."[445]

One father of a wayward teenager contacted his former mission president—his hero—when his son fell into heartbreaking transgression.

> I talked with the president for a long time. Here was a man whom I had learned to love and trust thirty years earlier. He, too, had struggled with one of his children for a time, and he explained how he and his wife had endured the challenge. Now they were on the other end of things. His child had made a courageous and thorough change, and most importantly, their relationship was stronger than ever. The president is a man as Christlike as anyone I have ever known. Because he has always tried to be like Jesus and do what Jesus would do, he is my hero. I want to be like him in every way. When he gave me counsel, I was willing to listen and to follow. And I [have not been] disappointed—what the president told me to do is working.

Just as we seek counsel from heroes, we need to be the heroes our children will eventually turn to. Parents are thus given a heroic work to do; their lives should emulate Christ so that they might "illuminate . . . God"[446] to their children. Although wayward children may ridicule their parents' Christlike example, even if they stray to Plutonian distances, they cannot fully break free of the gravitational force (sealing power) that holds them in their parents' orbit. Wayward children are always tethered to their *sun* who emulates the *Son.* By means of a righteous parent's example, the Holy Ghost will testify to these children that Jesus is the Christ and that the gospel is true. Speaking to parents concerning emulation, Elder Boyd K. Packer said, "Where is your

---

445 Alma 13:2.
446 Neal A. Maxwell, "Encircled in the Arms of His Love," *Ensign,* November 2002.

power? It is in the power of example,"[447] and, as Elder Sterling W. Sill said, "The power of example is the greatest power in the world."[448] If wayward children will not listen to our words, our testimony will nevertheless be delivered to them through the power of the Holy Ghost by means of our example.

Jennifer, a recently single mother, recounted the splintering effect that her divorce had on her children. Each one suffered from the trauma, and some left the Church completely. She remained active, attended her meetings alone every week, and faithfully served in a seemingly insignificant calling. Over the years, Jennifer's example worked on her children. Without uttering a word about religion, she modeled a Christlike character that trumpeted her testimony. One by one her children returned and repented, and now they are all active and married in the temple. When Jennifer emulated the Savior, she gained power to rescue her children.

CHARITY SUFFERS LONG

As with Jennifer's example, sometimes the wait for repentance is long. To suffer long with someone is to suffer [allow] him the right to exercise his agency. To suffer long is to suffer with him as we watch him suffer the consequences of his actions, even when those consequences do not motivate him to change. To suffer long is to patiently pray that perhaps a change of heart might occur that could drive the wayward soul to the Savior, who has suffered for him.

When we serve "one of the least" of God's children, who may be temporarily *least* because of his poor choices, the Lord counts our service to the child as if we had done that service unto the Savior.[449] And God rewards our sacrifice with an incredible return—"an hundredfold."[450] Truly, He is the most generous paymaster.

President Kimball, quoting Elder Orson F. Whitney, wrote,

No pain that we suffer, no trial that we experience is wasted. It ministers to our education, to the

447 Boyd K. Packer, *Conference Report*, October 1963, 64.
448 Sterling W. Sill, *Conference Report*, April 1960, 68.
449 See Matthew 25:40.
450 Matthew 19:29.

development of such qualities as patience, faith, forti-
tude and humility. All that we suffer and all that we
endure, especially when we endure it patiently, builds
up our characters, purifies our hearts, expands our
souls, and makes us more tender and charitable, more
worthy to be called the children of God . . . and it is
through sorrow and suffering, toil and tribulation, that
we gain the education that we come here to acquire and
which will make us more like our Father and Mother in
heaven.

Then President Kimball concluded, "Suffering can make saints
of people as they learn patience, long-suffering, and self-mastery. The
sufferings of our Savior were part of his education."[451]

After years of suffering their children's drug problems, alcohol use,
verbal abuse, rebellion, sexual exploits, broken marriages, attempted
suicides, and occasional jail time, a California couple wrote,

The Lord has always been there for us. For the last
twenty years, we have attended the temple regularly
and always put our children's names on the prayer roll.
The Lord has been so good to our children, too. He has
saved their lives on numerous occasions—multiple car
wrecks, drug overdoses, and suicide attempts. Each time
they were rescued miraculously. We have wondered if
the Lord was preserving them until they could make
their way back home. Remarkably, there are signs. In
the last two years they have done an *about-face,* and
both started attending church. One has become temple
worthy and the other is close behind.

When our ability to suffer long is tried beyond our apparent
limit to endure, and when we search our souls for something more
to give, only to find an empty reservoir, we can take comfort in Elder
Maxwell's perspective on the godlike qualities we are gaining: "The

---

451 Spencer W. Kimball, *Faith Precedes the Miracle,* 98.

dues of discipleship are high indeed, and how much we can *take* so often determines how much we can then *give!*"[452]

CHARITY IS KIND

Often, parents of wayward children suffer from wounded egos. We feel as though we have failed the child, the Lord, and ourselves. We feel as though we are distancing ourselves from God rather than moving toward Him. We wonder about our acceptability as we watch our weaknesses and failings paraded before us.

But as we contemplate our own weaknesses, we are less inclined to be judgmental of others and are more inclined toward kindness and compassion. When one mother was asked to contribute to this book, she wrote of how these terrible feelings can be turned into more productive emotions:

> I have had many thoughts running through my mind. I came to realize that I am not as far away from the pain of those years as I thought I was. Long ago, I carefully wrapped up those worst years in mental batting and stored them away deeply in the back of my mind. I never wanted to access them again. [Though] I have never ever blamed Heavenly Father for any of this, I have always felt I was the one who failed, and my greatest emotion has been feelings of letting Him down. It is [the source of] my worst pain that I could not provide my children whatever it was that they needed to stay on the straight and narrow. I would have given my life to do that. It has left me with mammoth guilt and terrible feelings of failing them.
>
> [However,] on the other hand, my experience has given me great understanding and empathy for those going through this kind of struggle and pain [both as parents and troubled youth]. It has made me look at young people who are struggling, and try to really see what they're going through and why. There are

---

452 Neal A. Maxwell, "Patience," *Ensign,* October 1980.

so many who are in serious pain. They make poor choices, then don't know what to do, so they sink down in desperation. If I can help them, I do. I try to listen and help them talk things out.

Quoting the Prophet Joseph Smith, Wallace H. Goddard suggested a kind way to measure parental success in terms of the softening of our hearts:

> Joseph Smith said, "The nearer we get to our Heavenly Father, the more we are disposed to look with compassion on perishing souls; we feel that we want to take them upon our shoulders, and cast their sins behind our backs. My talk is intended for all this society; if you would have God have mercy on you, have mercy on one another" (*Teachings of the Prophet Joseph Smith*, 241). Notice that this is expressed as a direct relationship: "The nearer we get . . . the more we are disposed."[453]

That is, as we move closer to God, we develop more compassion. And the inverse is true: as we feel more compassion, we know that we are getting closer to God.

Compassion is a "deep awareness of the suffering of another coupled with the wish to relieve it."[454] To feel compassion is to feel as Jesus feels, to develop the ability to sense another's pain and to seek to carry or remove it. When we are in pain, we cry out, "Does anyone know how I feel?" And the compassionate Christ replies, "I know exactly how you feel, and I can do something about it."

> And he shall go forth, suffering pains and afflictions and temptations of every kind; and this that the word might be fulfilled which saith he will take upon him the pains and the sicknesses of his people.

453 Wallace H. Goddard, "Taking the Measure of Our Progress," MeridianMagazine.com

454 *American Heritage Dictionary*, "Compassion."

> And he will take upon him death, that he may loose the bands of death which bind his people; and he will take upon him their infirmities, that his bowels may be filled with mercy, according to the flesh, that he may know according to the flesh how to succor his people according to their infirmities.[455]

As we have discussed, Jesus' ability to feel compassion and to extend compassionate help increased from "grace *to* grace" by his extending "grace *for* grace."[456] Because He feels what we feel, He is motivated to help. Over and over in the scriptures we see Him helping others by reason of His compassion.

- Compassion moved Him to appoint twelve Apostles: "But when he saw the multitudes, he was moved with compassion on them, because they fainted, and were scattered abroad, as sheep having no shepherd."[457]
- Compassion moved Him to heal the blind: "So Jesus had compassion on them, and touched their eyes: and immediately their eyes received sight, and they followed him."[458]
- Compassion moved Him to heal the leper: "And Jesus, moved with compassion, put forth his hand, and touched him, and saith unto him . . . be thou clean."[459]
- Compassion moved Him to release a man from Satan's grasp: to the once-afflicted man, the Savior said, "Go home to thy friends, and tell them how great things the Lord hath done for thee, and hath had compassion on thee."[460]

---

455 Alma 7:11–12.
456 D&C 93:12–13; emphasis added.
457 Matthew 9:36.
458 Matthew 20:34.
459 Mark 1:41.
460 Mark 5:19.

- Compassion moved Him to restore a dead son
  to his grieving mother. "And when the Lord saw
  her, he had compassion on her, and said unto her,
  Weep not. And he came and touched the bier: and
  they that bare him stood still. And he said, Young
  man, I say unto thee, Arise."[461]

The more we become like Christ, the more we feel compassion and consequently feel an increase in our ability to help.

Compassion, like the other virtues we have discussed, is unique to God; Satan cannot duplicate it. The virtue of compassion defines true Saints, who are willing "to bear one another's burdens, that they may be light; Yea, and are willing to mourn with those that mourn; yea, and comfort those that stand in need of comfort."[462]

Compassion and mercy are companion virtues that reach out to the perishing soul in pity rather than in judgment. Nephi rejoiced that God was a being who had a fullness of this virtue: "Thou art merciful, thou wilt not suffer those who come unto thee that they shall perish!"[463] James, the Lord's brother, one who likely knew Jesus well, offered the following insight: "The Lord is very pitiful, and of tender mercy."[464] Can our children say that of us?

To become like God, we must replace anger, resentment, and judgment with mercy, kindness, and compassion. Peter wrote, "Be ye all of one mind, having compassion one of another, love as brethren, be pitiful, be courteous: Not rendering evil for evil, or railing for railing: but contrariwise blessing . . ."[465]

We simply cannot teach wayward souls about Christ and His love and healing power unless we exemplify Christ and His compassion. They must see Christ reflected in those who profess to believe in Him; otherwise they will not seek Him. Someday, when their wayward lives begin to unravel and their road leads them to dead ends, they will search for a safe place to land where charity, mercy, and compassion abound. The greatest

---

461 Luke 7:13–14.
462 Mosiah 18:8–9.
463 1 Nephi 1:14.
464 James 5:11.
465 1 Peter 3:8–9.

sermon that we might ever teach is our emulation of Christ's compassion: "Be ye kind one to another, tenderhearted, forgiving one another, even as God for Christ's sake hath forgiven you."[466]

Charity Does Not Rejoice in Iniquity: Embracing Forgiveness

Our capacity to forgive is linked to our capacity to love; and our capacity to love is linked to our capacity to become like God. Perhaps more than any other virtue, forgiveness—our willingness to thoroughly and "frankly forgive,"[467] as did Nephi—demonstrates redeeming, reconciling, Christlike love.

Forgiveness is a spiritual gift that is obtained by asking for it "with a sincere heart, with real intent"[468] (that is, with the *real intention* to forgive). Parents of wayward children often face a number of people they must forgive: their children, judgmental onlookers, and themselves. Often, fasting and requesting a priesthood blessing to obtain this spiritual gift is helpful. Receiving a priesthood blessing has another benefit; through the power of the priesthood, the adversary may be detected and cast away, for it is often the adversary who blunts our ability to forgive and buffets us with the miserable effects of carrying a grudge. Both the recipient and the priesthood holder can profit from the Lord's counsel on casting out the "dark spirits" of Satan's influence: "This kind goeth not out but by prayer and fasting."[469]

Job is a powerful and interesting lesson on forgiveness. Job was an ancient priest and judge who was highly respected and very wealthy. He was doing everything right when everything went wrong. In an instant, he lost his seven sons and three daughters. Then he lost his wealth and his health. When he was cast from his home to take up residence near the city's refuse pile, he was separated from his wife—possibly one of his hardest trials. Then three of his friends (and later a fourth) came to comfort him. They were so astonished at his condition and appearance that they could not utter a word but rather sat with him in silence for seven days, "for they saw that his grief was very great."[470] Then the

---

466 Ephesians 4:32.
467 1 Nephi 7:21.
468 Moroni 10:4.
469 Matthew 17:21.
470 Job 2:13.

unimaginable happened—Job's friends turned against him and accused him of sin. They imagined that nothing short of misdeeds and flaws in his character could produce such misery. Surely, they said, Job was now reaping the reward for his poor choices and bad conduct.

Job, however, was not a sinner "deserving" of his trials. Are we the same, undeserving of the trials that come with a wayward child? Nevertheless, in our case, we often play both the roles of the martyr *and* his accusing friends; we berate ourselves and take responsibility when children stray from the path of righteousness. Often, our quick assumption is that we're suffering because of our own shortcomings. While there may be an element of truth to that statement (and if there is, we ought to quickly repent), our shortcomings typically pale in comparison to the child's use of agency. Nevertheless, we are prone to errantly assign personal blame as though we could read the mind of God. We are quick to judge ourselves harshly, and thereby we become our own worst enemies, much like Job's judgmental friends, who were willing to accuse Job while he was suffering.

Amazingly, despite all the false accusations and abuse, Job maintained his integrity. He knew that sin was not the cause of his affliction. Obviously, Job knew the Lord well enough to know that he was right before the Lord. If escaping his circumstance were as easy as admitting to a mistake, Job would have gladly done so. But he had received no such divine communication, so he was duty-bound to maintain his integrity and wait for the Lord to deliver him.

In the end, the Lord vindicated Job when the Lord chastised Job's friends. Speaking to one of them, Eliphaz, the Lord said, "My wrath is kindled against thee, and against thy two friends: for ye have not spoken of me the thing that is right, as my servant Job hath." Then, in an extraordinary gesture to reach out to the friends and invite them to repent (and the result would become Job's ultimate test), the Lord commanded Eliphaz and the friends, "Therefore take unto you now seven bullocks and seven rams, and go to my servant Job, and offer up for yourselves a burnt offering; *and my servant Job shall pray for you: for him will I accept:* lest I deal with you after your folly." [471]

The final trial of Job was forgiveness! After all that had happened to him, after all the abuse, could he now pray for his friends? Yes. And the

---

471 Job 42:7–8; emphasis added.

result was astounding: "And the LORD turned the captivity of Job, when he prayed for his friends: also the LORD gave Job twice as much as he had before."[472] Through the powerful act of forgiveness, Job's captivity was turned; through the powerful act of forgiveness, Job was able to rescue and reclaim his friends; and through the powerful act of forgiveness, the Lord restored to Job twice as much as he had had before.

At some point, and perhaps at many points along the way, we will have to forgive our wayward child, other judgmental people, and ourselves. And, as President Kimball stated, if we are able to forgive sincerely, we are "near to perfection."[473] Our reward for having made this sacrifice—for forgiveness is a sacrifice of pride—will be much more than what was required of us in order to forgive: twice as much in the case of Job, and even more in other cases. In the early days of the restored Church, the suffering, forgiving Latter-day Saints were told, "And again, if your enemy shall smite you the second time, and you revile not against your enemy, and bear it patiently, your reward shall be an hundredfold."[474]

The reward comes from having learned to be like God. In his study of such, struggling to comprehend the boundaries of forgiveness, Peter asked Jesus, "Lord, how oft shall my brother sin against me, and I forgive him? till seven times? Jesus saith unto him, I say not unto thee, Until seven times: but, Until seventy times seven."[475] That is, we cannot become sons and daughters of God without being able to forgive without limitation. To emphasize this point, the Lord taught a parable that reveals something we must learn in order to become like Him—the capacity and desire to forgive endlessly, even when sins are severe and enormous:

> Therefore is the kingdom of heaven likened unto a certain king, which would take account of his servants.
>
> And when he had begun to reckon, one was brought unto him, which owed him ten thousand talents.

---

472 Job 42:10.
473 Spencer W. Kimball, *The Teachings of Spencer W. Kimball*, 204.
474 D&C 98:25.
475 Matthew 18:21–22.

But forasmuch as he had not to pay, his lord commanded him to be sold, and his wife, and children, and all that he had, and payment to be made.

The servant therefore fell down, and worshipped him, saying, Lord, have patience with me, and I will pay thee all.

Then the lord of that servant was moved with compassion, and loosed him, and forgave him the debt.[476]

We are part of the kingdom of heaven; we are the servants of the King who will take account of us. Our debt to sin is massive; we cannot pay it. The demands of justice are unbearable. His patience with and mercy toward us are what we plead for. Because the King is compassionate, He is willing to loose us from our burden and forgive our debt. But if we will not extend the same courtesy to another debtor, as the parable later details, we kindle the wrath of the King, who will deliver us to the tormentors until we pay all that was originally due.[477] Our casually forgiving someone will not suffice; we must do so from our heart, the most sensitive and tender part of our soul. We cannot truly forgive and hold anything back. If we are not willing to do this, we commit the "greater sin."[478]

Because the trait of forgiveness defines Jesus, and because we must develop this principle of salvation to become like Him, He gives us multiple opportunities to learn it in mortality, primarily with those whom we love the most. Forgiveness is one of the greatest tests of discipleship. Being willing to forgive speaks to our desire to become like Christ, for by forgiving we lay the groundwork for the sinner's redemption. The Christlike Saint seeks to redeem and reclaim while Satan seeks to captivate and destroy; one reason that we withhold forgiveness is to hold the sinner in a form of spiritual *bondage*. That is a reason why refusing to forgive is such a serious sin. We simply cannot be Saints and do the work of Satan on any level. On the other hand, sincere forgiveness closes the door on Satan, who would use the unsettled issue to destroy our souls.

---

476 Matthew 18:23–27.
477 See Matthew 18:34.
478 D&C 64:9.

"Forgiving" Charity Is Not Puffed Up or Envious, Neither Does It Vaunt Itself
We all have an abundance of what will hurt us and canker our
souls—too much envy, too much pride, too much animosity. Joseph
Smith taught that the sacrifice of all things, good and bad, is what is
required for perfection and eternal life.[479] When the rich young man
asked Jesus how he could obtain eternal life, Jesus told him to keep
the commandments. The young man stated that he was fulfilling
that requirement and asked, "What lack I yet?" Jesus invited him to
become perfect by selling his possessions, distributing the proceeds to
the poor, and following Him. The Lord's invitation required that the
young man trust that, in sacrificing, he would receive more treasure
in heaven than his worldly sacrifice represented. An attitude of faith
is what the young man lacked. And he went away sorrowing.[480] The
young man's riches were not the issue; what he *lacked* was. What he
lacked was faith; what he had too much of was holding him back
from becoming perfect—in this case, the love of money.

Those who refuse to sacrifice anything which might hold them back
can "hardly enter into"[481] the kingdom of heaven. When Jesus' disciples
heard Him teach this doctrine, "they were exceedingly amazed, saying,
Who then can be saved? But Jesus beheld their thoughts, and said unto
them, With men this is impossible; but *if they will forsake all things for
my sake,* with God whatsoever things I speak are possible."[482]

What does this mean? We may be holding onto an abundance
of something that is prohibiting us from progressing toward exaltation—a grudge, for example. What we *lack* is the faith and love
to forgive. But we have a choice: we can choose to have either our
grudge or eternal life, but we can't have both. Because the sacrifice
of all things is necessary for eternal life, we must sacrifice everything,
even our sins, if we truly want it. As king Lamoni cried out to the
Lord, "I will give away all my sins to know thee, and that I may be
raised from the dead, and be saved at the last day."[483]

---

479 Joseph Smith, *Lectures on Faith,* 6:7.
480 See Matthew 19:16–22.
481 Matthew 19:23.
482 JST—Matthew 19:25–26; emphasis added.
483 Alma 22:18.

As Jesus taught, the ultimate perfection of forgiveness is the ability to love and do good to our *enemies,* which can be defined as those with whom we have enmity: "Love your enemies, bless them that curse you, do good to them that hate you, and pray for them who despitefully use you."[484] Such forgiveness is the goal as well as the sign of the steady completion of the perfection process. If we can forgive even our enemies, we are truly free.

Once we have set our minds on forgiving, spiritual gifts are unleashed to aid us. Much like the payment of tithing unleashes financial and spiritual blessings, so does seeking to forgive open the windows of heaven. These spiritual gifts help us grow from one capacity to another until we can forgive perfectly. Then, like Alma, we forget the pain of former sins (our sins *and* other people's sins), and rancor is replaced with charity, which allows us to see others and ourselves as Jesus does.

Hurt turns to love; hatred to pity. We want for the offender what Christ wants: to reclaim and exalt them. As we seek to forgive, the Lord helps us take the long view of things; eternal life is the goal, and we cannot achieve it saddled with a burden that is viewed by God as greater than the sinner's. But if we can learn to forgive perfectly, our effort is accepted by the Lord as a sacrifice that will be rewarded an hundredfold. From the outset of the process to forgive, the Lord invites us to come and follow Him.[485] This is His invitation and His guarantee to keep us completely safe while we open our hearts and make the sacrifice of forgiveness.

CHARITY BELIEVES, BEARS, ENDURES, AND HOPES ALL THINGS

"Nothing could be as frightening as an impatient God," an institute student wrote. Who could believe in a God whose patience wanes or whose love is limited? Patience is not only waiting for the Lord, it is also anticipating His deliverance with "a perfect brightness of hope."[486] Therefore, through the process of righteous waiting we learn godlike patience. We could suggest that patience is waiting *for* someone, that patience is waiting *with* someone, and that patience is waiting *upon,* or serving, someone. Patience also requires faith, which is often developed

---

484 3 Nephi 12:44.
485 See Matthew 19:21.
486 2 Nephi 31:20.

by the trial of patience. Elder Maxwell taught, "Patience is tied very closely to faith in our Heavenly Father. Actually, when we are unduly impatient, we are suggesting that we know what is best—better than does God. Or, at least, we are asserting that our timetable is better than his. Either way we are questioning the reality of God's omniscience."[487]

Elder Maxwell notes, "Sometimes that which we are doing is correct enough but simply needs to be persisted in—patiently—not for a minute or a moment but sometimes for years."[488] Regarding patience as it pertains to long-suffering, Elder Maxwell gave the following counsel as if directed specifically to parents of wayward children:

> If our patience is being tried, we might expect that our faith is also being tried; if our capacity for patience is increasing, we might also expect that our faith is increasing. In the eternal scheme of things, we cannot become as God without having developed the ability to demonstrate infinite patience with perfect faith. Therefore, it should come as no surprise that God would give us multiple opportunities to gain invaluable experience with patience and faith.[489]

The law of the harvest is this: *whatsoever ye sow, that shall ye also reap.*[490] Between *sowing* and *reaping* lies *enduring with patience.* Eventual triumph depends on what we do once the seed is sown.

Patient, faith-filled parents cling to the Lord's promise:

> Verily I say unto you my friends, fear not, let your hearts be comforted; yea, rejoice evermore, and in everything give thanks;
> Waiting patiently on the Lord, for your prayers have entered into the ears of the Lord of Sabaoth, and are recorded with this seal and testament—the Lord hath sworn and decreed that they shall be granted.

---

487 Neal A. Maxwell, "Patience," *Ensign*, October 1980.
488 Ibid.
489 Ibid.
490 See D&C 6:33.

> Therefore, he giveth this promise unto you, with an immutable covenant that they shall be fulfilled; and all things wherewith you have been afflicted shall work together for your good, and to my name's glory, saith the Lord.[491]

If patience and faith are companions, so are patience and agency. When we lose our patience, we reveal an ugly side of us. Elder Maxwell said, "We are plainly irritated and inconvenienced by the need to make allowances for the free agency of others. In our impatience . . . we would override others. . . . When we are unduly impatient, however, we are, in effect, trying to hasten an outcome when acceleration would abuse agency."[492] And that is something that neither God nor someone hoping to one day become a god would do.

Patience, faith, long-suffering, and endurance are inseparably connected to God's *timing*. "It is in length of patience, and endurance, and forbearance, that so much of what is good in mankind and womankind is shown."[493]

In the case of righteous parents, the idea of accepting divine timing speaks to the level of faith that they have developed over years of righteous living.

Patient Charity Is Not Easily Provoked, Neither Does It Behave Unseemly
In Doctrine and Covenants 121, the Lord gave Joseph Smith invaluable counsel concerning the priesthood which might also be applied to parents.[494] Parents who have the faith to patiently wait for the Lord's timing are those who are striving *not* to set their hearts "upon the things of this world, and aspire to the honors of men"; neither do they attempt to "cover [their] sins, or gratify [their] pride or [their] vain ambition." To exercise such patience and faith, they have learned that the "rights of the priesthood are inseparably connected with the powers of heaven, and that the powers of heaven cannot be controlled nor handled only upon the principles of righteousness." To

---

491 D&C 98:1–3.
492 Neal A. Maxwell, "Patience," *Ensign*, October 1980.
493 "Talks to Young Men," *Improvement Era*, September 1903.
494 See D&C 121:33–46.

such parents, who have righteously responded to the Lord's call, the filthy waters that roll about them cannot forever "remain impure"; neither can the powers of heaven be forever staid. Things *will* change. Nothing can "hinder the Almighty from pouring down knowledge [and blessings] from heaven upon [their] heads."[495]

Such parents move forward in righteousness because they know that sanctifying themselves is the one thing they *can* do to affect the situation. In patience, they resist applying "unrighteous dominion" or exercising "control or dominion or compulsion upon the souls of the children of men, in any degree of unrighteousness," because they know that "the heavens withdraw themselves; the Spirit of the Lord is grieved; and when it is withdrawn, Amen to the priesthood or the authority of [those parents]."[496] That is, if they heatedly pursue unrighteous dominion or control in a way that offends the Spirit, their connection with heaven is severed, their righteous example is injured, and their relationship with the child is damaged. Nothing good can come from unrighteously compelling a soul to change.

Rather, Godlike patience demands trusting in the Lord's timing through enduring and loving "by persuasion, by long-suffering, by gentleness and meekness, and by love unfeigned; by kindness, and pure knowledge [knowing and seeing as God knows and sees], which shall greatly enlarge the soul without hypocrisy, and without guile."[497]

Patience, then, is the delicate balance of honoring agency and "reproving betimes with sharpness [clarity and swiftness] when moved upon by the Holy Ghost"[498]—but only then. And if reproving is necessary, the Lord demands "showing forth afterwards an increase of love toward him whom thou hast reproved, lest he esteem thee to be his enemy; that he may know that thy faithfulness is stronger than the cords of death."[499]

Then comes the reward of patience. As we grow in the principles of patience, charity, and virtue, our "confidence [begins to] wax strong in the presence of God; and the doctrine of the priesthood

---

495 D&C 121:33, comments added.
496 D&C 121:37, comments added.
497 D&C 121:41–42, comments added.
498 D&C 121:43, comments added.
499 D&C 121:43–44.

[begins to] distil upon [our] soul as the dews from heaven."[500] The Holy Ghost becomes more fully our constant companion, and we begin to gain increasing power to govern our kingdom in right-eousness and truth. Amazingly—and this is our ultimate faith in the Lord's timing—all good things begin to flow unto us "without compulsory means."[501] That is, by the power of our righteousness, as described above, and not by force, bad things will improve and good things will flow to us.

Charity Never Faileth

Of all the qualities that could describe God, the Apostle John chose love. "God is love."[502] Satan cannot duplicate love; he can only offer lust, covetousness, envy, and fleeting pleasure. Consequently, true love is not born of sin, and substitutes for love cannot produce happiness.[503] Because love originates with God, "every one that loveth is born of God, and knoweth God."[504]

Implicit in the virtue of love is a feeling of safety—a powerful idea for parents: "There is no fear in love; but perfect love casteth out fear."[505] On the other hand, limited love engenders fear, and fear "hath torment." We are warned, "He that feareth is not made perfect in love."[506] That is, a child who should be enjoying perfect love but who has reason to question his parents' love will feel fear and torment in the relationship. Moreover, if a parent withholds love while bearing testimony of the love of God, that parent "is a liar,"[507] and needs to repent and rethink his relationship with God and the child, because the Lord states, "If ye have not charity, ye are nothing."[508]

John explains that loving God and loving a child are indivisible: "And this commandment have we from him, That he who loveth

---

500 D&C 121:45.
501 D&C 121:46.
502 See 1 John 4:16.
503 See Alma 41:10.
504 1 John 4:7.
505 1 John 4:18.
506 Ibid.
507 1 John 4:20.
508 Moroni 7:46.

God love his brother [or child] also."[509] Sometimes love needs to be jumpstarted, whether our love for the child or the child's love for us. God presented a pattern for this process: "We love [God], because he first loved us."[510] Likewise, when we love a child first, we encourage his love in return. And when we love God, He gives us love—the gift of charity—that we can give to our children.

When I was a new missionary, I had a companion whom I despised. He and I were complete opposites. I could not hide my loathing. Soon, our missionary work came to a halt. My only goal was to endure until a transfer came. One morning I awoke to see my companion fully dressed in a suit, sitting on a stool, shining my shoes. My heart was softened and my anger fled. How could I dislike someone who served me? Thereafter, many of our differences dissolved, and those that remained were overshadowed by love. Amazingly, when we began to love each other, our missionary success increased. All from a simple act of love. My companion took the initiative and the risk and loved me first.

Love cannot abide when contention or competition is present. Rather, love thrives on cooperation. When we contend, we step into Satan's territory. "For verily, verily I say unto you, he that hath the spirit of contention is not of me, but is of the devil, who is the father of contention, and he stirreth up the hearts of men to contend with anger, one with another. Behold, this is not my doctrine, to stir up the hearts of men with anger, one against another; but this is my doctrine, that such things should be done away."[511] While there must be household rules, we must avoid contending with or criticizing our wayward children. Love simply cannot exist under such conditions. No one was ever forced into goodness. Acknowledging choice while lovingly setting fair and natural consequences for choice preserves love and promotes cooperation, which, together, form a safe environment to which the child might return.

Elder Bruce C. Hafen wrote of the benefits of patient love, quoting both President Kimball and Sterling Ellsworth on the topic:

---

509 1 John 4:21.
510 1 John 4:19.
511 3 Nephi 11:29–30.

As Sterling Ellsworth wrote:

"Children need love like fish need water. If [because of what happens at home or in other relationships during childhood] they don't get the real thing, they reach for love substitutes such as food, sexual self-gratification, and pornography. Some love substitutes are even worse. . . .

"When true love is given to a child, he grows up sensitive to his own identity. . . . He doesn't need to go looking for love because his 'love bucket' is full" (Sterling Ellsworth, *Latter-day Plague*, 19–20).

If the search for "love substitutes" is indeed at work in a child's rebellion, the truly attentive parent may, with great effort over a period of time, begin to restore some of the love, the attention, and the security the child may have missed—whatever the cause. . . .

As President Spencer W. Kimball taught: "Jesus saw sin as wrong but also was able to see sin as springing from deep and unmet needs on the part of the sinner. This permitted him to condemn the sin without condemning the individual" (Spencer W. Kimball, *The Teachings of Spencer W. Kimball*, 481).[512]

A father from Idaho wrote about the redeeming love he and his wife showed toward their wayward son:

> When my wife, Marie, and I became acquainted with the principles in this book, we began to pray with more fervency for our son Spencer, who was in his mid-twenties. We examined our lives, attended the temple, and fasted with more frequency and purpose. In short, we centered in on our covenants and put forth as much effort as possible to put those covenants to work.

---

512 Bruce C. Hafen, *Covenant Hearts*, 116–17.

Because Spencer was the type of boy who would stubbornly hold to his destructive and rebellious lifestyle until the bitter end, we knew that he would not consider changing until he reached rock bottom. As Marie and I talked about Spencer and prayed for guidance, we were impressed to pray for two things: that Spencer would get to rock bottom as soon as possible, and that a good girl would come into his life, because we knew he would do anything for love.

Over the next few months we saw signs of change in Spencer. He began to think about deep subjects, and he began to question all sorts of life issues. We were impressed the Holy Ghost was working upon him without his knowing. Additionally, he met a fine young woman, and he began to think about life in terms of responsibility and long-term commitment.

Then one day the foundation collapsed underneath Spencer; it always does when your foundation is built upon sand. Everything that he had been putting off with creditors and the legal system came crashing down around him. If this had happened a few months earlier, Marie and I would have panicked. But because we had been praying for him to hit bottom, we saw the hand of the Lord. Now we needed to know how the Lord wanted us to respond.

As we prayed together and individually, we received impressions about our various roles. Astonishingly, I was told that I should keep my mouth shut and let my wife do the talking. My interactions with Spencer always ended with his becoming defensive, but when Marie talked to him, he would soften. More justice was not what he needed right now; mercy was what he needed, and my wife had a talent in that area.

After Marie and I agreed upon a strategy, we took it to the Lord. When we prayed, I received another impression. I realized that I had not fully trusted the Lord in the past. I had always felt that I had to do everything alone. Now I realized that there was a team involved in dealing with Spencer, and Marie and I were only two of the players. The Lord, the Holy Ghost, and angels (who we felt were deceased relatives) were the other team members. Marie was to take the assignment of expressing love to Spencer and offer relief; I was to verify what she said; and our heavenly team would bear testimony and take over. I felt the Spirit whisper, "The greatest sermon that Marie and you will preach today is your example. Let us do [any other] preaching." I felt a bit strange that I had almost no role, but I realized that the Lord was calling the play.

When Marie and I met with Spencer and discussed his situation, he was scared, confused, and humble. Marie did what she does best: she expressed her sincere love for him and told him that she believed in him. Then she pulled out the checkbook and wrote out a check with no strings attached, setting him free. At her gesture of unconditional love, the once defiant, proud Spencer broke down and sobbed. He couldn't hold back. He could no longer maintain his rebellious attitude. The love of his mother broke his heart and rendered him contrite. Her love had liberated him.

Now he was able to open up about his love for this girl, but he could not imagine that she could love him in return because of his baggage. What did he have to offer? he asked. He thought he was the scum of the earth. Marie would not accept his words. "Anyone who gets my boy must be the very best," she said. "She must love and cherish you as I do." Then Marie asked Spencer to invite the girl to our home for dinner.

Throughout that marvelous experience, we said nothing about Spencer's lifestyle and we made no demands. We only showed mercy. With his foundation collapsing, we knew that a new foundation needed to be built, and that foundation was unconditional love. If I had been left to myself, I would have started with the walls or ceiling, but Marie had the spiritual gift to set a proper foundation. That's the first step that may be comprised of many until we get our son back. But working with our heavenly partners, we now have the faith that we will be able to build upon that foundation a house that will never fall.

The heavenly teamwork experienced by Spencer's father is available to all of us striving to exemplify Christlike love and patience. Consider this final experience of a father in Orem, Utah:

> I am the problem solver in the family. When something or someone needs fixing, I spring into action. But despite my best efforts, I could not "fix" my son. Jeremy seemed intent on self-destruction: bad friends, long hair, sloppy clothes, alcohol, experimentation with drugs, sexual problems, dropping out of school, etc. Jeremy was out of control and in a tailspin that I could not "fix." One night, in desperation, I went to my knees and pleaded with the Lord for help. Suddenly, a quiet question formed in my mind: "What would you do if Jeremy had the flu?" My answer was immediate: "I would stay with him, love him, and try to make him comfortable until the sickness ran its course." And then came the divine instruction: "Think of this as the flu. Stay with Jeremy and make him comfortable in your love while the spiritual sickness runs its course." For the first time, I felt relief. My son was spiritually sick, but it would pass, and the Physician was working with him. I couldn't heal Jeremy—that was the Physician's job—but I could love him and make him comfortable until the sickness passed. As I ended my prayer, a final impression entered my mind: "I know how you feel; you are not alone. Jeremy is my son, too."

The pure love of Christ is marked by patience—charity waits. Patience says, "I will wait *with* you, I will wait *for* you, and I will wait *upon* you." In other words, regardless of your situation, *I will wait.* Elder Angel Abrea said, "We are not talking . . . about a passive patience which waits only for the passing of time to heal or resolve things which happen to us, but rather a patience that is active, which makes things happen. Such was the patience Paul described in his epistle to the Romans when he used the words 'by patient continuance in well doing' (Rom. 2:7)."513

Ultimately, like all other virtues of God, charity is a gift of the Spirit. To obtain and develop it, we must "pray unto the Father with all the energy of heart, that [we] may be filled with *this* love."514 The effort to obtain this love and to love this way is worth the price, for in a world where everything fails, the great promise of charity is that "charity *never* faileth."515

---

513 Angel Abrea, "Patience in Affliction," *Ensign,* May 1992; emphasis removed.
514 Moroni 7:48; emphasis added.
515 Moroni 7:46; emphasis added.

Chapter 9

THE SAVING POWER OF PRIESTHOOD ORDERS AND ORDINANCES

*Without the ordinances thereof, and the
authority of the priesthood, the power of godliness is not
manifest unto men in the flesh.*

—*D&C 84:20–21*

LEE, A FATHER FROM IDAHO, attributed his children's change to a growing appreciation of temple worship.

> My wife, Jeannie, and I have a large family. All our children are active in the Church except two. Why these two, we do not know. A few years ago, when my wife and I felt the family hemorrhaging and did not know how to stop it, a good friend approached me with a question. "Have you put the temple to work for you?" I had no idea what he meant. Jeannie and I had always attended the temple, and, over the years, we had heard teachers and Church leaders speak of the temple's power and promise great blessings. But I had never considered how to access that power to obtain the blessings. My friend challenged me to fast and go to the temple "as a student," praying for further light and knowledge. He pointed out scriptures to me that indicate the power of the temple covenants and ordinances. He told me that I had been given all the tools that I needed to help my family if I would just learn to use them.

I admit that I had never thought of temple service beyond fulfilling an assignment to do work for the dead. But Jeannie and I were so desperate that we were willing to try anything. Within the week, we decided to fast and go to the temple to pray for instructions. I can still remember that day in the temple. I don't think I had ever paid so close attention to the temple ceremony. Later, when my wife and I prayed, we had a profound experience. Suddenly, it was as though all the lights turned on. Scripture after scripture raced through our minds, all of them connected to the common fabric of the temple.

For the next weeks and months, we pored over the scriptures seeking more information. We were astonished that there was a mountain of information we had missed. We felt as though we were reading the scriptures for the first time. Line upon line, we formulated a plan to try and help our children by implementing temple principles. We realized that prophets had applied these same principles to call back and bless their people, and because God is a consistent God, we could expect the same results.

Thereafter, Jeannie and I made the temple central to our worship. We attended more often and with a new purpose—to receive more instructions and to seek blessings for our children. We came to realize that all priesthood ordinances are principles of power that have intended and practical uses. To access that power, a person must make and keep sacred covenants. Amazingly, as Jeannie and I focused more on the temple, we noticed changes beginning to occur in our wayward children. Their rough exterior softened. Their tough defensive armor began to show cracks. Thoughts began to enter their minds that caused them to ask us penetrating questions. Unanticipated kindnesses were shown to them from Church members, which caused them to feel gratitude. They began to feel more keenly the consequences of their actions. They began to communicate with us more, and in a noncombative way.

We are still in the process; we haven't gotten them home yet. But we notice enough positive evidence that we are sure that it is only a matter of time. Now, when Jeannie and I pray, we feel more empowered to ask for and receive an answer, and more empowered to ask for help from heaven. We had never before realized the power of the temple, but now we are sure that as we continue to apply its principles, we will eventually reclaim our children.

ADAM AND EVE SET THE EXAMPLE

There is great power in the temple—power to ask for and receive blessings. Adam and Eve exemplified the pattern of asking and receiving. Finding themselves estranged from God, they offered mighty prayer at an altar in a temple setting to seek for reconciliation and for knowledge and power in order to be brought back into God's presence. Angels were immediately dispatched to observe Adam and Eve's obedience as our first parents endured testing over a period of time. Then, when God had determined that they had qualified for the blessings they were seeking, the veil was rent and heavenly messengers appeared providing deliverance, knowledge of God, power to ask Him questions directly, and power to return to His presence. This is a journey that every fallen person must make. No power except the Melchizedek Priesthood can bring an individual to God and teach that individual how to ask for and receive the revelation required to successfully make the journey.

As Adam and Eve approached God in mighty faith and prayer, they received His assurance that a Savior would redeem them and their children. As Abraham and Sarah approached God in mighty faith and prayer, they received the new and everlasting covenant with the promise that this covenant would be offered to their family as a perpetual right [516]—the right to all gospel blessings, including eternal marriage with the promise of eternal posterity. These parents—Adam and Eve and

---

516 Bruce R. McConkie, *Mormon Doctrine,* "New and Everlasting Covenant," 529.

Abraham and Sarah—should be the models for every husband and wife. The blessings they secured for us, their children, culminate in the temple. Like them, we should seek the blessings associated with the temple so that we might be able to petition heaven in mighty prayer and secure the promise of the Savior's grace and the blessings of the new and everlasting covenant for our family.

Now that Adam and Eve had repented and were redeemed, they were empowered to become the messengers of redemption to their children. Working with God and angels, they labored all their days to teach their family the plan of salvation. They gained the power to do this redemptive work through temple covenants and ordinances. Once they were endowed with that knowledge and power, they were better able to help rescue their children from the effects of the Fall and to bring them back into the presence of God.[517] By the Savior's power of redemption and resurrection, and by the power of the new and everlasting covenant, we are rescued from our fallen state and then empowered to help with the work of redemption among our family and others.

THE PRIESTHOOD'S PROCESS OF SALVATION TAUGHT BY PROPHETS

The prophets have taught these truths about the process of salvation: "Now this Moses plainly taught to the children of Israel in the wilderness, and sought diligently to sanctify his people that they might behold the face of God."[518] What did Moses plainly teach the people? According to the Doctrine and Covenants, he taught the following principles:

> And this greater priesthood administereth the gospel and holdeth the key of the mysteries of the kingdom, even the key of the knowledge of God.
>
> Therefore, in the ordinances thereof, the power of godliness is manifest.
>
> And without the ordinances thereof, and the authority of the priesthood, the power of godliness is not manifest unto men in the flesh;

---

517 See John A. Widstoe, *Program of the Church*, 78.
518 D&C 84:23.

For without this no man can see the face of God,
even the Father, and live.[519]

In summary, he instructed that a person must sanctify himself to
come close to God and that the Melchizedek Priesthood has two grand
functions: (1) It enables men to administrate the kingdom of God, and
(2) It gives them the ability, through priesthood ordinances, to exercise
power to receive personal revelation from God, power to learn about
God, and the power to see God. These ordinances lead to the increased
ability to ask God directly for knowledge and blessings. Let me suggest
a possible explication of what these verses are teaching us:

- What are "the mysteries of the kingdom"? Things
  that only can be learned through personal revelation.
- What is the "key of the knowledge of God"? The
  temple covenants and ordinances—*keys*—which,
  when exercised in righteousness, open the door to
  revelation from God, about God, and ultimately
  introduce us to God.
- What is the "power of godliness"? It is the receipt of
  the patriarchal order of the priesthood, the highest
  order of the Melchizedek Priesthood, which a
  husband and wife enter into as part of the marriage
  sealing. This order, which includes all other
  temple blessings, gives a couple all of the necessary knowledge and power to become *godly*, or like
  God, including the power to bind their children
  to themselves and the power to help save them.
  Additionally, inherent in the patriarchal order of
  the priesthood is the power of eternal lives.
- How is the "power of godliness" manifested, or
  how does it function? Through the "ordinances
  thereof"—that is, through the temple ordinances.
- What is the ultimate purpose of the "power of godliness"? To enable men to see the face of God and live

---

519 D&C 84:19–22.

forever in the family unit—to be where He is, to do
His works, to live His lifestyle, and to know Him,
which is to be like Him in every way.[520]

Therefore, it is in the temple where covenants, ordinances, knowledge, and power pertaining to the priesthood (including the patriarchal order of the priesthood) are received and ultimately *made sure.* Clearly, for both men and women, temple blessings contain a treasury of knowledge and power which enable them to ask for and receive blessings, especially in behalf of those they love.

Speaking of temple blessings as containing the greater power to ask and receive, Sister Bathsheba Smith, second general president of the Relief Society, said, "When speaking in one of our general fast meetings, [Joseph Smith] said that we did not know how to pray to have our prayers answered. But when I and my husband had our endowments . . . Joseph Smith presiding, he taught us the order of prayer."[521] Sister Smith was not talking about prayer as a sequence of steps, but rather as a power flowing from a priesthood order.

Previously, we discussed prayer's increased potency as we combine it with obedience and sacrifice—essential elements of sanctification. In this chapter, we will build on those principles as we discuss the powerful connection between prayer, priesthood, and the temple.

MELCHIZEDEK—A MODEL FOR PARENTS

Melchizedek means "king of righteousness."[522] The *Encyclopedia of Mormonism* describes Melchizedek as an "example of righteousness and the namesake of the higher priesthood," and states that Melchizedek "represents the scriptural ideal of one who obtains the power of God through faith, repentance, and sacred ordinances, for the purpose of inspiring and blessing his fellow beings."[523] That this righteous man gained power from heaven to rescue his wicked people and turn them

---

520 See D&C 132:24.
521 Bathsheba Smith, *Juvenile Instructor* 27, 1 June 1892, 345.
522 Hebrews 7:2.
523 *Encyclopedia of Mormonism,* "Melchizedek," 879–880.

back to God so that they in turn could obtain heaven[524] should be of primary interest to parents of wayward children.

By what power did Melchizedek accomplish this monumental work? The answer to this question is our key to being able to do the same.

Melchizedek was both the king (leader of the kingdom) and high priest (leader of the Church) of Salem,[525] which was the later location of Jerusalem. Melchizedek is described as "a man of faith, who wrought righteousness; and when a child he feared God, and stopped the mouths of lions, and quenched the violence of fire."[526] His people, which we assume would have included his family, had "waxed strong in iniquity and abomination; yea, they had all gone astray; they were full of all manner of wickedness."[527] We parents immediately appreciate Melchizedek's dilemma. What Melchizedek needed to rescue his people was both priesthood authority and priesthood power.

By righteousness Melchizedek qualified to be ordained to the priesthood. He "exercised mighty faith, and received the office of the high priesthood according to the holy order of God."[528] Now he was authorized by God to work redeeming miracles among his wicked people. But power in the priesthood comes by sanctification. Therefore, Melchizedek sanctified himself and gained great power to bless others. By the power of the priesthood, he gave blessings, preached repentance, and administered the priesthood ordinances "that thereby [through these ordinances] the people might look forward on the Son of God . . . for a remission of their sins, that they might enter into the rest of the Lord."[529] As a result of his efforts, Melchizedek was able to successfully call his people back to God: "And behold, they did repent; and Melchizedek did establish peace in the land in his days."[530] Melchizedek became known as "the Prince of peace,"[531] which, of

---

524 See JST Genesis 14:34.
525 See Genesis 14:18.
526 JST Genesis 14:26.
527 Alma 13:17.
528 Alma 13:18.
529 Alma 13:16.
530 Alma 13:18.
531 JST Genesis 14:33.

course, is a title also attributed to Abraham[532] and Jesus Christ. The titles *King of Righteousness* and *Prince of Peace* are representative of what a Melchizedek Priesthood holder should strive to become. Ultimately, because of the righteousness and priesthood of Melchizedek, his "people wrought righteousness, and obtained heaven,"[533] which is exactly what we parents want for our children. In striving to obtain these blessings for our children, we can look to Melchizedek as he looked to Christ:

> So righteous and faithful was Melchizedek in the execution of his high priestly duties that he became a prototype of Jesus Christ (Heb. 7:15). The Book of Mormon prophet Alma said of him, "Now, there were many [high priests] before him, and also there were many afterwards, but none were greater" (Alma 13:19). The Doctrine and Covenants states that Melchizedek was "such a great high priest" that the higher priesthood was called after his name. "Before his day it was called *the Holy Priesthood, after the Order of the Son of God.* But out of respect or reverence to the name of the Supreme Being, to avoid the too-frequent repetition of his name, they, the church, in the ancient days, called that priesthood after Melchizedek, or the Melchizedek Priesthood" (D&C 107:2–4; italics in original).[534]

Today, a worthy man may have the authority of the Melchizedek Priesthood conferred upon him, but he cannot enter into "the highest order of the Melchizedek Priesthood [which] is patriarchal authority"[535] unless he is married in the temple. Elder Bruce R. McConkie said, "Celestial marriage is an 'order of the priesthood.'"[536] By receiving the patriarchal priesthood, a man becomes a type of Melchizedek,

---

532 See Abraham 1:2.
533 JST Genesis 14:34.
534 *Encyclopedia of Mormonism*, "Melchizedek," 879–880.
535 Ibid., "Patriarchal Order of the Priesthood," 1067.
536 Bruce R. McConkie, *A New Witness for the Articles of Faith*, 312.

that is, a *king of righteousness* and a *priest* unto God. Following this pattern, a righteous Melchizedek Priesthood holder, as a king, has the authority to reign in righteousness over his kingdom (family), as did King Melchizedek. Also, a righteous Melchizedek Priesthood holder is a priest unto the Most High God. Like Melchizedek, that man now has the power to preach repentance, give blessings, and bring his family to the saving priesthood ordinances "that thereby [they] might look forward on the Son of God . . . for a remission of their sins, that they might enter into the rest of the Lord."[537] As a king and a priest, a Melchizedek Priesthood holder has the power to establish peace in his family, which peace is the "rest of the Lord." Thus he becomes a prince of peace to his wife and children.

Likewise, because the priesthood power to which we are referring is of the patriarchal order received in the temple, it is available to both men and women. Elder James E. Talmage said,

> In the sacred endowments associated with the ordinances pertaining to the House of the Lord, woman shares with man the blessings of the Priesthood. When the frailties and imperfections of mortality are left behind, in the glorified state of the blessed hereafter, husband and wife will administer in their respective stations, seeing and understanding alike, and co-operating to the full in the government of their family kingdom. Then shall woman be recompensed in rich measure for all the [cultural and historical] injustice that womanhood has endured in mortality. Then shall woman reign by Divine right, a queen in the resplendent realm of her glorified state, even as exalted man shall stand, priest and king unto the Most High God. Mortal eye cannot see nor mind comprehend the beauty, glory, and majesty of a righteous woman made perfect in the celestial kingdom of God.[538]

---

537 Alma 13:16.
538 James E. Talmage, "The Eternity of Sex," *Young Woman's Journal 25*, October 1914, 602–603; comments added.

Of course a man cannot become a king unless he has a queen, and vice versa, and they together have a kingdom. As men become kings and priests by entering into this order of the priesthood, women become queens and priestesses in that same order. Together they partake of the temple priesthood ordinances and are thus jointly empowered to do the work of Melchizedek among their family—their kingdom.

> It was this "order" [of the priesthood], coupled with faith, that gave Melchizedek the power and knowledge that influenced his people to repent and become worthy to be with God. . . . Those ordained to this order were to "have power, by faith," and, according to "the will of the Son of God," to work miracles. Ultimately, those in this order were "to stand in the presence of God" (JST Gen. 14:30–31). *This was accomplished by participating in the ordinances of this order.*[539]

THE HOLY PRIESTHOOD AFTER THE ORDER OF THE SON OF GOD

The blessings given to Abraham flow to us by and through the Melchizedek Priesthood. What the ancients called entering into the order of the Son of God is today called entering into the fullness of the Melchizedek Priesthood. This can only happen in the temple. Both worthy men and women enter into this highest order of the priesthood in the temple.

The "order of the Son of God" centers on God's promise to Adam to provide a Savior to redeem him and his children[540] from their fallen condition and give them all the necessary laws and ordinances of the gospel to empower and teach them how to regain God's presence. This was the plan of salvation, and it was to be administered by "the order of the Son of God." This *order* of the priesthood contained the power that Adam sought to bless his family and "bring them into the presence of God."[541] President Benson was asked how Adam

---

539 *Encyclopedia of Mormonism,* "Melchizedek," 879–880; emphasis added.
540 See Alma 13:2.
541 See Joseph Fielding Smith, ed., *Teachings of the Prophet Joseph Smith,* 159.

brought his family into the presence of the Lord. His answer was that Adam ministered unto his family the priesthood order of the Son God. That is, they entered into a temple and received their blessings.[542] Likewise, we obtain the power to bring our children into the presence of God by going to the house of the Lord and entering into "the order of the Son of God" by means of the ordinances, including eternal marriage when the opportunity arises. Let's discuss the differing orders of the priesthood so we might better understand the unique saving power of each.

THE RESTORATION OF PRIESTHOOD ORDERS AND POWERS

Joseph Smith said, "All Priesthood is Melchizedek, but there are different portions or degrees of it."[543] That is, there is but one priesthood, which is Melchizedek, and it is "the highest and holiest Priesthood, and is after the order of the Son of God, and all other Priesthoods are only parts, ramifications, powers and blessings belonging to the same, and are held, controlled, and directed by it."[544] The Melchizedek Priesthood has a variety of *orders,* among which are Aaronic, Melchizedek, and Patriarchal. Each of these priesthood orders needed to be restored. The earliest recorded reference to priesthood restoration was in 1823, when Moroni appeared to Joseph Smith and prophesied, "I will reveal [restore] unto you the Priesthood by the hand of the Elijah."[545] But to which order of the priesthood was Moroni referring?

The restoration of the priesthood began on May 15, 1829, with the appearance of John the Baptist, who restored the Aaronic Priesthood. Shortly thereafter, in June 1829, it is assumed, Peter, James, and John restored the Melchizedek Priesthood, including the "keys of the kingdom of God,"[546] which authorizes men to perform the ordinances of salvation and commissions them to preach the gospel of salvation throughout the world. Now the Aaronic and

---

542 See Ezra Taft Benson, "What I Hope You Will Teach Your Children about the Temple," *Ensign,* August 1985.

543 Joseph Smith, *The Teachings of the Prophet Joseph Smith,* 180.

544 Joseph Fielding Smith, ed., *Teachings of the Prophet Joseph Smith,* 166–167.

545 D&C 2:1.

546 Ezra Taft Benson, "What I Hope You Will Teach Your Children about the Temple," *Ensign,* August 1985.

Melchizedek priesthoods had been restored, but in 1823, Moroni
had prophesied that Elijah would come and reveal yet another priesthood order—the *patriarchal order of the Melchizedek Priesthood.*
Joseph Smith learned that this priesthood order could not be restored
without a temple. When the Prophet was expounding on these three
priesthood orders, he made the following statement concerning the
patriarchal order of the priesthood: "[This] Priesthood is Patriarchal
authority. Go to and finish the temple, and God will fill it with
power, and you will then receive more knowledge concerning this
priesthood."[547]

Shortly after the dedication of the Kirtland Temple, on April
3, 1836, Elijah appeared to Joseph Smith and Oliver Cowdery and
committed to them the keys of the patriarchal order of the priesthood, which had power "to turn [seal] the hearts of the fathers to the
children, and the children to the fathers."[548] This patriarchal order of
the priesthood is entered into by husbands and wives when they are
sealed in the temple. The patriarchal order is, in the words of Elder
James E. Talmage, "a condition where 'woman shares with man the
blessings of the Priesthood,' where husband and wife minister, 'seeing
and understanding alike, and cooperating to the full in the government of their family kingdom' (James E. Talmage, Young Woman's
Journal 25, October 1914, 602–603). A man cannot hold this priesthood without a wife, and a woman cannot share the blessings of this
Priesthood without a husband, sealed in the temple."[549]

To turn the hearts of parents and children to each other is, according
to Joseph Smith, the same as *sealing* their hearts together: "Elijah shall
reveal the covenants to *seal* the hearts of the fathers to the children, and
the children to the fathers."[550] "In order to facilitate this linkage, Elijah
revealed, 'the covenants of the fathers in relation to the children, and the
covenants of the children in relation to the fathers.'"[551] That is, Elijah
revealed the sealing keys of the priesthood whereby covenants and

---

547 Joseph Smith, *History of the Church,* 5:554–555.

548 D&C 110:15.

549 *Encyclopedia of Mormonism,* "Patriarchal Order of the Priesthood," 1067.

550 Joseph Fielding Smith, ed., *Teachings of the Prophet Joseph Smith,* 323;
    emphasis added.

551 B. H. Roberts, *History of the Church,* 5:530.

ordinances are bound on earth and in heaven, and therefore they carry "efficacy, virtue, or force in and after the resurrection from the dead."[552]

But Elijah's mission was greater still; Elijah's charge was also to restore the "fulness of the priesthood," which includes the fullness of the temple covenants and the "ordinances of the house of the Lord."[553] Therefore, the Lord commanded the Saints to build a temple for the purpose of endowing them with power from on high: "Yea, verily I say unto you, I gave unto you a commandment that you should build a house, in the which house I design to *endow* those whom I have chosen with *power from on high.* . . ."[554] To *endow* means "to equip or supply . . . to place, receive . . . bestow . . . provide."[555] When a college receives an endowment, the principal is typically placed in a fund where it spins off income perpetually—the endowment is structured to give continually. Just so, God endows us in the temple with knowledge and power that bless us eternally. By relying upon the Lord's endowment and by growing in our understanding of it, we receive greater and greater power to bless our family and others.

Of the connection of the endowment to the fullness of the priesthood, Elder Bruce R. McConkie wrote, "It is *only through the ordinances* of his holy house that the Lord deigns to 'restore again that which was lost unto you, or which he hath taken away, even *the fulness of the priesthood.*'"[556] And Joseph Smith said, "If a man gets a fulness of the priesthood of God he has to get it in the same way that Jesus Christ obtained it, and that was *by keeping all the commandments and obeying* all the ordinances of the house of the Lord."[557]

Elijah's appearance in the Kirtland Temple was preceded by the appearances of the Savior, Moses, and Elias. That Moses and

---

552 D&C 132:7.

553 Joseph Fielding Smith, ed., *Teachings of the Prophet Joseph Smith*, 308.

554 D&C 95:8; emphasis added.

555 *American Heritage Dictionary*, "Endow."

556 Bruce R. McConkie, *Mormon Doctrine*, "Restoration of the Gospel: 10. Temple Ordinances," 637; emphasis added.

557 Joseph Fielding Smith, ed., *Teachings of the Prophet Joseph Smith*, 308; emphasis added.

Elias came and restored keys should hold enormous significance for parents. Moses committed the keys of the gathering of both the dead and the living of the family of Israel. This suggests that individually we are now in possession of the priesthood capacity to gather our families "from the four parts of the earth"[558]—an interesting statement when considered in the context of wayward family members who have strayed. For what purpose is the gathering of families? Elder McConkie wrote, "Israel gathers for the purpose of building temples in which the ordinances of salvation and exaltation are performed for the living and the dead."[559] On an individual level, this statement suggests that we now have power to gather or call our family to the temple to receive the crowning ordinances of salvation.

Elias, whose office is that of forerunner,[560] appeared after Moses and "committed the dispensation of the gospel of Abraham, saying that in us and our seed all generations after us should be blessed."[561] President Joseph Fielding Smith, explaining this, said, "Elias came, after Moses had conferred his keys, and brought the gospel of the dispensation in which Abraham lived. *Everything that pertains to that dispensation, the blessings that were conferred upon Abraham, the promises that were given to his posterity, all had to be restored,* and Elias, who held the keys of that dispensation, came."[562] This is the power to organize families into eternal units. That is, because of Elias, our children and grandchildren can now be blessed with the gospel of Abraham (the new and everlasting covenant), which is the right to receive the priesthood, all gospel blessings, ordinances, and sealings, including eternal marriage and eternal life. This right flows to our children because we, like Abraham, Isaac, Jacob, and their wives, have entered into the Abrahamic covenant or are living worthy of that future blessing.

Joseph Fielding McConkie wrote of the next step in the restoration of saving ordinances: "Simply stated, Elijah was sent in 1836 to reveal keys of the priesthood and sealing powers that had not yet been

---

558 D&C 110:11.
559 Bruce R. McConkie, *A New Witness for the Articles of Faith*, 539.
560 See *Encyclopedia of Mormonism*, "Elias," 449.
561 D&C 110:12.
562 Joseph Fielding Smith, *Doctrines of Salvation*, Volume 3, 127.

fully operational in this dispensation. Elijah restored the keys whereby families organized in the patriarchal order through the powers delivered by Elias could be bound and sealed for eternity."563 Why is the patriarchal priesthood important to us? Because patriarchal priesthood is *family* priesthood, and entering into this order of the priesthood directly affects and eternally empowers both fathers and mothers to do the work of redemption among their posterity. President Joseph Fielding Smith said, "Through the power of *this priesthood which Elijah bestowed,* husband and wife may be sealed, or married for eternity; children may be sealed to their parents for eternity; thus the family is made eternal, and death does not separate the members. *This is the great principle that will save the world from utter destruction.*"564

Imagine Elias and Elijah laying their hands upon your head to give you a priesthood blessing. Elias speaks first and offers you the same covenant of the gospel that Abraham received—the new and everlasting covenant. When you agree to its terms, Elias blesses you with everything that was promised to Abraham: you and your posterity now have the eternal right to the priesthood, the gospel, and eternal life. Central to these blessings is the promise that your marriage will become eternal and that you will have eternal posterity. Additionally, you are promised, as was Abraham, that you and your posterity will receive a promised land in this world and a promised inheritance in the celestial world to come. Now that you have entered into the new and everlasting covenant, which includes the new and everlasting covenant of marriage,565 Elijah confirms these blessings with a *seal* that cannot be broken. Then, as a final blessing, because you have proven faithful at all hazards, he blesses you with the *fulness of the priesthood,* which in the ultimate sense means your being sealed up to eternal life; that is, Elijah makes everything that has been done *more sure.*566 Now, because of your righteousness, Elijah extends to you a promise for your children, which is in addition to the promise made by Elias. The promise is this: *as you turn your heart to your children, their hearts will turn to you and the Abrahamic covenant that you*

563 Joseph Fielding McConkie, *Joseph Smith: The Choice Seer,* 187.
564 Joseph Fielding Smith, *Doctrines of Salvation,* Volume 2, 118; emphasis added.
565 See D&C 131:2.
566 See Joseph Fielding Smith, ed., *Teachings of the Prophet Joseph Smith,* 337–338.

have made. Because you have received the fullness of the priesthood, you now have more power to ask for a *turning* (a conversion opportunity) to happen, subject to Heavenly Father's will and your children's agency. Elijah's blessing guarantees that no matter what happens in time or eternity, these children are yours. Then, when Elias and Elijah finish their blessing upon your head, the Savior receives you into His embrace. You are home at last, and your spouse and your children are there with you.

Of the interwoven tapestry of the restoration of the priesthood, Joseph Fielding McConkie wrote,

> Joseph Smith taught that ultimate salvation is found only in the eternal union of man and woman. Every priesthood, grace, power, and authority restored to the Prophet Joseph Smith centers in the salvation of the family. Peter, James, and John restored the Holy Priesthood, thereby authorizing men to perform the ordinances of salvation; Elias restored the ordinance of eternal marriage and the promise of an endless seed; and Elijah restored the sealing power and the fulness of the priesthood by which husband, wife, and children are bound eternally. These doctrines build on the assurance of the Book of Mormon that the resurrection is corporeal and thus that women will be resurrected as women and men as men, the bond of their love ever intact. Thus, as baptism is the gate to the strait and narrow path leading to eternal life, eternal marriage becomes the door through which all who inherit that glory must enter. None enter alone. The man and the woman must stand side by side. Couples in turn must be bound in eternal covenant with their righteous progenitors and with their posterity. In that eternal and restored system we know as The Church of Jesus Christ of Latter-day Saints, salvation is a family affair.[567]

---

567 Joseph Fielding McConkie, *Joseph Smith: The Choice Seer*, 193–194.

Joseph Smith said, "How shall God come to the rescue of this generation? He will send Elijah the Prophet . . . *Elijah shall reveal the covenants to seal* the hearts of the fathers to the children, and the children to the fathers."[568] Personalizing this statement by the Prophet, we might ask, "How shall God rescue *our* children?" And the answer is, "He will send Elijah to our children to reveal to them their parents' covenants, which have the power to seal their hearts to ours." That is, by virtue of our covenants, the spirit of Elijah reaches out to our children to reveal to them our covenants and seal or turn their hearts to ours.

RIGHTEOUSNESS AND PRIESTHOOD POWER

Elder Russell M. Nelson said, "A distinction . . . exists between priesthood authority and priesthood power. When ordained to an office in the priesthood, one is granted authority. But power comes from exercising that authority in righteousness."[569] A man who sanctifies himself has greater power in the priesthood than a man who does not; a man or woman who sanctifies himself or herself by honoring his or her temple covenants has greater power to ask for and receive blessings than a man or woman who does not; a husband and wife who sanctify themselves in the patriarchal order of the priesthood have greater power to bless their family than a couple who does not.

Ann, a mother in Utah, wrote of her experience with the temple and its incredible power to save her children:

> For many years, I had been feeling like I did not go to the temple often enough. Because my husband was traveling in his work, I was alone many evenings of the week, so I decided that it would be a good time to volunteer as an ordinance worker.
>
> When the temple matron's counselor took me on a tour of the temple and explained my duties, she invited me to put my own name on the temple prayer roll, as well as the names of my children. I should do

---

568 Joseph Fielding Smith, ed., *Teachings of the Prophet Joseph Smith,* 323; emphasis added.

569 Russell M. Nelson, "Personal Priesthood Responsibility," *Ensign,* October 2005.

this each week, she said, and I would receive special blessings for my temple service. She couldn't possibly have known that I was also struggling with how to help my two teenage sons, who had gotten into drugs and associated evils, including a debilitating depression affecting their self-worth. It seemed that every good thing I had tried to instill in my sons was thrown out the window when they got into drugs.

I served in the temple for six years. My boys' names were on the temple's prayer rolls every single day during those years. I watched as small miracles happened to them until, eventually, they found the gospel. My youngest boy found a girl who helped him pull out of his problems and work toward a temple marriage. She and her family were able to encourage my boy when he would no longer listen to me. Today, both boys are married and sealed to wonderful girls. There is no doubt in my mind that my efforts to cleanse myself, learn, and serve in the house of the Lord brought these miracles and helped my sons choose to come back into full fellowship with the Lord. The blessings that came to my children and me far outweighed the blessings of service that I gave as a temple worker.

The requirement to sanctify ourselves to obtain greater power in the priesthood hearkens back to the Lord's commandment to abide in Him, *the true vine.*

> I am the true vine, and my Father is the husbandman.
>
> Every branch in me that beareth not fruit he taketh away: and every branch that beareth fruit, he purgeth it, that it may bring forth more fruit.
>
> Now ye are clean through the word which I have spoken unto you.
>
> Abide in me, and I in you. As the branch cannot bear fruit of itself, except it abide in the vine; no more can ye, except ye abide in me.

I am the vine, ye are the branches: He that abideth in me, and I in him, the same bringeth forth much fruit: for without me ye can do nothing.

If a man abide not in me, he is cast forth as a branch, and is withered; and men gather them, and cast them into the fire, and they are burned.

If ye abide in me, and my words abide in you, ye shall ask what ye will, and it shall be done unto you.

Herein is my Father glorified, that ye bear much fruit; so shall ye be my disciples.[570]

We, the branches, grow from the true vine and draw our nourishment from it. Note in Jesus' teaching that the branches are already producing, but the husbandman (God) wants them to produce more. To that end, He begins to prune—to "purge and purify." The branches must endure this purging and purifying process if they hope to gain greater strength to produce more fruit. The husbandman cuts from the branch anything that saps its strength, and he carefully directs the growth so that that branch can perform optimally. For a while the branch may look (and probably feel) pitiful and barren. It might not produce much fruit for a season. But the husbandman knows that in time the purging and purifying procedure will cause the branch to bring forth more than it ever has. Remaining attached to the true vine and enduring the purging are the keys.

Here is Christ's promise: as long as we, the branches, remain in Christ and He in us, our nourishment and strength will never fail. "Ye shall ask what ye will, and it shall be done unto you."[571] Parents of wayward children have urgent things to ask of Christ. To the degree that we are *in* Him and He is *in* us, and to the degree that we submit to the Father's process of sanctification, we are promised that we can draw strength from the true vine to ask for and receive blessings.

Like the analogy of the true vine and its branches, "the rights of the priesthood are inseparably connected with the powers of heaven." It is our degree of righteousness that measures the strength of our connection to the powers of heaven—"the powers of heaven cannot be

---

570 John 15:1–8.
571 John 15:7.

controlled nor handled only upon the principles of righteousness."[572]
Therefore, the Father purges and purifies us to bring forth more fruit;
that is, as we become more righteous, we receive more priesthood
power.

SEEDS OF THE COVENANT PLANTED BY PARENTS AND PROGENITORS
As we have learned, one of the greatest powers of the priesthood is the
patriarchal power to "plant in the hearts of the children the promises
made to the fathers" with the assurance that "the hearts of the children shall turn to their fathers."[573] This *planting* and *turning* is often
associated with genealogical work, which is part of Elijah's mission.
But President Harold B. Lee added that the spirit of Elijah also
"applies just as much on this side of the veil . . . . So, the hearts of you
fathers and mothers must be turned to your children right now, if you
have the true spirit of Elijah, and do not think that it applies merely
to those who are beyond the veil."[574]

When we parents offer prayer, *patriarchal prayer*, in behalf of our
children, who are the children of the covenant,[575] we turn our hearts to
them and effectively seek for heavenly help to plant in their hearts the
seeds of our covenants and testimonies. This suggests that our *patriarchal prayer* literally opens the door for our children's grandparents and
other forefathers and foremothers—perhaps even back to Abraham and
Sarah, Isaac and Rebekah, Jacob and Rachel, and Adam and Eve—to
come forth and plant the seeds of their covenants and testimonies in
the children's hearts. After all, these children are theirs too.

By the power of the Holy Ghost, this planting is often accomplished by angels, who are the children's ancestors. As we have
stated, President Joseph F. Smith said, "When messengers are sent
to minister to the inhabitants of this earth, they are not strangers,
but from the ranks of our kindred, friends, and fellow-beings and
fellow-servants."[576] Seen or unseen, these ancestral angels plant in the

---

572 D&C 121:36.

573 D&C 2:2.

574 Harold B. Lee, quoted in Robert L. Millet's *When a Child Wanders*, 120.

575 See 3 Nephi 20:26.

576 John A. Widtsoe, ed., *Gospel Doctrine: Selections from the Sermons and Writings
     of Joseph F. Smith*, 435.

children's hearts tiny seeds of recollection—faint remembrances of the children's premortal covenants. The seeds of those memories are held in place by the power of the fathers' covenants and sealings. Our children may have forgotten the truth; or they may believe the gospel but doubt their desire and ability to live it—whatever is the case, one thing is certain: our children know the truth. Both in this life and in countless ages past, they have heard the truth declared by their nearest and most distant progenitors. Now they just need to remember and courageously respond; they need to *turn their hearts* back. And the probability is that they will. The priesthood power manifested in mighty patriarchal prayer sets in motion this *planting* from both sides of the veil, and holds the seed of covenant and testimony in place until it grows to the point that it will likely turn the children back to the Lord and to us, their parents.

Priesthood Ordinances Provide Guidance, Protection, and Strength to Endure and Overcome

Endowed parents can draw upon the power of their priesthood covenants and ordinances to protect, guide, and strengthen their children and themselves.

Because of the priesthood's power to ward off and shield us from danger, the Lord revealed that we must receive the priesthood endowment in order to escape the tempter: "And that ye might *escape the power of the enemy,* and be gathered unto me a righteous people, without spot and blameless—Wherefore, for this cause I gave unto you the commandment that ye should go to the Ohio; and there I will give unto you my law; and *there you shall be endowed with power from on high.*"[577]

Of the priesthood's power to protect and to guide, President Harold B. Lee taught, "The temple ceremonies are designed by a wise Heavenly Father, who has revealed them to us in these last days as a *guide and a protection throughout our lives.* . . . We talk of security in this day, and yet we fail to understand that here on this Temple Block we have standing the holy temple wherein we may find *the symbols by which power might be generated that will save this nation*

---

577 D&C 38:31–32; emphasis added.

from destruction. Therein may be found the fulness of the blessings of the Priesthood."[578] Certainly, if the guidance of the temple covenants and ordinances can save the nation from destruction, it can save our children.

Moreover, priesthood temple covenants and ordinances give us the strength to endure tribulation and come off conqueror. Elder Robert D. Hales said, "The steadying arm of the Lord reaches us through the ordinances of His holy temples. Said the Prophet Joseph Smith . . . 'You need an endowment, brethren, in order that you may be prepared and able to overcome all things.' How right he was! *Being blessed with the temple covenants and endowed with power [makes] it possible for the Latter-day Saints to endure tribulation with faith."*[579]

Clearly, the blessings of protection, guidance, strength, and victory flow from honoring temple covenants and ordinances.

THE LANGUAGE OF PRIESTHOOD POWER

There is a vast difference between the way men and God work. To accomplish most things in life, mankind must exert physical effort, whereas God works by faith and the power of words.[580] In *Lectures on Faith,* Joseph Smith taught of the power of the word of God:

> We understand that when a man works by faith, he works by *mental exertion* instead of physical force. It is *by words,* instead of exerting his physical powers, with which every being works when he works by faith. God said, "Let there be light: and there was light." Joshua spake and the great lights which God had created stood still. Elijah commanded and the heavens were stayed for the space of three years and six months, so that it did not rain: he again commanded and the heavens gave forth rain. All this was done by faith. And the Saviour says: "If you have faith as a grain of mustard seed, say to this mountain, 'Remove,'

---

578 Harold B. Lee, *Decisions for Successful Living,* 141; emphasis added.
579 Robert D. Hales, "Faith through Tribulation Brings Peace and Joy," *Ensign,* May 2003; emphasis added.
580 See Bruce R. McConkie, *A New Witness for the Articles of Faith,* 176–177.

and it will remove; or say unto this sycamine tree, 'Be ye plucked up, and planted in the midst of the sea,' and it shall obey you" (Gen. 1:3, Josh. 10:12–13, 1 Kgs. 17:1; 18:1, 41–45, Matt. 17:20, Luke 17:6). *Faith, then, works by words; and with these its mightiest works have been, and will be, performed."*[581]

The Nephite prophet Jacob said, "For behold, by the *power of his word* man came upon the face of the earth, which earth was created by the *power of his word*. Wherefore, if God being able to *speak* and the world was, and to *speak* and man was created, O then, why not able to command the earth, or the workmanship of his hands upon the face of it, according to his will and pleasure?"[582] Clearly, there is power in God's words.

The word of God must be spoken with God's authority, and as "priesthood power is the . . . authority delegated by God to act in His name,"[583] therefore the word of God is *priesthood language*.

> And so great was the faith of Enoch that he led the people of God, and their enemies came to battle against them; *and he spake the word of the Lord,* and the earth trembled, and the mountains fled, even according to his command; and the rivers of water were turned out of their course; and the roar of the lions was heard out of the wilderness; and all nations feared greatly, *so powerful was the word of Enoch, and so great was the power of the language which God had given him.*[584]

Other prophets have testified of the power of priesthood language, the word of God:

- Paul: "Through faith we understand that the worlds were framed *by the word of God*, so that

---

581 Joseph Smith, *Lectures on Faith,* 7:3; emphasis added.
582 Jacob 4:9; emphasis added.
583 James E. Faust, "Power of the Priesthood," *Ensign*, May 1997.
584 Moses 7:13; emphasis added.

things which are seen were not made of things which do appear."[585]

- Moroni: "Who shall say that it was not a miracle that *by his word* the heaven and the earth should be; and *by the power of his word* man was created of the dust of the earth; and *by the power of his word* have miracles been wrought?[586]

- Nephi: "Now ye know that Moses was commanded of the Lord to do that great work; and ye know that *by his word* the waters of the Red Sea were divided hither and thither, and they passed through on dry ground."[587]

The words of God flow from the *Word*[588] or the *Word of God's Power*[589] or the *Word of God*[590]—Jesus Christ. Everything must be done in His name. At the time of ordination, Melchizedek Priesthood holders have the name of Jesus Christ "put upon them" so that they may represent Him and speak the *word of God* by the use of *His name*. The Lord explained to Abraham, "Behold, I will lead thee by my hand, and I will take thee, *to put upon thee my name, even the Priesthood.*"[591] In the temple—and here is the key—men and women are taught specific words of God (sacred priesthood language) under the covenant of nondisclosure and dedicated, proprietary use. Elder McConkie said, "The greatest blessings are reserved for those who obtain 'the fulness of the priesthood,' meaning the fullness of the blessings of the priesthood. *These blessings are found only in the temples of God.*" Then quoting Joseph Smith, he continued, "'There are certain key words and signs belonging to the priesthood which must be observed in order to obtain the blessing.'"[592]

---

585 Hebrews 11:3; emphasis added.
586 Mormon 9:17; emphasis added.
587 1 Nephi 17:26; emphasis added.
588 See John 1:1.
589 See Moses 1:32.
590 See Revelation 19:11–16.
591 Abraham 1:18; emphasis added.
592 Bruce R. McConkie, *Mormon Doctrine*, "Melchizedek Priesthood," 482; emphasis added.

We must learn to authoritatively speak those words of God in righteousness to effect miracles, as did the prophets. Herein is power to petition blessings from heaven in behalf of our children. Joseph Smith said, "A man can do nothing for himself unless God direct him in the right way; and *the Priesthood is for that purpose.*"[593] As we grow in our understanding of priesthood language, doors will open that we might likewise do the mighty works associated with such language. This, then, is the language of power for *"the salvation of the children of men"*[594]—our children!

President Benson summarized the previous points in a simple but profound statement:

> The temple ceremony was given by a wise Heavenly Father to help us become more Christlike. The endowment was revealed by revelation and can be understood only by revelation. The instruction is given in *symbolic language.* The late Apostle John A. Widtsoe taught, "No man or woman can come out of the temple endowed as he should be, unless he has seen, beyond the symbol, the mighty realities for which the symbol stands."[595]

KEYS OF THE PRIESTHOOD

No power is greater than priesthood power to rescue the wayward and bring them to Christ. Therefore, everything we can learn about the priesthood increases our faith and ability to seek redeeming blessings. The fullness of the priesthood is only available by righteously receiving and living *all* of the temple covenants and ordinances. These covenants are presumed to be the keys of salvation, as found only in the temple. President Ezra Taft Benson said,

> Even though the Aaronic Priesthood and Melchizedek Priesthood had been restored to the

---

593 Joseph Fielding Smith, ed., *Teachings of the Prophet Joseph Smith*, 364; emphasis added.

594 D&C 128:11.

595 John A. Widstoe quoted, and President Benson, in Ezra Taft Benson's *The Teachings of Ezra Taft Benson*, 250–251; emphasis added.

earth, the Lord urged the Saints to build a temple to receive the *keys* by which this order of priesthood could be administered on the earth again, "for there [was] not a place found on earth that he may come to and restore again that which was lost . . . *even the fulness of the priesthood*" D&C 124:28).[596]

In the revelation quoted by President Benson, the Lord speaks of both the "fulness of the priesthood" and of "keys." The term *keys* has several meanings. Typically, the term is used to describe the directing power of the priesthood. In that sense, "many keys were restored . . . by heavenly messengers to the Prophet Joseph Smith and Oliver Cowdery. The keys of the kingdom of God on earth are held by the apostles. The president of the church, who is the senior apostle, holds all the keys presently on earth and presides over all the organizational and ordinance work of the Church (D&C 107:8–9, 91–92). He delegates authority by giving the keys of specific offices to others (D&C 124:123)."[597]

In another sense, the term *keys* refers to a "means of access," or "something that secures or controls entrance."[598] "Holders of the Melchizedek Priesthood are said to have 'the keys of the Church,' 'the key of knowledge,' and 'the keys of all the spiritual blessings of the church' (D&C 42:69; 84:19; 107:18), while belonging to the Aaronic Priesthood are 'the keys of the ministering of angels, and of the gospel of repentance, and of baptism by immersion for the remission of sins' (D&C 13:1; 84:26)."[599] In the case of temple keys, these keys unlock the doors of revelation and power—important *keys* for parents.

Of keys received by individuals in the temple, Brigham Young taught, "Then go on and build the temples of the Lord, that you may receive the endowments in store for you, and *possess the keys of the eternal Priesthood,* that you may receive every word, sign, and token, and be made acquainted with the laws of angels, and of the kingdom

---

596 Ezra Taft Benson, *The Teachings of Ezra Taft Benson*, 249; emphasis added.
597 *Encyclopedia of Mormonism*, "Keys of the Priesthood," 780–781.
598 Dictionary.com, "Key."
599 *Encyclopedia of Mormonism*, "Keys of the Priesthood," 780–781.

of our Father and our God, and know how to pass from one degree to another, and enter fully into the joy of your Lord."[600]

Worthy men and women are endowed with keys of revelation to personally save their children, others for whom they have a stewardship, and themselves. Blaine Yorgason suggests, then, that the term *keys,* in this sense, is synonymous with temple ordinances. Quoting from Doctrine and Covenants section 84, he wrote, "'This greater priesthood . . . holdeth the *key* of the mysteries of the kingdom, even the *key* of the knowledge of God. Therefore *in the ordinances thereof* [and where are most of our ordinances found?], the power of godliness is manifest.'"[601] That is, while priesthood *authority* is conferred and made operational by delegated administrative keys, priesthood *power* comes by becoming godly—and true godliness cannot be achieved without the keys or ordinances of the priesthood. Neither can the highest level of revelation be achieved. Brigham Young said, "The Priesthood is given to the people and *the keys thereof,* and, when properly understood, they may actually unlock the treasury of the Lord, and receive to their fullest satisfaction."[602]

Would not attaining these powers be the desire of every parent who struggles with a wayward child? And yet, these powers, which enhance our ability to ask for and receive blessings, are within reach as we learn and apply the temple covenants and ordinances. On April 28, 1842, six days before the endowment was first given, Joseph Smith told the Relief Society that he was about to deliver *"the keys of the Priesthood to the Church,* and said that the faithful members of the Relief Society should receive them with their husbands, that the Saints whose integrity has been tried and proved faithful, *might know how to ask the Lord and receive an answer."*[603]

A subsequent revelation followed. Notice that these "keys" heighten our ability to "ask the Lord and receive an answer," especially with regard to the salvation of our loved ones on either side of the veil.

---

600 Brigham Young, *Discourses of Brigham Young,* 395–396; emphasis added.
601 Blaine Yorgason, *I Need Thee Every Hour,* 363; emphasis added.
602 Brigham Young, *Discourses of Brigham Young,* 131; emphasis added.
603 Joseph Fielding Smith, ed., *Teachings of the Prophet Joseph Smith,* 226; emphasis added.

Now the great and grand secret of the whole matter, and the *summum bonum* of the whole subject that is lying before us, consists in obtaining the powers of the Holy Priesthood. *For him to whom these keys are given there is no difficulty in obtaining a knowledge of facts in relation to the salvation of the children of men, both as well for the dead as for the living.*"[604]

The "living" would include our children. Clearly, temple keys are keys to salvation.

---

604   D&C 128:11; emphasis added.

Chapter 10
THE POWER OF GATHERING IN THE LORD'S NAME

For where two or three are gathered together in my name,
there am I in the midst of them.

—*Matthew 18:20*

THE SCRIPTURES ARE REPLETE WITH commandments for the Saints to be one. It applies to Apostles, husbands and wives, families, Church organizations and units, and the everyday disciple of Christ. The commandment has a blessing attached, a blessing that lends great power to all who seek to obey it—whether they be civilly married couples, couples sealed in the temple, single parents who can access the faith of those around them, or even children striving to ignite the faith of their parents. Though much of this chapter will focus on couples, many of the principles and promises can be applied to all who yearn for the return of a loved one to the path of righteousness.

THE POWER OF ONENESS
President Gordon B. Hinckley taught this incredible principle with a promise: "When you are united, your power is limitless. You can accomplish anything you wish to accomplish."[605] Jesus taught His disciples in Jerusalem concerning the power of unity, and then He taught that principle anew in this dispensation: "Verily, verily, I say unto you, as I said unto my disciples, where two or three are gathered

---

605 Gordon B. Hinckley, "Your Greatest Challenge, Mother," *Ensign,* November 2000.

together in my name, as touching one thing, behold, there will I be in the midst of them—even so am I in the midst of you."[606]

Oneness is exemplified throughout the gospel. The Godhead is comprised of three distinct individuals, whose united purpose makes them one. They should be our model. We become *at one* with God through the *At-one-ment* of Jesus Christ, and it is through His *At-one-ment* that we become one[607] and joint-heirs with Him.[608]

Another example of oneness is Zion. Individuals who create of their relationship a *Zion* are of "one heart and one mind," and remarkably, this environment results in an interesting effect, which has far-reaching consequences—that of economic equality or the idea of "no poor among them."[609] Beyond the economic implications, which are Zion's least requirement, "no poor" also means *no poor in spirit*—that is, no spiritually or emotionally poor. No lack at all—something stressed-out parents of the wayward can appreciate! Consider the effects of the righteous Nephites' oneness after Christ's coming:

> And there were no contentions and disputations among them, and every man did deal justly one with another. . . .
>
> And the Lord did prosper them exceedingly in the land . . . [and they] . . . were blessed according to the multitude of the promises which the Lord had made unto them. . . .
>
> And they had all things common among them; therefore there were not rich and poor, bond and free, but they were all made free, and partakers of the heavenly gift.
>
> And it came to pass that there was no contention in the land, because of the love of God which did dwell in the hearts of the people.
>
> And there were no envyings, nor strifes, nor tumults, nor whoredoms, nor lyings, nor murders, nor

---

606 D&C 6:32.
607 See Bruce R. McConkie, *The Mortal Messiah,* Volume 1, 131.
608 See Romans 8:17.
609 Moses 7:18.

any manner of lasciviousness; and surely there could
not be a happier people among all the people who had
been created by the hand of God. . . .

    They were in one, the children of Christ, and heirs
to the kingdom of God.

    And how blessed were they![610]

Imagine inserting the words *the family* in place of *them, they,
the people,* or *the land.* Other scriptural accounts describe the power
of oneness in relation to its converting power. Alma and Amulek
became one and helped to convert many wicked Nephites. The
sons of Mosiah became one and were the instruments in converting
thousands of bloodthirsty Lamanites. Alma's grandsons, Nephi and
Lehi, became one and helped convert yet more thousands of the
unrepentant. So how can we access the power of gathering in the
Lord's name for our wayward loved ones, even if we are single parents
or acting without the faith or support of our spouse?

Unity of Faith through Purpose, Action, Fasting, and Prayer
President Henry B. Eyring promised us that the wayward would
return as a reward of our unrelenting efforts. In many cases, he said,
God would call back our children (and one could certainly apply
this to other loved ones) through those who are called to serve in the
Church.[611] Clearly, we should actively use the resources of the Church,
family, and trusted and influential friends in applying our faith on
behalf of our loved ones. Joseph Smith said, "The greatest temporal and
spiritual blessings which always come from faithfulness and concerted
effort, *never attended individual exertion or enterprise.*"[612]

    Caring friends, family, bishoprics, teachers, and other relevant local
Church presidencies should be invited to participate in influencing,
fasting, and praying for our loved ones. Unity in purpose and action is
made even more holy and influential through prayer. For instance, in
the presence of six Elders, the Prophet Joseph Smith received a revelation that, in part, speaks to the subject of the power of multiple voices

---

610 4 Nephi 1:2, 7, 11, 3, 15–18.
611 See Henry B. Eyring, "The True and Living Church," *Ensign,* May 2008.
612 Joseph Smith, *Teachings of the Prophet Joseph Smith,* 183; emphasis added.

united in prayer. Because they were gathered in the Lord's name and united in prayer, the Lord was in their midst and invited them to ask for and receive blessings: "Lift up your hearts and be glad, for *I am in your midst,* and am your advocate with the Father; and it is his good will to give you the kingdom. And, as it is written—Whatsoever ye shall ask in faith, *being united in prayer* according to my command, ye shall receive."[613] Then the Lord blessed them with what they were praying for because "it is given unto you that ye may understand, *because ye have asked it of me and are agreed.*"[614] That is, they had unitedly agreed, and, as if with one voice, they had asked in faith.

This is the principle Alma the Elder applied in rescuing his wayward son. Notice in the angel's words how others joined with Alma in his quest:

> And again, the angel said: Behold, the Lord hath heard *the prayers of his people,* and also the prayers of his servant, Alma, who is thy father; for he has prayed with much faith concerning thee that thou mightest be brought to the knowledge of the truth; therefore, for this purpose have I come to convince thee of the power and authority of God, that the prayers of his *servants* might be answered according to *their* faith.[615]

Then, when Alma the Younger had his experience with the angel, his father gathered those same people to help ensure the experience became one of conversion:

> And he caused that a *multitude* should be gathered together that they might witness what the Lord had done for his son, and also for those that were with him.
>
> And he caused that the *priests* should assemble themselves together; and they began to fast, and to pray to the Lord their God that he would open the

---

613 D&C 29:5–6; emphasis added.
614 D&C 29:33; emphasis added.
615 Mosiah 27:14; emphasis added.

mouth of Alma, that he might speak, and also that his limbs might receive their strength—that the eyes of the *people* might be opened to see and know of the goodness and glory of God.[616]

Lastly, as touched on earlier, accessing the power of the unified faith of thousands through the temple prayer rolls, and of the faith and help of those across the veil, whom we help when we do the work for the dead, we can effectively *gather* in the Lord's name as we strive for the salvation of our children and loved ones, knowing that Christ's grace and power is thus in our midst and we are His.

ONENESS AS COUPLES

Consider the scripture in Doctrine and Covenants 38:27, which reads, "I say unto you, be one; and if ye are not one ye are not mine." Certainly this scripture applies to husband and wife. By definition of their marriage covenant, they are (or should be) one. This principle of gathering in the Lord's name has power to invite Him and thereby invokes extraordinary power when exercised in righteousness.

The Lord takes seriously the oneness that should exist in marriage, even when that marriage is not yet a temple marriage. He states emphatically that it is simply "not good that the man should be alone"; man needs and is incomplete without "an help meet."[617] Clearly, the condition of aloneness is "not good" and so critical to our salvation that it requires the sacrifice of all former relationships and self to rectify.

Speaking of the quality of *oneness* created by the partnership of marriage, President Hinckley said the following:

> In His grand design, when God first created man, He created a duality of the sexes. The ennobling expression of that duality is found in marriage. One individual is complementary to the other. As Paul stated, "Neither is the man without the woman, neither the woman without the man, in the Lord" (1 Cor. 11:11).

616 Mosiah 27: 21–22; emphasis added.
617 Moses 3:18.

There is no other arrangement that meets the divine purposes of the Almighty. Man and woman are His creations. Their duality is His design. Their complementary relationships and functions are fundamental to His purposes. One is incomplete without the other.[618]

In the oneness of a Zion marriage, where God has made two people one, and where the husband and wife have worked to knit their hearts and minds as one in purpose, there is simply no lack. The Nephites achieved this same oneness after the visitation of the resurrected Christ.

The oneness of a husband and wife in marriage can result in the same, unparalleled happiness, blessings, and abundance the Nephites experienced. More importantly, those who come in contact with such a couple, children included, are leavened by the couple's oneness until all within their gravitational pull become one. In the same way that Jesus Christ and Heavenly Father are one, which oneness enables Jesus to draw all men to Him,[619] so we parents, by our oneness, gain power to draw our children to us if we keep the full requirements of covenant marriage.

Synergy Versus Antagonism

The stress that comes in dealing with a wayward child can result in either antagonism or synergy between parents. Because the "war" with their child can be long and severe, parents can either harden their hearts against each other or soften them and unite in an unbreakable union of purpose. Using the people of Nephi as an example of this very principle, Elder Boyd K. Packer noted,

> The same testing in troubled times can have quite opposite effects on individuals. Three verses from the Book of Mormon, which is another testament of Christ, teach us that "they had wars, and bloodsheds, and famine, and affliction, for the space of many years.

---

618 Gordon B. Hinckley, "The Women in Our Lives," *Ensign*, November 2004, 84.
619 See 3 Nephi 27:14–15.

"And there had been murders, and contentions, and dissensions, and all manner of iniquity among the people of Nephi; nevertheless for the righteous' sake, yea, because of the prayers of the righteous, they were spared.

"But behold, because of the exceedingly great length of the war between the Nephites and the Lamanites many had become *hardened* . . . [but also due to the] great length of the war . . . many were *softened* because of their afflictions, insomuch that they did humble themselves before God, even in the depth of humility"(Alma 62:39–41, italics added).[620]

Afflictions can push parents apart, when in actuality afflictions are designed to weld us together. A young woman who had endured yet another miscarriage was told in a blessing, "This experience will weld you and your husband together forever." We might ask, "But aren't they bound by marriage?" Or even, "Aren't they already sealed in the temple?" Yes, but they were not as yet *welded.* Both triumphing over the furnace of affliction and living worthy of the Holy Spirit of Promise are required to make a sealing *sure.*

When it comes to antagonism, we cannot factor out Satan, the father of antagonism, who seeks to tear us apart. Elder M. Russell Ballard said, "When evil wants to strike out and disrupt the essence of God's work, it attacks the family. It does so by attempting to disregard the law of chastity, to confuse gender, to desensitize violence, to make crude and blasphemous language the norm, and to make immoral and deviant behavior seem like the rule rather than the exception."[621] Joseph Smith taught this frightening reality: "In relation to the kingdom of God, the devil always sets up his kingdom at the very same time in opposition to God."[622] Imagine, on that joyful day when we were married, the devil also set up a kingdom to oppose us! Remaining unaware of that fact and neglecting to fight back can ruin us. Of this fact, President George Q. Cannon taught,

---

620 Boyd K. Packer, "The Mystery of Life," *Ensign,* November 1983.
621 M. Russell Ballard, "Let Our Voices Be Heard," *Ensign,* November 2003, 18.
622 Joseph Fielding Smith, ed., *Teachings of the Prophet Joseph Smith,* 365.

> If any man or woman expects to enter into the
> celestial kingdom of our God without being tested
> to the very uttermost, they have not understood the
> Gospel. If there is a weak spot in our nature, or
> if there is a fiber that can be made to quiver or to
> shrink, we may rest assured that it will be tested. Our
> own weaknesses will be brought fully to light, and in
> seeking for help, the strength of our God will also be
> made manifest to us.[623]

With so much at stake, we cannot allow that which President
Thomas S. Monson called "hidden wedges"[624] to form cracks in our
relationship while expecting to save others.

Oneness has a synergistic effect. *Synergy* refers to the phenomenon
in which two or more agents acting together create an effect greater
than the sum of the individual agents. For example, if one thread can
hold five pounds before it breaks, two threads woven together might
be predicted to hold twice as much—ten pounds. But, because of the
effect of synergy, the two threads woven together can actually hold
twenty pounds! Richard Eyre describes synergy this way: "If person A
alone is too short to reach an apple on a tree and person B is too short
as well, once person B sits on the shoulders of person A, they are more
than tall enough to reach the apple."[625]

Disturbingly, the opposite of synergy, *antagonism,* can result in
two agents effectively working against each other, thus achieving *less*
in combination than the individuals could achieve separately.

The Lord commanded us to be one and to share each other's
burdens: "And be you afflicted in all his afflictions, ever lifting up your
heart unto me in prayer and faith, for his and your deliverance."[626]
Oneness brings deliverance! But because we live in a fallen world where
we are subject to the temptations of Satan, duality and conflict often
retard unity and peace. We must quickly recognize and rectify such a

---

623 George Q. Cannon, *Messages of the First Presidency of The Church of Jesus Christ
     of Latter-day Saints*, Volume 3, 27.
624 Thomas S. Monson, "Hidden Wedges," *Liahona*, July 2002.
625 Richard Eyre, "Synergicity," MeridianMagazine.com.
626 D&C 30:6.

condition; synergy must replace antagonism for unity and strength to reenter the relationship. An antagonistic relationship simply cannot produce the power necessary to rescue wayward children.

Elder Bruce C. Hafen related the story of Nicole and Geoff, a couple experiencing antagonism in their marriage.

> A few years after their temple marriage, Geoff began losing interest in the Church, which left Nicole feeling spiritually very alone. . . .
>
> As she searched for guidance, Nicole ran across a book about the Atonement . . . "and [her] life changed." Instead of continuing to worry about her husband's choices, she gave priority to putting her own "spirituality back on track." She prayed for changes in her marriage, in her husband's choices, and in her own choices. She was surprised when the changes didn't come in big ways, but they eventually did come—"in the most subtle ways and through obedience to promptings." Then, she wrote, "last Sunday, with no forewarning and with no apparent catalyst, Geoff woke up and casually announced he was coming to church."
>
> She had learned to stop working on trying to force his Church activity. Rather, she had focused on being "faithful regardless of others' decisions" and on making herself "the kind of wife and person that Geoff wants to be with forever."[627]

David Whitmer, a close friend of Joseph Smith, related an enlightening experience that happened while the Prophet was translating the gold plates:

> He [Joseph] was a religious and straightforward man. He had to be; for he was illiterate and could do nothing himself. He had to trust in God. He could not

---

627 Bruce C. Hafen, *Covenant Hearts,* 128–129.

translate unless he was humble and possessed the right feelings towards everyone. To illustrate so you can see: One morning when he was getting ready to continue the translation, something went wrong about the house and he was put out about it. Something that Emma, his wife, had done. Oliver and I went upstairs and Joseph came up soon after to continue the translation but he could not do anything. He could not translate a single syllable. He went downstairs, out into the orchard, and made supplication to the Lord; was gone about an hour—came back to the house, and asked Emma's forgiveness and then came upstairs where we were and then the translation went on all right. He could do nothing save he was humble and faithful.[628]

The principle is clear: *heal your relationship first, and then you can heal others.*

The Power of Love

The first step in healing our relationships is through practicing Christlike love. True love between a husband and wife gives them the power to effectively seek and secure blessings from heaven and to rescue their wayward children. President Joseph F. Smith said, "Charity, or love, is the greatest principle in existence."[629] The Apostle John wrote: "Beloved, let us love one another: for love is of God; and every one that loveth is born of God, and knoweth God." Restated, the man or woman who does not love well does not know God well: "He that loveth not knoweth not God; for God is love."[630] Therefore, the more like God we become, the more love we have to give, and the more love we have to give, the more power we have to save others.

Craig and Janice, parents from New Mexico, spoke candidly about the impact their wayward daughter had on their relationship and how the rekindling of their love saved their marriage from destruction.

---

628 B. H. Roberts, *History of the Church*, Volume 1, 131.
629 Joseph F. Smith, *Conference Report*, April 1917, 4.
630 1 John 4:7–8.

Agency is that wonderful gift that is full of promise and risk. When our daughter Andrea, exercised her agency to sin, she reacted by feeling dirty and worthless. Because she couldn't forget the deed, she imagined that she couldn't be forgiven. She was too embarrassed to talk to the bishop and begin the repentance process. But as quiet as she wanted to keep the deed, secrets have a way of getting out. Soon, members of the ward snubbed Andrea. In my opinion, this is a form of persecution. The snubbing had a spiraling effect—she no longer felt comfortable at church, so she quit attending, which caused her to lose the Spirit.

We were divided as to how to help Andrea. My husband wanted to press Andrea to repent quickly, because living with unrepentant sin can be disastrous. I agreed, but I wanted to take the nurturing approach and keep the relationship intact. Unfortunately this caused a lot of conflict and contention between us. Not only was this not helpful to Andrea, but it kept us from comforting each other at a very traumatic time. The adversary is so clever. We wanted the same thing, but we thought it needed to be done in two exactly different ways. That distraction pulled us away from each other and from Andrea.

Craig made the first gesture of reconciliation. Love notes and flowers started appearing at unexpected times. He planned a short romantic trip together, and he made sure that weekly date nights were sacred. He took more opportunities to compliment me on my appearance, and he continually expressed his gratitude that I was his wife. Even more important, he told me that I was a good mother, and gave me specific evidences. That was so comforting to me at a time when I was feeling like a failure. He asked for my opinion on dealing with Andrea, and he really considered what I had to say. We shared ideas and came up with a unified plan. All of this endeared him to me in a way that I had never experienced before. I was actually grateful for the adversity because it pulled us together in a remarkable, loving way. Of course, I could not let his loving gestures go unreciprocated. The more he gave the more I wanted to give back to him. Being loving is so wonderful.

We still struggle with Andrea, but the loving unity of our marriage seems to be bringing her around. Home is now the safe place that she needs to deal with her problems. She knows that her parents love each other, and she knows that we love her. We hope that the few narrow-minded people at the ward will someday soften their position, but for now we try to put all our energy into our relationship. We are certain that love and unity will eventually prevail.

Parents who are truly united in love have saving power that is perhaps only exceeded by the saving power of God. Thus it behooves parents to recommit to each other and tap into the incredible power of unified love.

What Is "True Love"?

There is a vast difference between being *in love* and being *loving*. True love is built on the three pillars of complete loyalty, complete sacrifice, and complete trust. Moreover, true love is patient. As we have discussed, patience promises, "I will wait for you; I will wait with you; I will wait upon you." True love is being *loving*, which is being charitable, and charity is the "pure love of Christ."[631] Charity is not so much a *feeling* as it is a *principle of power* that can lift and save.

H. Wallace Goddard observed that charity has three meanings: *love from Christ, love for Christ, love like Christ*. The process of loving begins when we feel Jesus reaching after us (love *from* Christ).

---

631 Moroni 7:47.

> Somewhere along the path the miracle of His love breaks down our resistance. As we begin to understand His goodness and redemptiveness, we are changed. We are filled with a profound awe and gratitude for Him. We experience the stirrings of hope. Without this conversion, we are nothing spiritually (1 Cor. 13:2; 2 Ne. 26:30; Moro. 7:44, 46; D&C 18:19). As the amazing truth of His unrelenting love pierces our hearts, we are led to the second kind of charity, *love for Christ.* "We love him, because he first loved us" (1 Jn. 1:19). . . . As soon as we glimpse His love for us we instinctively love Him in return. We fall at His feet and bathe them with tears of gratitude. Why would He do all He has done to love and rescue my flawed soul? Why??? The answer is charity. As we feel the love from Him and for Him, we naturally *love like Him.* We become saviors on Mount Zion with Him.[632]

Interestingly, a temple marriage—especially one that is built upon the foundation of charity—is called a saving ordinance.[633] Temple marriage saves a man and a woman. Marriage is one of the greatest evidences of God's salvation. In an act of unequalled charity, He snatches two individuals from their fallen condition, introduces them to each other as His beloved son and daughter, and invites them to experience His exalted meaning of love and thus partake of the fullness of His glory. Through marriage God saves the couple, they save each other, and others are saved in the process. Amazingly, by means of the couple's saving marriage, their progenitors now experience a higher manifestation of salvation, for "they without us cannot be made perfect."[634]

Likewise, future generations are saved by the couple's marriage. As children are born into this union, they are saved by the love and the covenants of their parents. Therefore, by the couple's entering into the saving relationship of marriage, the children become the focal point of eternity for untold generations past and future.

---

632 H. Wallace Goddard, *Drawing Heaven into Your Marriage,* 111.
633 See Bruce R. McConkie, *Mormon Doctrine,* "Celestial Marriage," 117–118.
634 D&C 128:15.

"The Family: A Proclamation to the World" states that husbands and wives, by virtue of their marriage vows, have a solemn obligation to love and care for one another.[635] As couples continue to court and care for one another, they ensure their love will never die. Likewise, to keep their love vibrant, husbands and wives might try applying two keys of courting: anticipate the needs of their companion, then surprise and delight with constant acts of love. It has been said that children can receive no greater gift than being reared by parents who love each other.

Surely there can be nothing greater than the love that Heavenly Father has for our Heavenly Mother. A husband wrote about his contemplation of this idea and how it helped him to be a better partner:

> After three and a half decades of marriage, I was one day distressed by the realization that, as much as I loved my wife, my level of love for her paled in comparison to the love that Heavenly Father has for His wife. His love is perfect love; mine is not. Therefore, I realized that I had a ways to go. Because charity is a spiritual gift, I began to pray that I could learn to love my wife as Heavenly Father loves His wife. Every time I prayed, I received the same answer, *Do more for your wife.* Love, I learned, is a feeling that has expression and grows by loving actions. If I wanted to love more, I needed to do more, and I needed to do all this for no selfish expectation, and only for the pure purpose of expressing love. Whereas worldly love often diminishes with time, charitable love increases until it becomes perfect and becomes like the love shared by our Heavenly parents. Do I love my wife more now than when we married in 1972? Much more. Why? Because over the years we have shared so many loving experiences. My love for her is not perfect, but I am determined

---

635 See "The Family: A Proclamation to the World."

that it will be, and that is sure to be a wonderful journey.

To Love First

How does love grow? It grows as we love someone first. "Herein is love, not that we loved God, but that he loved us . . . We love him, because he first loved us."[636] We love first, and then love is returned. As we discussed in chapter seven, it is an oft-repeated scriptural formula that has many applications: "Blessed are the merciful: for they shall obtain mercy."[637] Elder Boyd K. Packer said it this way: "As you give what you have, there is a replacement, with increase!"[638] Love is returned by someone's loving first; love increases by being loving; love cleaveth unto love like "light cleaveth unto light."[639] This love, a saving love, is charity, which *never faileth*. John Greenleaf Whittier wrote, "I'll lift you, and you lift me, and we'll both ascend together." Of course, loving first is fraught with risk. Love shown might not be returned immediately. Sometimes it may seem like it will never come.

Elder Maxwell explained that parents often extend love that is not reciprocated. He quoted Edith Hamilton as saying, "'When love meets no return the result is suffering and the greater the love the greater the suffering. There can be no greater suffering than to love purely and perfectly one who is bent upon evil and self-destruction. That was what God endured at the hands of men' (*Spokesman for God*, 1936, 112)." Elder Maxwell explained that the pain that we feel provides us an appreciation for the Savior, which appreciation we might not otherwise gain.[640]

Nevertheless, love we must, for only love unfeigned has the power to rescue a wayward soul. If we want to love our wayward children back, we must start by better loving God and our spouse, which increases our capacity to love. Then we are in a position to better love the "unlovable" child. Often, we will need to show love for the

---

636 1 John 4:10, 19.
637 Matthew 5:7.
638 Boyd K. Packer, "The Candle of the Lord," *Ensign*, January 1983.
639 D&C 88:40.
640 Edith Hamilton quoted, also Elder Maxwell, in Neal A. Maxwell's "Enduring Well," *Ensign*, April 1997.

child before he shows love to us, and we must persist in that love until love breaks down every barrier between us, melts the child's heart, embraces him in an unbreakable bond, and finally leads him home. Professor Rex A. Skidmore has said, "Parents need to remember that a youth is never so much in need of understanding as when he is non-approachable and never so much in need of love as when he is unlovable."[641]

Love Perfected

Being loving to our spouse is not only an expansive principle, it is a perfecting one that draws God near. "If we love one another, God dwelleth in us, and his love is perfected in us."[642] Moreover, by loving acts we are endowed with an added measure of the Holy Ghost: "Hereby know we that we dwell in him, and he in us, because he hath given us of his Spirit."[643] As we abide in this cycle of loving and receiving love, our love eventually becomes perfect: "God is love; and he that dwelleth in love dwelleth in God, and God in him. Herein is our love made perfect."[644]

Significantly, the only other person besides God whom a man is commanded to love with all his heart is his wife: "Thou shalt love thy wife with all thy heart, and shalt cleave unto her and none else."[645] Our model is Christ, who frequently refers to Himself as the Bridegroom,[646] and we, being part of His Church, are symbolically His bride.[647] In Hosea, He is the forgiving, compassionate, nurturing Husband, and elsewhere He is the Good Shepherd, who gives His life for those whom He loves.[648] This quality of love is that which yokes us to Him, an important principle considering the fact that He, by covenant, is an important third partner in our marriage; He is as essential to us as we are to each other. Our marriage simply cannot be

---

641 Rex A. Skidmore, "What Part Should the Teen-ager Play in the Family?" *Improvement Era*, January 1952.
642 1 John 4:12.
643 1 John 4:13.
644 1 John 4:16–17.
645 D&C 42:22.
646 See Matthew 9:15.
647 See Isaiah 62:5.
648 See John 10:11.

sanctified, and we cannot grow in the principle of love, without Him. In the case where we are in a struggling marriage in which our spouse does not seem willing to work with us in increasing love, or where a spouse does not believe in gospel principles, we may still rely on the amazing power of love—freely given by us—to powerfully affect the relationship and us individually. This is one reason why we do not need to fear one-sided love.

No Fear in Love

Perhaps one of the greatest benefits of loving is ceasing to be afraid: "There is no fear in love; but perfect love casteth out fear." If our circumstance is causing us fear, we might consider reexamining the foundation upon which our love is built, "because fear hath torment. He that feareth is not made perfect in love."[649] We must regroup by being loving, and love will be returned with increase. As love grows, we will feel our level of fear decrease. This love is the love of God, giving us peace and ameliorating the risks of unreturned mortal love.

Love—The Greatest Power

Love—perfect love—is the greatest power in the universe. Love motivates God to do all that He does. The greatest expression of His love is to give and redeem life. He invites His children to experience His type of life, for therein is His joy made full.[650] By following His example—giving life and redeeming life—our joy is also made full.[651] Therein is the perfection of and hope for our love. Therein are children given, and therein are children saved.

POWER IN THE SEALING OF THE HOLY SPIRIT OF PROMISE

Though love is powerful, it requires a sealing of that love—in the temples of our God—to fully and finally save our children and cement our marriages. For single parents and those wishing to be sealed in the temple, this can be a painful reminder. However, though this section deals specifically with the power given to married couples who are sealed in the temple, many of its principles apply to singles,

---

649 1 John 4:18.
650 See 3 Nephi 17:20.
651 See Alma 26:11.

single parents, those working for eternal union with less-active spouses, and children who are praying for their wayward parents. Faith and grace allow us to act as if we were in possession of that which we lack and to do all that we can do with the assurance that the Lord will make up the difference. Attesting to the truth of this comforting fact, President Lorenzo Snow said,

> There is no Latter-day Saint who . . . will lose anything because of having failed to do certain things when opportunities were not furnished him or her. . . . If a young man or a young woman has no opportunity of getting married, and they live faithful lives up to the time of their death, they will have all the blessings, exaltation, and glory that any man or woman will have who had this opportunity and improved it.[652]

President Spencer W. Kimball also addressed this issue, saying that faithful members would "not be deprived of any blessings which they might have received if they had lived up to all of the commandments with which they could comply."[653] Considering these statements, we might worry about whether those promises apply to us if we had the opportunity of marriage but have since gotten divorced, or if we originally married outside the temple. The answer gives us great hope. Prophets have made it abundantly clear that even the vilest of sinners (a phrase not applied lightly) have repented and gained all blessings through their subsequent faithfulness. So it seems obvious that the mistakes of our youth, our poor choices, and even our sins, can be repented of and ameliorated through the grace of Christ. Though natural consequences may sometimes make life more difficult and complex, the Lord is ever merciful regarding our spiritual progression. Current righteousness and the keeping of all covenants we have made to this point will give us access to the promises and power of the gospel.

If this is the case, then why is a review of the value of temple marriage important? We can be comforted by an examination of these blessings of such marriage, and we can be inspired to keep our eyes

---

652 Lorenzo Snow, *Teachings of Lorenzo Snow*, 138.
653 Spencer W. Kimball, *The Teachings of Spencer W. Kimball*, 542.

on the goal. When one finally has or again has the opportunity to fall in love, that love between a husband and a wife—through a temple marriage—solidifies the initial sealing of their marriage covenant into an unbreakable *welding link.* They become one in word, purpose, and deed, and that ultimate and final kind of unity is necessary to obtain the celestializing blessings of heaven in behalf of their children. While our temple experience teaches us that the sealing of parents is provisional and based on subsequent obedience,[654] we also become aware that no such qualifying language is used when a child is born in the covenant or when a child born outside the covenant is later sealed to his parents. This suggests that the Lord intends for the child to belong to the parents forever. President Joseph Fielding Smith said, "Those born under the covenant, throughout all eternity, are the children of their parents. Nothing except the unpardonable sin, or sin unto death, can break this tie. If children do not sin as John said, 'unto death,' the parents may still feel after them and eventually bring them back near to them again."[655] The prophets have stated repeatedly that the calling of parent is one from which we are never released.[656] Such is the incredible power of the sealing ordinance. The covenants made and the sealing pronounced on parents married in the temple creates a *patriarchal hold* that secures children to their parents forever, pulling them into that covenant.

Thus, for a man and a woman, the ultimate goals of love are to enter into the new and everlasting covenant of marriage, then persist in that covenant until their marriage is sealed by the Holy Spirit of Promise. The Holy Spirit of Promise is a "name-title used in connection with the sealing and ratifying power of the Holy Ghost."[657] Great power devolves upon a husband and wife who have married in the temple and lived worthily so that the Holy Spirit of Promise can validate their marriage. Elder Bruce C. Hafen wrote,

> A covenant marriage in the highest sense will begin
> as a temple marriage. When the partners are then

---

654 See Bruce R. McConkie, "Celestial Marriage," *Mormon Doctrine,* 117–18.
655 Joseph Fielding Smith, *Doctrines of Salvation,* Volume 2, 90.
656 See M. Russell Ballard, "Let Our Voices Be Heard," *Ensign,* November 2003.
657 Bruce R. McConkie, *Mormon Doctrine,* "Holy Spirit of Promise," 361.

sufficiently righteous, the marriage will be sealed by the Holy Spirit of Promise (D&C 132:7), "which the Father sheds forth upon all those who are just and true" (D&C 76:53). Such a marriage will then be not only eternal in duration but also celestial in quality, for it will be a marriage that partakes of God's quality of life.[658]

President James E. Faust made one of the clearest statements on the subject: "When the covenant of marriage for time and eternity, the culminating gospel ordinance, is sealed by the Holy Spirit of promise, *it can literally open the windows of heaven for great blessings to flow to a married couple who seek for those blessings.*"[659]

This highest manifestation of gospel blessings is contingent upon our faithfulness to our covenants. Although marriage is an important step toward exaltation, it is not the *ultimate* step. Elder Bruce R. McConkie wrote, "It should be clearly understood that these high blessings are not part of celestial marriage. 'Blessings pronounced upon couples in connection with celestial marriage are conditioned upon the subsequent faithfulness of the participating parties.'"[660] As we discussed before, if a man and a woman marry in the temple, thereby entering into the patriarchal order of the priesthood, and then remain worthy so that their marriage is sealed by the Holy Spirit of Promise, they are given greater power from on high to ask for and receive the highest blessings. These blessings include power to gather or call back their family to Christ (keys restored by Moses), power to organize their family into an eternal, celestial unit, including power to ensure that each family member receives all the blessings of the new and everlasting covenant (keys restored by Elias), and power to have all those blessings *sealed* so that these blessings might endure forever (keys restored by Elijah).

Speaking of these great blessings that flow to the children by the power of their parents' temple sealing, Joseph Fielding Smith wrote,

---

658 Bruce C. Hafen, *Covenant Hearts*, 77.

659 James E. Faust, "The Gift of the Holy Ghost—A Sure Compass," *Ensign*, April 1996; emphasis added.

660 Joseph Fielding Smith, quoted in Bruce R. McConkie's *Mormon Doctrine*, "Calling and Election Sure," 110.

"These keys hold the power to *seal husbands and wives for eternity* as well as for time. They hold the power to seal children to parents, the key of adoption, by which the family organization is made intact forever. *This is the power which will save the obedient from the curse in the coming of the great and dreadful day of the Lord. Through these keys the hearts of the children have turned to their fathers.*"661

So the key to rescuing our wayward children lies not only in our striving to be unified, but to be unified with respect to our covenants and increasing commitment to the sacrifices required when we receive the gifts of gospel blessings. Elder Russell M. Nelson wrote, "As you obey each of God's commandments, your holiness will fortify the foundation of your fathers' faith. When the two of you are together spiritually, one plus one is clearly greater than two."662

Following is a story of a Nevada couple who followed this advice. When James was a teenager, he set about to self-destruct in record time. Thomas and Alyssa, his parents, were helpless to halt or alter his determination. A bad group of friends introduced him to alcohol and, later, tobacco. When he began to fail badly in school, Thomas and Alyssa tried to help him with a tutor, but James soon lost all interest. Later, he dropped out of school, and later still, when Thomas and Alyssa had laid out a simple set of rules that James would not abide, they asked him to live elsewhere. By that time, he was using and selling drugs, stealing from his parents, and having frequent run-ins with the law. At one point, James was incarcerated for a year, but when he was released he continued with his destructive behavior.

To deal with the problem, Thomas and Alyssa did something remarkable: they pulled together as a couple. They renewed their marriage by frequent dating and trips. They increased their temple attendance, and they put more energy into their couple prayers. In the midst of one of the worst trials of their lives, they reacted by loving each other and God more.

Throughout these years of intense stress and heartbreak, Thomas and Alyssa kept in contact with James and assured him of their love for him. Thomas said, "Alyssa and I didn't know what else to do. In the beginning, we prayed because that was all we could think to do.

---

661 Joseph Fielding Smith, *Doctrines of Salvation*, Volume 2, 119; emphasis added.
662 Russell M. Nelson, *The Power within Us*, 113.

But over time, we discovered that parental prayer is a sort of *right* God gives fathers and mothers. We didn't even know that we had such a right until we noticed our prayers being answered in miraculous ways."

At one critical moment, James had moved to a new city and had no place to room. His parents knew that his decision would make or break him. His history had been to live with the lowlifes of society—jobless and hard partying alcoholics and drug users. Now he was faced with a similar decision, and Thomas and Alyssa went to their knees. They pled with Heavenly Father to help James find an LDS person to live with. Within the week, James called and said that he had made a friend of a returned missionary who had invited him to be his roommate. James stayed with this young man until his next crisis.

Later, James called his father and announced that he and a woman with whom he had been having an affair were going to buy a condo so they could live together. Despite Thomas's stern counsel discouraging this, James had stubbornly made up his mind and once again announced that he was going to do things his way. Thomas and Alyssa went to their knees and prayed that something would happen to give James another choice.

Within the week, James called to tell his parents that the woman had broken up with him. He was hurt, but he had begun to date an LDS girl. Within a short period of time, James and the girl fell in love and wanted to get married. She had set her sights on a temple marriage, and that made James reconsider his life. He asked his father to give him a blessing. James went to his bishop, confessed, and gave up all his bad habits. The young woman was willing to wait for James as he completed the repentance process, and after a year, they were married in the temple. Of this miracle, Thomas and Alyssa say, "Couples may not know the power that God puts into their hands. A couple that has truly become one can sincerely pray for their children, and miracles will happen. That oneness calls forth a power we had never thought possible."

Thus, although love may motivate a man and woman to enter into marriage, only God has the power to truly make them one. Moroni revealed to Joseph Smith the sobering fact of why this welding link—a temple sealing and subsequent sanctification—must be in place to make a couple (and their progenitors and children) one: so that "the whole earth [would not] be utterly wasted at [the Lord's] coming."[663] Robert L. Millet gives us further insight into this idea of the earth's being wasted:

> Why would the earth be wasted at his coming? Because the earth would not have accomplished its foreordained purpose of establishing on its face a family system patterned after the order of heaven. If there were no sealing powers whereby families could be bound together, then the earth would never "answer the end of its creation" (D&C 49:16). It would be wasted and cursed, for all men and women would be forever without root or branch, without ancestry or posterity.[664]

With the merciful gift and commandment of having our marriages start across the temple altars, righteous parents are made one by God and sealed together with His unbreakable welding link. Then, as they faithfully persevere in their covenants, the Holy Spirit of Promise seals their marriage more surely so that the welding link that was set in place at the altar will never fail.

The children who issue forth from this union—or who are sealed into it—are *surely* secured to their parents by virtue of that same, *sure* weld. Despite their rebellion, they cannot break free. The power of their parents' oneness, which was set in place by God and made sure by the Holy Spirit of Promise, has the power to hold onto the children and eventually reel them back.

---

663 D&C 2:3; comments added.
664 Robert L. Millet, *When a Child Wanders,* 100–101.

Section 3
HOPE

Chapter 11

PROMISES TO PARENTS

The tender mercies of the Lord are over all those whom
he hath chosen, because of their faith, to make them mighty, even
unto the power of deliverance.

—*1 Nephi 1:20*

AS A MAN OR WOMAN of God sanctifies him or herself and strives to move forward in faith against adversity, the Lord will eventually present the right circumstance for deliverance. Nephi stated as much in 1 Nephi 3:7, and despite several failed attempts to retrieve the brass plates, he continued to sanctify himself, trying to keep the commandment he'd been given until the Lord presented a solution.[665] Likewise, we parents have been given commandments to bear children,[666] to teach them to honor and respect their parents,[667] to prepare them for baptism,[668] to teach them the gospel and bring them up in light and truth,[669] to teach them to pray and walk uprightly before the Lord,[670] and to correct them in a spirit of love.[671] Clearly, if God gives us one of His children, He expects us to deliver the child back to Him in a redeemed condition. The parable of the talents teaches us that—whatever God

---

665 See 1 Nephi 3–4.
666 See Genesis 1:28.
667 See Mosiah 13:20.
668 See D&C 68:25–28.
669 See D&C 93:40–42.
670 See D&C 68:28.
671 See D&C 121:43.

entrusts to us, we are under obligation to return to Him with increase.[672] Therefore, when we, like Nephi, encounter resistance and obstacles while rearing God's children, we, like Nephi, should set a straight course. We must sanctify ourselves and move forward in faith with the assurance that the Lord will eventually present a solution that leads to deliverance. The Lord's promise is that, if we do this, He will open "an effectual door."[673]

The restored gospel provides us power that we can draw upon to fulfill our divine parental charge. President James E. Faust acknowledged that, "Satan's pervasive snares are increasing, and raising children is becoming harder,"[674] but the Brethren have also made it clear that the Lord has restored priesthood keys that are available to each worthy parent—keys to gather together the family for the purpose of administering the gospel blessings, and keys to have those blessings sealed upon their heads for time and eternity.[675]

As President Boyd K. Packer said, "We cannot overemphasize the value of temple marriage, the binding ties of the sealing ordinance, and the standards of worthiness required of them. *When parents keep the covenants they have made at the altar of the temple, their children will be forever bound to them.*"[676] As mentioned earlier, President Henry B. Eyring confirmed such ideas in an April 2008 general conference session. He prophesied of several significant events in our future, one of those being the *increasing* return of wayward children as a reward for parents' unrelenting efforts. He indicated that if we never give up, neither will God give up, and in many cases, where our children seem unresponsive to us, God will call back our children through those who are called to serve in the Church.[677]

This eternal bond is like a tether that holds children to their parents' orbit by the force of the sealing ordinance's gravitational pull.

---

672 See Matthew 25:14–28.

673 See D&C 118:3.

674 James E. Faust, "Dear Are the Sheep That Have Wandered," *Ensign*, May 2003.

675 See Bruce R. McConkie, *A New Witness for the Articles of Faith*, 539.

676 Boyd K. Packer, "Our Moral Environment," *Ensign*, May 1992; emphasis added.

677 See Henry B. Eyring, "The True and Living Church," *Ensign*, May 2008.

This idea is suggested by Joseph Fielding McConkie and Craig Ostler in a discussion of Abraham's description of Kolob: Kolob is the "first creation, nearest to the celestial, or the residence of God;"[678] it is "set nigh unto the throne of God, to govern all those planets which belong to the same order as that upon which [Abraham stood]"[679]—therefore Kolob represents Jesus Christ.[680] Notice that Kolob's daily rotation is equal to one thousand earth years.[681] Also notice that the rotation speed of all other celestial bodies increases in proportion to their distance from Kolob.[682]

In a BYU Education Week presentation on the Book of Abraham, Wayne Brickey suggested that this phenomenon indicates that Christ, like Kolob, moves slowly to ensure that He leaves no one behind, not even the "wandering stars."[683] This is a significant idea as it concerns the process of redemption. Often, the time required to draw a *wandering star* back into a safe orbit is long. The Savior has lots of time. In the meantime, we are assured that He, like Kolob, has every wandering star in His gravitational grasp. Joseph Fielding Smith wrote of God the Father's equal grasp on His children: "The Father has never relinquished his claim upon the children born into this world. They are still his children."[684]

Here is a list of just some of the extraordinary promises—some previously quoted in this book and some new—that have been made to parents of wayward children. Please note that although many of these promises are in reference to those who have been sealed in the temple, the promises are by no means exclusive to that qualification. The overriding criteria of these promises are the personal making and keeping of covenants with God and persistence in personal sanctification. This allows the principle of grace to be applied. Grace makes it possible to obtain the Lord's promises after we do all that we can; the

---

678 Abraham, Facsimile 2, Figure 1 explanation.

679 Abraham 3:9.

680 See Joseph Fielding McConkie and Craig J. Ostler, "Kolob and Christ—Abraham 3:1–17," *Revelations of the Restoration*, 1000.

681 Abraham 3:4.

682 Abraham 3:6–9.

683 Jude 1:13.

684 Joseph Fielding Smith, *Doctrines of Salvation*, Volume 1, 316.

Lord then makes up the difference.[685] We are never penalized for our lack of opportunity to make temple covenants when we live worthy of those promised future blessings.

THE PROPHETS' PROMISES

Joseph Smith

When a seal is put upon the father and mother, it secures their posterity, so that they cannot be lost, but will be saved by virtue of the covenant of their father and mother.[686]

I have a declaration to make as to the provisions which God hath made to suit the conditions of man—made from before the foundation of the world. What has Jesus said? All sin, and all blasphemies, and every transgression, except one, that man can be guilty of, may be forgiven; and there is a salvation for all men, either in this world or the world to come, who have not committed the unpardonable sin, there being a provision either in this world or the world of spirits. . . . *Every man who has a friend in the eternal world can save him.* . . . And so you can see how far you can be a savior. . . .

Hence the salvation of Jesus Christ was wrought out for all men, in order to triumph over the devil; *for if [that salvation] did not catch [a man] in one place, it would in another*; for he stood up as a Savior.[687]

There is never a time when the spirit is too old to approach God. All are within the reach of pardoning mercy.[688]

---

685 See LDS Bible Dictionary, "Grace," 697.
686 Alma P. Burton, ed., *Discourses of the Prophet Joseph Smith*, 151.
687 Joseph Fielding Smith, ed., *Teachings of the Prophet Joseph Smith*, 356–57; emphasis added.
688 Ibid., 191.

Our Heavenly Father is more liberal in His views, and boundless in his mercies and blessings, than we are ready to believe or receive.[689]

Brigham Young

Let the father and mother, who are members of this Church and Kingdom, take a righteous course, and strive with all their might never to do a wrong, but to do good all their lives; if they have one child or one hundred children, if they conduct themselves towards them as they should, binding them to the Lord by their faith and prayers, I care not where those children go, they are bound up to their parents by an everlasting tie, and no power of earth or hell can separate them from their parents in eternity; they will return again to the fountain from whence they sprang.[690]

Wilford Woodruff

I tell you when the prophets and apostles go to preach to those who are shut up in prison . . . thousands of them will there embrace the gospel. They know more in that world than they do here.[691]

Lorenzo Snow

When the gospel is preached to the spirits in prison, the success attending that preaching will be far greater than that attending the preaching of our elders in this life. I believe there will be very few indeed of those spirits who will not gladly receive the gospel when it is carried to them. The circumstances there will be a thousand times more favorable.[692]

---

689 Joseph Fielding Smith, ed., *Teachings of the Prophet Joseph Smith,* 257.
690 Brigham Young, *Discourses of Brigham Young,* 208.
691 G. Homer Durham, ed., *The Discourses of Wilford Woodruff,* 152.
692 Lorenzo Snow, *The Teachings of Lorenzo Snow,* edited by Clyde J. Williams, 98.

God has fulfilled His promises to us, and our prospects are grand and glorious. Yes, in the next life we will have our wives, and our sons and daughters. If we do not get them all at once, we will have them some time. . . . You that are mourning about your children straying away will have your sons and your daughters. If you succeed in passing through these trials and afflictions . . . you will, by the power of the Priesthood, work and labor, as the Son of God has, until you get all your sons and daughters in the path of exaltation and glory. This is just as sure as that the sun rose this morning over yonder mountains. Therefore, mourn not because all your sons and daughters do not follow in the path that you have marked out to them, or give heed to your counsels. Inasmuch as we succeed in securing eternal glory, and stand as saviors, and as kings and priests to our God, we will save our posterity.[693]

Joseph F. Smith

Jesus had not finished his work when his body was slain, neither did he finish it after his resurrection from the dead; although he had accomplished the purpose for which he then came to the earth, he had not fulfilled all his work. And when will he? Not until he has redeemed and saved every son and daughter of our father Adam that have been or ever will be born upon this earth to the end of time, except the sons of perdition. That is his mission. *We will not finish our work until we have saved ourselves, and then not until we shall have saved all depending upon us; for we are to become saviors upon Mount Zion, as well as Christ. We are called to this mission.*[694]

693 Lorenzo Snow, *The Teachings of Lorenzo Snow,* 195.

694 Joseph F. Smith, *Gospel Doctrine: Selections from the Sermons and Writings of Joseph F. Smith,* 442; emphasis added.

Orson F. Whitney

You parents of the wilful and the wayward! Don't give them up. Don't cast them off. They are not utterly lost. The Shepherd will find his sheep. They were his before they were yours—long before he entrusted them to your care; and you cannot begin to love them as he loves them. They have but strayed in ignorance from the Path of Right, and God is merciful to ignorance. Only the fulness of knowledge brings the fulness of accountability. Our Heavenly Father is far more merciful, infinitely more charitable, than even the best of his servants, and the Everlasting Gospel is mightier in power to save than our narrow finite minds can comprehend.[695]

The Prophet Joseph Smith declared—and he never taught more comforting doctrine—that the eternal sealings of faithful parents and the divine promises made to them for valiant service in the Cause of Truth, would save not only themselves, but likewise their posterity. Though some of the sheep may wander, the eye of the Shepherd is upon them, and sooner or later they will feel the tentacles of Divine Providence reaching out after them and drawing them back to the fold. Either in this life or the life to come, they will return. They will have to pay their debt to justice; they will suffer for their sins; and may tread a thorny path; but if it leads them at last, like the penitent Prodigal, to a loving and forgiving father's heart and home, the painful experience will not have been in vain. Pray for your careless and disobedient children; hold on to them with your faith. Hope on, trust on, till you see the salvation of God.[696]

---

695 Orson F. Whitney, *Conference Report*, April 1929, 110.
696 Ibid.

James E. Faust

A principle in this statement that is often overlooked is that they must fully repent and "suffer for their sins" and "pay their debt to justice." I recognize that now is the time "to prepare to meet God" [Alma 34:32]. If the repentance of the wayward children does not happen in this life, is it still possible for the cords of the sealing to be strong enough for them yet to work out their repentance? In the Doctrine and Covenants we are told, "The dead who repent will be redeemed, through obedience to the ordinances of the house of God,

"And after they have paid the penalty of their transgressions, and are washed clean, shall receive a reward according to their works, for they are heirs of salvation" (D&C 138:58–59). . . .

Mercy will not rob justice, and the sealing power of faithful parents will only claim wayward children upon the condition of their repentance and Christ's Atonement. Repentant wayward children will enjoy salvation and all the blessings that go with it, but exaltation is much more. It must be fully earned. The question as to who will be exalted must be left to the Lord in His mercy.

There are very few whose rebellion and evil deeds are so great that they have "sinned away the power to repent" [Alonzo A. Hinckley, in Conference Report, Oct. 1919, 161]. That judgment must also be left up to the Lord.[697]

John J. Carmack

In 1919 at general conference, Alonzo A. Hinckley, then president of the Deseret Stake of Zion, quoted Elder James E. Talmage of the Quorum of the Twelve Apostles as follows: "I promise the Saints

---

697 James E. Faust, "Dear Are the Sheep That Have Wandered," *Ensign*, May 2003.

in the Deseret stake of Zion that if their lives are such that they can look their sons and daughters in the face, and if any of them have gone astray, that the parents are able to say, 'It is contrary to my instruction and my life's example; it is against every effort of love, long suffering, faith, prayer and devotion that that boy or girl has gone,'—I promise you, fathers and mothers, that not one of them shall be lost unless they have sinned away the power to repent" (in *Conference Report*, October 1919, 161). Balm and hope abound in that counsel. We may not understand exactly how Elder Talmage's counsel will come to pass in this life, but we can understand that there is more to the relationship of righteous parents and their children than we fully understand in this life and more help available with the problems that arise in that relationship than we grasp with our worldly logic. We are not alone in our struggle to save and preserve the sealing between us and our children.[698]

Gordon B. Hinckley

I leave my blessing upon you. May there be . . . a sense of security and peace and love among your children, precious children every one of them, even those who may have strayed. I hope you don't lose patience with them; I hope you go on praying for them, *and I don't hesitate to promise that if you do, the Lord will touch their hearts and bring them back to you with love and respect and appreciation.*[699]

"Be Not Afraid, Only Believe"

Jairus was a Jewish ruler who besought Jesus to save his dying daughter.[700] His story could be applied to any parent whose child is

---

698 John J. Carmack, "When Our Children Go Astray," *Ensign*, February 1997.
699 Gordon B. Hinckley, *Church News*, 2 September 1995, 4.
700 See Mark 5:21–43.

spiritually dying. Jairus's twelve-year-old daughter was at the point of death, and gratefully Jesus, the only one who could save her now, was coming. When Jairus saw Jesus, he rushed to Him and "fell at his feet, and besought him greatly."[701] No time for introductions, Jairus cried, "My little daughter lieth at the point of death; I pray thee, come and lay thy hands on her, that she may be healed; and she shall live."[702]

Of the father's distress, Ted Gibbons noted,

> We feel this father's great faith and confidence in this appeal. His girl was dying. *Jesus could heal her if He would.* He had healed others . . . had [even] done so from a distance.
>
> [But] their journey was interrupted by the touch of the woman with the issue of blood, and as the Savior finished speaking with her, someone from the bedside of the child came looking for her father and said to him, "Thy daughter is dead: why troublest thou the Master any further?" (Mark 5:35).
>
> Imagine the pain caused by those words. Christ had healed the sick. . . . But this was no longer a matter of sickness; the child was dead. *"Why troublest thou the master any further?"*[703]

Jairus must have buckled under the weight of the news. But notice what Jesus did: *"As soon as Jesus heard the word that was spoken, he saith unto the ruler of the synagogue [Jairus], Be not afraid, only believe."*[704] Jesus would not allow a negative, alternative voice to damage Jairus's faith. In effect, Jesus said to him, "Don't listen to that voice. What the voice is saying is not true. It is *not* too late. Focus on me, and let's go to your house and save the child. The damsel is not dead, but sleepeth!"[705] And when they arrived, Jesus took the child

---

701 Mark 5:22–23.

702 Mark 5:23.

703 Ted Gibbons, *Nowhere Else to Go* (unpublished manuscript in author's possession).

704 Mark 5:36; emphasis added.

705 See Mark 5:39.

by the hand and commanded, "Damsel, I say unto thee, arise. And straightway the damsel arose, and walked."[706]

Jesus gave the same never-too-late message to grieving Martha at the death of her brother, Lazarus: "Jesus said unto her, I am the resurrection, and the life: he that believeth in me, though he were dead, yet shall he live."[707] Even now, though Lazarus had lain in the grave four days and all evidence pointed to his complete and unalterable demise, *though he were dead, yet would he live!* Although Martha was distraught, she remained focused on the Savior and His saving power: "But I know, that even now, whatsoever thou wilt ask of God, God will give it thee." And Jesus confirmed her faith in Him: "Jesus saith unto her, Thy brother shall rise again."[708]

And Lazarus did rise again. Jesus "cried with a loud voice, Lazarus, come forth. And he that was dead came forth, bound hand and foot with graveclothes: and his face was bound with a napkin. Jesus saith unto them, Loose him, and let him go."[709] This story has obvious spiritual implications.

We must never listen to the alternative voices or imagine that it is too late. If we persist in sanctifying ourselves, one day the Savior will come as He did to Jairus's daughter, lay His hands on our children as it were, and they will live. President Howard W. Hunter said, "Whatever Jesus lays his hands upon lives. If Jesus lays his hands upon a marriage, it lives. If he is allowed to lay his hands on the family, it lives."[710] We must believe that the Savior can call out a wayward child, as He did Lazarus, who might be decaying in the tomb of spiritual death, and *though he be dead,* yet the child will emerge alive. Although the child might be bound with the graveclothes of sin, the Savior will say, "Loose him, and let him go." The promises made by the Lord's prophets of such deliverance are sure. To participate in God's plan of deliverance, we must sanctify ourselves and follow the direction of the Spirit.

Consider the following account of one father's once-wayward boy:

---

706 Mark 5:41–42.
707 John 11:25; emphasis added.
708 John 11:22–23.
709 John 11:43–44.
710 Howard W. Hunter, "Reading the Scriptures," *Ensign,* November 1979.

Our son was dead; spiritually dead, that is. Where does one begin to describe the deep sadness and the feelings of total helplessness and loss? Even these words do not adequately describe the emotional [black hole] that surrounded and imprisoned my wife and me as we watched our son rapidly and undeterred set out to destroy not only his life but also his eternal salvation and divine appointment.

Jeff's downward slide started in his teenage years. I still can't believe it happened, but if it can happen to Jeff it can happen to anyone. My wife and I had loved our only son, indulged him, and wanted him to have every opportunity to be happy and feel good about himself. Jeff was the all-American boy. . . . He was also a basically good kid, although he sometimes struggled with self-worth and often associated with friends who were not the best examples. During his teenage years, he began to change; he became arrogant, selfish, and argumentative. He learned to get his way by using his anger to intimidate and exasperate us. He portrayed himself as a victim. Nevertheless, he [still generally] seemed to want to do good things, and he even encouraged one of his best friends to go on a mission. Jeff helped his friend prepare by reading scriptures with him before school. His friend was older and entered the MTC three months before Jeff's nineteenth birthday.

That inspired Jeff and he started working with the bishop to prepare his mission papers. But after several meetings with the bishop, he stomped into the house offended one night because the bishop hadn't shown up for their appointment. For some reason, this hurt Jeff deeply. He imagined that the bishop didn't really love or care about him.

That single event tipped Jeff over, and he decided not to serve a mission. Thereafter, Jeff lost interest in the Church and started questioning Church policy and the validity of its doctrines. He stopped attending his church meetings and fulfilling priesthood assignments. Because he was the leader of his band of friends, who were not very active, he persuaded them to also abandon their mission plans. He began to disregard all Church standards, and he started hanging out with a rough group that frequented R-rated movies and stayed out until all hours of the night. He began coming home smelling of smoke and alcohol. Then he declared himself to be agnostic.

Because Jeff was a likable, natural leader, he attracted other misfits. He brought them to our home, freely shared our food with them, and relentlessly argued with us about our rules and standards. Soon, we had to ask him to either follow our rules or live elsewhere. This angered him, but he moved out and shacked up with people who could only be described as the dregs of society. Now he was so entrenched in this debased lifestyle that he went out of his way to fight against and live opposite to every ideal and value of the Church.

Jeff began using pot and other drugs and driving under the influence. Drugs were readily available at his workplace and from his associates. . . . He engaged in gratuitous sex with his girlfriend. He began stealing from stores to get things that he wanted. When he was broke, which was often, he would drop in on us for some quick food—and, of course, he brought his drug-using friends with him and expected us to feed them. He got a tattoo on his arm, earrings, and studs in his tongue. He would arrogantly walk into the house with his friends and proudly flaunt his newly acquired attire, piercings, and opinions. He would poke fun at the Church and its standards and express how liberated he felt now that he had adopted beliefs that aligned with his behavior.

It was all we could do to not retch and cry. I wanted to slap him and shake him from this evil state. I wondered, *Where did my loving boy go?* Every once in a while, I would try to calmly point out the flaws of his lifestyle and the blessings of righteous living, but he always became irate. It was as though he was possessed. He was truly past feeling. Our hearts were broken. We loved him so deeply and hurt so much for him. We greatly feared for his salvation. Our beloved son was dying, and there seemed to be nothing that we could do.

My wife and I prayed hard, night and day. We came to appreciate how Alma the Elder must have felt as he prayed for his son. We wondered, *If Alma the Elder could pray for something dramatic to provide his son an opportunity to change, could we not do the same?* We didn't care how the opportunity came—a visitation from an angel or just for Jeff to hit bottom—all we wanted was for something to happen to shake him loose [from Satan's hold].

Then one night, my wife had a strong impression that we needed to stop preaching to him, acting disappointed about his choices, and looking down on him and his friends, and simply love him. So that is exactly what we started to do. A change in us had to happen before a change in our son could occur. That was not a comforting thought, but one that we embraced nevertheless. Thereafter, when Jeff would criticize our lifestyle, beliefs, or the Church, we would smile, acknowledge his opinion, then ask why he felt that way or gently change the subject. My wife welcomed his friends into our home and offered them food. Being the saint that she is, she actually hoped that they might feel the Spirit in our home. On the other hand, I found it very hard to show love in this way. I had to bite my tongue on many occasions. I tried to take cues from my wife, who comes by the gift of charity more easily. She was able to genuinely radiate love to Jeff and his friends. Over time, as I watched her, I had the impression she was the angel that I had been praying for. In the end, she became the agent that made Jeff's change possible.

Until that ordeal, I had never been able to comprehend exquisite pain and exquisite joy. Now, we had experienced both extremes. Years before, we had prayed for a son to come into our family, and when we were blessed with him, we had tried to love him unconditionally. We had nurtured, taught, sacrificed for, and tried to raise him to be a valiant child of God. Then, watching him plummet down to depths so low that he became unrecognizable caused pain worse than death. When Jeff should have been serving a mission for the Church, he was fighting against it. In fact, I call those two years his "Mission to Hell." The answer to our prayers and the change that took place in Jeff's life are incomprehensible to me now.

A series of significant events took place as if orchestrated from above. These events had a profound influence on our son. First, Jeff's missionary friend was set to return, which started Jeff thinking about their relationship. With Jeff's new lifestyle, how would he renew a friendship that was supremely important to him? This concerned Jeff and made him think more seriously about his choices.

Next, Jeff attended a rock concert, where he and some friends were smoking pot and doing mushrooms. He passed in and out of consciousness while he was listening to the music and under the influence of the drugs. He felt out of control, and he remembered thinking that imminent death was a possibility. He reported that every time he [tried to focus on] the music, he would loose consciousness again. But every time he held onto the thought of family, he would stay present and not succumb. He struggled between the two worlds. He survived, and he realized that he had been spared. After the concert, these thoughts continued to play in the back of his mind.

Finally, at work, someone secretly placed on his desk a piece of paper that outlined the difference in behaviors between a person who chose Christ and a person who chose Satan. He noted that all the behaviors listed on Satan's column were exactly what he was doing. For some reason this conflict played right in front of him and struck a nerve. He started crying uncontrollably and couldn't stop for a long time.

A few days passed, and when his friend returned from his mission, he and Jeff began to hang out. Jeff was still quite moved by his recent experiences and was primed for a change. He and his friend had long talks that resulted in spiritual moments. The walls of rebellion finally tumbled down. One night, in tears, Jeff came home with his returned missionary friend and another friend and asked me for a priesthood blessing. I was floored. The once-proud Jeff now stood before me genuinely broken-hearted and of a contrite spirit. He wanted God's forgiveness. He pled for my wife's and my forgiveness. He wept freely in our arms, expressing love, gratitude, and remorse. In the blessing I felt impressed to express to him his Savior's undying love, His awareness of Jeff's circumstances, and His promise of total forgiveness. Jeff received a spiritual witness of the truth of those statements.

From that day forward, Jeff asked us to be patient with him while he tried to change. Each day he gave up a different vice. From the moment of the blessing, he never took another illicit drug or engaged in any sexual behavior. He stopped smoking one day and gave up alcohol the next. Having been previously disfellowshipped, Jeff started meeting with his new bishop to restore his membership standing and his priesthood. Our once-wayward boy is home at last!

Seeing him now, I want to cry out with the prodigal son's father, "This my son was dead, and is alive again; and was lost, and is found!"(See Luke 15:32.)

As this story illustrates, our children are bound to us through our keeping of righteous covenants—whether they come back to the fold in this life or the next. As President Joseph Fielding Smith said, "Those born under the covenant, throughout all eternity, are the children of their parents. Nothing except the unpardonable sin, or sin unto death, can break this tie. If children do not sin as John says, 'unto death,' the parents may still feel after them and eventually bring them back near to them again."[711] May we have the patience and faith to "feel after them" until the time of their redemption.

---

711 Joseph Fielding Smith, *Doctrines of Salvation,* Volume 2, 90.

Chapter 12
ALL THINGS ARE POSSIBLE

*Wherefore, whoso believeth in God might with surety hope
for a better world . . . which hope cometh of faith, maketh an anchor
to the souls of men, which would make them sure and steadfast, always
abounding in good works, being led to glorify God.*

—Ether 12:4

IF THE SCRIPTURES TEACH US anything, they teach us that Israel's God
will not let Israel go,[712] despite her bouts of waywardness. The Lord
is always reaching out to her. Robert L. Millet surmises rightly that
"What is true of a nation is equally true of individuals. Few of us in
this life will[,] through our sins[,] place ourselves beyond the pale of
saving grace."[713] Can we imagine that the Savior, innocent of sin,
who had assumed the staggering weight of the demands of justice
until vessels broke and blood seeped from every pore of His suffering
body, who had submitted Himself to brutal beatings, to unconscio-
nable humiliation, to arrogant injustice, to the torture of a thirty-
nine-lash scourging,[714] to the horror of being stripped and stretched
violently upon a cross, to being victimized by brutish soldiers who
drove thick spikes through His palms, wrists, and feet, to suffering the
blinding pain of being raised up to hang, full body weight, from those
spikes until He allowed death to overwhelm Him—can we imagine
that after the Redeemer had paid that immeasurable price to ransom

712 See Isaiah 49:16.
713 Robert L. Millet, *When a Child Wanders*, 146–147.
714 Bruce R. McConkie, *Sermons and Writings of Bruce R. McConkie*, 209.

every individual, that He would lose interest in a sinner, give up, or stop short of His rescuing effort?

THE WORTH OF A SOUL

"Remember the worth of souls is great in the sight of God."[715] Just how valuable is one wayward soul? Jesus answered: "Are not five sparrows sold for two farthings, and not one of them is forgotten before God? But even the very hairs of your head are all numbered. Fear not therefore: ye are of more value than many sparrows."[716] How could the worth of "many sparrows" compare to the worth of one child of God? Moreover, if God's attention is drawn to individual birds, is it not much more riveted upon His children? "Are ye not much better than they?"[717] Elder Neal A. Maxwell said,

> Fortunately, God is preoccupied with His children. We (and what we may become) are His work and glory. (Moses 1:39.) All that He does is for our benefit. (2 Ne. 26:24.) As George MacDonald said of God, "He lays no plans irrespective of His children." "Worlds and suns and planets," wrote MacDonald, are but "a portion of His workshops and tools for the bringing out of righteous men and women to fill His house of love."[718]

Of stars and sparrows and saving souls, Elder Maxwell further taught that we, by divine appointment, have been sent to earth at this time in history to succeed.[719] "The same God that placed that star in a precise orbit millennia before it appeared over Bethlehem in celebration of the birth of the Babe has given at least equal attention to placement of each of us in precise human orbits so that we may, if we will, illuminate the landscape of our individual lives, so that our

---

715 D&C 18:10.

716 Luke 12:6–7.

717 Matthew 6:26.

718 Neal A. Maxwell, *Meek and Lowly,* 12.

719 See Neal A. Maxwell, "Encircled in the Arms of His Love," *Ensign,* November 2002.

light may not only lead others but warm them as well."[720] Further, Elder Maxwell said, "The Prophet Joseph Smith declared that God, 'before [the earth] rolled into existence . . . contemplated the whole of the events connected with the earth. . . . [God] knew . . . the depth of iniquity that would be connected with the human family, their weakness and strength . . . the situation of all nations and . . . their destiny . . . and [He] has made ample provision [for mankind's] redemption.'" We imperfect parents are part of God's "ample provision." We do our best to shine and serve in our assigned orbits, knowing, as Elder Maxwell concluded, "that we are encircled 'in the arms of [His] love' (D&C 6:20)."[721]

Comparing the Stars to the Children of God

Elder James E. Talmage said, "What is a man in this boundless setting of sublime splendor? I answer you: Potentially now, actually to be, he is greater and grander, more precious in the arithmetic of God, than all the planets and suns of space."[722] Explicating that idea, one of the finest representations of God's individual concern for His children is found in the vision given to Moses in the Pearl of Great Price.[723] "Caught up into an exceedingly high mountain, [Moses] saw God face to face, and he talked with him."[724] In the vision that followed, God promised Moses that he would be allowed to see much of the workmanship of God's hands. As we shall see, God would draw a comparison between heavenly orbs and His children. Moses would need to remember this comparison in order to grasp the vision's significance. God began by saying, "Behold, thou art my son . . . and thou art in the similitude of mine Only Begotten. . . . And now, behold, this one thing I show thee."[725] The "one thing" the Lord showed Moses was this world. "And it came to pass that Moses looked, and beheld the world upon which he was created."[726] Moses

---

720　Neal A. Maxwell, *That My Family Should Partake*, 86.
721　Neal A. Maxwell, "Encircled in the Arms of His Love," *Ensign*, November 2002.
722　James E. Talmage, quoted in Hugh B. Brown's *Continuing the Quest*, 209.
723　See Moses 1.
724　Moses 1:1–2.
725　Moses 1:4, 6–7.
726　Moses 1:8.

would soon come to understand the symbolism of this vision—God was going to compare the heavens to His children; or, in this case, God was comparing this *one world* with His one special son—*Moses.*

Then God opened Moses' eyes so he could see as God sees: "Moses beheld the world and the ends thereof, and all the children of men which are, and which were created; of the same he greatly marveled and wondered."[727] That is, Moses saw the beginning and end of the world's creation, including every soul that had lived or ever would live.

After the vision closed, and God left Moses to himself, Satan confronted him. Moses detected the devil, and, having overcome him by the name of the "Only Begotten," Moses called upon the name of God and experienced a second vision.[728] Once again, God drew individual attention to Moses—the *one*—whom God now blessed with assurance of exaltation: "Thou shalt be made stronger than many waters: for they shall obey thy command as if thou wert God. And lo, I am with thee, even unto the end of thy days; for thou shalt deliver my people [Israel] from bondage."[729] Note that this level of sanctification afforded Moses great strength to do the work of God and extraordinary power in using the name of Jesus Christ; Moses was also blessed with the personal ministration of Jesus Christ (the Second Comforter), and he was given power to deliver others; such is important knowledge for parents who strive to sanctify themselves to bless their children.

This additional endowment of power given to Moses opened the way for an additional endowment of knowledge with the continuation of the second vision. During the course of this vision Moses experienced a view of this *one* world.[730] "And it came to pass, as the voice was still speaking, Moses cast his eyes and beheld the earth."[731] As we will see, the metaphor had not changed—*one heavenly body as compared to one son.* In this second vision of the world, God allowed Moses to see what he had seen before, except now Moses was able

---

727 Moses 1:8.
728 See Moses 1:12–25.
729 Moses 1:25–26.
730 See Moses 1:25–27.
731 Moses 1:27.

to perceive both the world and all the souls of mankind *intimately,* even to the atomic level: "[Moses beheld] all of it; and there was not a particle of it which he did not behold, discerning it by the spirit of God."[732] Moses marveled that the children of God were as numerous as the "sand upon the seashore."[733] Note that whereas the symbolism had been *one son* [Moses] compared to *one earth,* the new comparable was *numerous children* compared to *numerous stars.* Now the vision expanded. God drew back the curtain so that Moses could see the workmanship of God's hands. Now Moses beheld "many lands; and each land was called earth" and "inhabitants" on those earths— "worlds without number."[734]

Worlds without Number

To understand the significance and vastness implied by the term *numberless,* let us examine what we know about the heavens. In 1983, even before the Hubble telescope and modern computer technology, we knew that the universe was immense; for instance, the National Geographic Society published a mind-boggling article and map of the known universe.[735] Our solar system, the editors explained, has a radius of 150 million kilometers, or .000016 light years. A light year is the distance light travels at—186,000 miles per second for a year, or 5,878,625,373,183.61 miles. Almost 6 trillion miles! Our solar system resides in the Milky Way Galaxy, which, by one estimate, has as many as one trillion stars like our sun. Our solar system's neighborhood—the twenty closest stars—has a radius of 20 light years, and this little neighborhood of stars lies on the outskirts of the vast Milky Way Galaxy, which has a radius of 50,000 light years. To illustrate the immensity of our galaxy, the sun, traveling at 220 kilometers per second, makes one revolution around the center of our galaxy every 230 million years!

As enormous as these numbers are, the Milky Way Galaxy is nevertheless a speck in the universal ocean. Consider this: our galaxy is one of a *cluster* of twenty nearby galaxies of like size, which cluster is called

---

732 Moses 1:27.
733 Moses 1:28.
734 Moses 1:29, 33.
735 Galaxy Map, *The National Geographic Society,* June 1983.

a "local group." The radius of this local group is two million light years. Similarly, local groups congregate in "local superclusters," which are the largest of celestial formations. Each local supercluster may comprise thousands of member galaxies. The local supercluster in which we reside has a radius of 75 million light years. As incredible as this fact may seem, nothing is more unfathomable than the fact that our local supercluster is but a mere speck in the known universe. And there is no visible end. What appeared as dots at the end of space twenty years ago have been identified as numerous superclusters with today's technology—"and thy curtains are stretched out still!"[736] If by means of modern telescopes we are able see to this extent, imagine what Moses was able to see by the power of God! And yet God had to limit this vision in order to keep Moses in the flesh.[737]

As we shall see, Moses' vision has a direct application to parents as they work with their children.

It All Comes Down to One.
Struggling to take it all in, "Moses called upon God, saying: Tell me, I pray thee, why these things are so, and by what thou madest them?"[738] That is, why do you do this and by whom do you do this? God postponed the answer. "For mine own purpose have I made these things. Here is wisdom and it remaineth in me."[739] Nevertheless, God was willing to tell Moses by whom He made these things: "And by the word of my power, have I created them, which is mine Only Begotten Son, who is full of grace and truth."[740] All the heavens were and are made by Jesus Christ! "And worlds without number have I created; and I also created them for mine own purpose; and by the Son I created them, which is mine Only Begotten."[741]

Now God did something very important, which was an essential lesson to Moses and should be to us—God brought Moses' attention

---

736 Moses 7:30.
737 Moses 1:5.
738 Moses 1:30.
739 Moses 1:31.
740 Moses 1:32.
741 Moses 1:33.

back to the *one:* this earth.[742] Despite the fact that there are innumerable worlds and innumerable inhabitants on those worlds, God's attention is on the *one.* Moses seemed content to receive what God wanted to reveal to him, and he began to press God for more information about *this* earth. God had told him by *whom* He accomplished His universal designs, but God had still not told Moses *why He did these things.* To answer Moses, God reviewed what He had shown Moses: this *one* earth resides among numberless hosts of heaven, but nevertheless God knows each earth intimately[743]—"they are mine."[744]

God was then ready to give Moses *the* answer. Now came God's grand secret, the reason for all creation and existence: "For behold, this is my work and my glory—to bring to pass the immortality and eternal life of man."[745]

It all comes down to the *one*—one person. Although God makes stars, it is not His primary business; He is in the business of redeeming His children. All creation points to the creation and redemption of the *one;* everything that God does is for the *one.* He said, "Remember the worth of souls is great in the sight of God."[746] He simply does not create anything, let alone children, with the expectation of failure.

While nothing trumps agency, God is nevertheless completely dedicated to His work, and when it comes to reclaiming and redeeming His children, there is simply no one better than God. Utilizing His complete arsenal of perfections—knowledge, power, love, etc.—He foresees every child's situation, prepares and provides a saving solution, endows that solution with power, and sets out in love to assemble every resource in heaven and on earth to rescue the *one.*

This is the God we believe in. This is the God of Adam, Enoch, Noah, Abraham, Moses, and Joseph Smith, and this is the God of whom President Gordon B. Hinckley bore testimony: "I want everybody in this hall tonight to realize that you each heard me say to you that I know that God our Eternal Father lives. I know that He lives. I know that He is a being of substance. I know that He is the great

---

742 See Moses 1:35.
743 See Moses 1:35.
744 Moses 1:37.
745 Moses 1:39.
746 D&C 18:10.

God of the universe. I know, however, that I am His child and that you are His children and that He will listen to and hear and answer our prayers."[747] With this confidence, President Hinckley was able to declare with prophetic authority, "We are winning, and the future never looked brighter."[748] How could he say this unless, with a prophet's view, he could see victory where now we might be anticipating defeat? President Hinckley's counsel was to follow the example of Moses—to move forward in faith, as did Israel, toward the sea, with the confidence that as we do so, it will part before us.[749] With that faith in the God of Israel, in Jesus Christ, who paid such an enormous price to rescue the *one*, we press forward toward our imposing sea with a "perfect brightness of hope,"[750] and we expect, as did Moses, that it will part and that the God of Israel will save our *one*. It is this same God of Israel who promised to "wipe away all tears,"[751] and to comfort all "them that mourn in Zion, to give unto them beauty for ashes, the oil of joy for mourning, the garment of praise for the spirit of heaviness."[752]

Attesting to this very fact, President James E. Faust wrote,

> We find solace in Christ through the agency of the Comforter, and the Savior extends this invitation to us: "Come unto me, all ye that labour and are heavy laden, and I will give you rest" (Matt. 11:28). The Apostle Peter speaks of "casting all your care upon him; for he careth for you" (1 Pet. 5:7). As we do this, healing takes place, just as the Lord promised through the prophet Jeremiah when He said "I will turn their mourning into joy, and will comfort them, and make them rejoice from their sorrow. . . . I have satiated the weary soul, and I have replenished every sorrowful soul"

---

747 Gordon B. Hinckley, "Inspirational Thoughts," *Ensign*, September 2007, 5.
748 Gordon B. Hinckley, "An Unending Conflict, a Victory Assured," *Ensign*, June 2007, 9.
749 See Gordon B. Hinckley, "An Unending Conflict, a Victory Assured," *Ensign*, June 2007, 4–9.
750 2 Nephi 31:20.
751 Revelation 7:17.
752 Isaiah 61:3.

(Jer. 31:13). And in the celestial glory, we are told that "God shall wipe away all tears from their eyes; and there shall be no more death, neither sorrow, nor crying, neither shall there be any more pain" (Rev. 21:4). Then faith and hope will replace heartache, disappointment, torment, anguish, and despair, and the Lord will give us strength, as Mormon said, that we "should suffer no manner of afflictions, save it were swallowed up in the joy of Christ" (Alma 31:38).[753]

PATIENCE FOR THE MIRACLE

Elder Neal A. Maxwell wrote, "Apparently it is necessary for us on occasion to be brought to a white-knuckles point of anxiety so as to be reminded, when rescued, of who our Rescuer is!"[754] This outstanding observation was brought home to me in the 1980 Holiday Bowl where Brigham Young University was pitted against Southern Methodist University. BYU entered the game with an 11–1 record, and SMU had an 8–3 record. BYU had overwhelmed its opponent with a powerful passing game orchestrated by quarterback Jim McMahon. But SMU had an explosive running offense led by Craig James and Eric Dickerson.

With four minutes left in the game, SMU scored to take a commanding 45–25 lead over BYU, which now appeared to be headed for yet another bowl loss. They simply could not handle SMU's offense. At this point of apparent hopelessness, my wife and I decided to spare ourselves the misery of watching BYU go down in defeat. We left our children with my mother and headed to a movie theater. When we returned, my mother met us at the door and excitedly announced that BYU had won. They had scored three touchdowns in the last two and a half minutes of the game. Thereafter, the game was to be called the "Miracle Bowl," and it has taken its place in history as one of the most exciting college bowl games ever played. And we had been too discouraged and impatient to see the miracle.

We were not alone. At the four-minute mark, most of the BYU fans had begun leaving the stadium when McMahon screamed that the

---

753 James E. Faust, "He Healeth the Broken in Heart," *Ensign*, July 2005.
754 Neal A. Maxwell, *Even As I Am*, 45.

game wasn't over yet. Very few believed him. Nevertheless, undaunted, he promptly threw a touchdown pass. This was followed by several more smart moves that decreased the gap in scores. After throwing two incomplete passes, McMahon then launched a "Hail Mary" into the end zone as time expired. What resulted was one of the most miraculous touchdowns in college football history. Then, with the score tied, BYU's Kurt Gunther kicked the extra point to give BYU a miraculous 46–45 victory. In the last two minutes and thirty-three seconds of the game, BYU scored 21 points—and we had missed it.

When all seems lost, we must not give up. President Benson said there is no question about the final outcome—righteousness will achieve victory.[755] Victory is in our future, even if that victory comes at the very last second. To achieve that victory, the Lord will call upon players on both sides of the veil. Our responsibility is to persevere by keeping one eye fixed on the goal and the other on what needs to happen today. Even if a child seems to be sinning away his salvation, we must never give up hope. Robert L. Millet wrote that though "there are limits, not necessarily to God's mercy but to the extent to which mercy can temper justice,"[756] nevertheless, there is still hope. He said, "I have a conviction that when a person passes through the veil of death, all those impediments and challenges and crosses that were beyond his or her power to control—abuse, neglect, immoral environment, weighty traditions, etc.—will be torn away like a film. Then perhaps that person shall, as President Woodruff suggested, see and feel things he or she could not see and feel before."[757]

Linda, a mother in Utah, wrote of clinging to hope, even up until the very last minute.

> My husband and I have five children. I learned from my two oldest to never give up. Our oldest son, Ben, started hanging with a bad group and drifted away from the Church. At one point, he told us that the Joseph Smith story was a load of baloney. He started smoking and experimenting with drugs. He stayed away from

---

755 See Ezra Taft Benson, "In His Steps," *Ensign*, September 1988.
756 Robert L. Millet, *When a Child Wanders*, 120–122.
757 Ibid., 126–127.

church for several years. We fasted and prayed for him constantly; we put his name in the temple religiously, and we tried to include him in family prayers and family home evening, as much as he would allow.

Once, at a regional conference, Elder Holland spoke and gave the congregation an apostolic blessing. He promised that if we as parents were faithful in all things, we would see our wayward children return. I remember weeping as I listened to his remarks. I prayed that his promise would be fulfilled.

Then, in 1998, our youngest child accidentally drowned. Ben was devastated; we all were. A month later, Ben phoned me and asked if I was sitting down. He announced that he had decided to go on a mission. I was speechless. He said that he had become so despondent over his brother's death that the only thing left to do was to pray. He told me that he had prayed all night and into the morning. Then he heard a voice as clear as a bell tell him to put his life in order and go on a mission. He moved home a few days later and began the repentance process to prepare to serve. At age twenty-two, he left for his field of service. Today he is married in the temple, has two beautiful children, and has graduated with a degree in business from BYU–Idaho.

Our second child, Paul, abandoned the Church in his junior year in high school when he started hanging around with a bad group of friends. This was uncharacteristic of Paul. He was the peacemaker in our home. He was always a sensitive and spiritual boy. Whenever my husband would give Paul a blessing, he would burst into tears. There was just something about him. But when he began to make poor choices of friends, he went from being an honor student to dropping out midway through that year. I watched with despair as he became more and more involved with drugs. He was arrested repeatedly, and went through the juvenile system. Most of the time the punishment was light, and he always bluffed his way through the drug counseling. Within the year, he moved out of our home and we rarely heard from him. Often, we had no idea where he was.

After Paul turned 18, he continued on his downward spiral. We prayed and prayed for him, and I fasted almost every Sunday. I recalled Elder Holland's promise, and I tried to be faithful in every way. Nevertheless, I found it hard not to question myself. I would constantly wonder what I had or had not done that had caused Paul to go down this path, but I never found any answers. Still, I beat myself up ruthlessly.

Paul finally reached a low point when he was sent to prison for an evaluation before sentencing. He spent three months in prison, twenty-three hours a day in a cell, and we could only have contact with him through letters. Over the course of those weeks, I noticed the tone of his letters change. He wrote and asked us to send him a set of scriptures. He read them from cover to cover. Soon, he was bearing his testimony in his letters. It was an amazing transformation. But his journey wasn't over. Next, he was sentenced to complete inpatient drug rehab, and he spent several months in the county jail waiting for a space to open up for him. While in jail, he attended the Church-sponsored meetings and he grew very close to the men and women who served there. He was finally admitted to the Salvation Army inpatient program, and he worked very hard to complete it.

When he was released, he did well for a few weeks, but then relapsed. Angry with himself for failing, he checked himself back into the program and worked even harder. He completely changed his life; he moved away from his old friends and started attending a singles' ward. There, he met a wonderful young woman, and they were married in the temple a little over a year ago. He continues to be involved with the LDS substance abuse program, and is often a facilitator at the meetings. He works with the young men in his ward, and has one of the strongest testimonies I've ever [heard].

As a parent, I have felt guilt, inadequacy, and failure during those days. So many times I felt that the Lord dealt me a bad hand and I wasn't up to the task. My husband and I counseled with our bishop many times, and even today I still question my parenting skills, but I never gave up and I will never give up. I continue to fast and pray for my children, and I know that miracles happen.

When Paul was in jail he wrote a touching poem. I think his sentiments might give hope to all parents who struggle with their wayward children.

The Person I Used to Be

As I sit in this cell
And I think about God
I see it's not really hell,
I've been brought back to the Rod.

So I'll hold on tight
Because falling away
Means not doing right
Like I did in those days.

When my will was important
And I did what I did,
It was from God's intent
For me that I hid.

But I've opened my eyes
Small miracles came
Now I see through the lies
And I take full blame.

Now I may have fooled others
And myself I've betrayed
And all that I have learned
Is that I should have stayed.

THE LAST HUMAN FREEDOM

In counseling parents of wayward children, Elder John K. Carmack found meaning and hope in the writings and ideas of war prisoner Viktor Frankl, particularly what Frankl called the "last human freedom":

> Every morning, parents whose children have gone astray face the stern test of whether they can continue to function, love, and serve as parents when faced with so much pain. I suggest they remember Viktor E. Frankl's survival as a Jew in a German concentration camp. Though only one prisoner in 28 survived, Viktor Frankl lived to write that a "man *can* preserve a vestige of spiritual freedom, of independence of mind, even in such terrible conditions of psychic and physical stress.
>
> "We who lived in concentration camps can remember the men who walked through the huts comforting others, giving away their last piece of bread. They may have been few in number, but they offer sufficient proof that everything can be taken from a man but one thing: the last of the human freedoms—to choose one's attitude in any given set of circumstances, to choose one's own way" (*Man's Search for Meaning,* 74–75).
>
> He added that prisoners facing the daily cruelty, savagery, and lack of respect for life and human dignity either perished or learned that *"it did not really matter what we expected from life, but rather what life expected from us"* (*Man's Search for Meaning,* 85). . . . [These prisoners] learned that nothing can be so bad as to ruin their inner peace and dignity. They discovered that proper attitudes gave them freedom from some of the ills they were having to endure. . . .

Parents often learn to survive themselves and become much stronger as they struggle to help and reclaim their wayward children. . . .

Do not give in to paralyzing feelings of guilt and hopelessness. Seek spiritual help and peace. Be strong and courageous. You will see it through.[758]

LIVING AFTER THE MANNER OF HAPPINESS

Consider the example of Nephi. After all he had gone through at the hands of his wayward loved ones, he was able to say that he lived after the manner of happiness.[759] This quality of life, as President Faust explained, is a product of absolute faith in Jesus Christ.[760] Because the Lord is who He is, our children are absolutely safe. Ted Gibbons describes our children's safety as their being "on belay."[761] As rock climbers scale dangerous mountains, the one leading the way anchors the rope so that it is secure; then he calls to the climber below: "You are on belay." That is, "You are safe to proceed and follow me; I've got the rope and you are secure." Our children are safe; the Savior has them on belay; although they might slip and crash into the sides of the mountain, they cannot fall. They are tethered to Jesus and bound to us by the power of the new and everlasting covenant. This is not to say that they cannot cut the rope by their exercise of agency, but one would have to choose to fall in the full light of truth. Our understanding of the resident powers in the plan of salvation allows us, like Nephi, to be at peace in the eye of the storm and live after the manner of happiness. The assurance of the Lord's being in control is the agent by which all Saints, from Adam to the present day, have been able to experience peace and happiness while enduring crushing trials.

IT'S GOING TO BE ALL RIGHT

The purpose of this book could be boiled down to this one statement: *it's going to be all right*. The Lord had provided a spiritual solution for

---

758 John K. Carmack, "When Our Children Go Astray," *Ensign*, February 1997.
759 See 2 Nephi 5:27.
760 See James E. Faust "Standing in Holy Places," *Ensign*, May 2005, 62, 67–68.
761 Ted Gibbons, *Nowhere Else to Go* (unpublished manuscript in author's possession).

waywardness. We are not impotent; we can pray for opportunities for our children to change. We have (or can develop) all the necessary tools to partner with heaven in bringing our children to a crossroads or in petitioning for a "conversion opportunity," as did Alma the Elder. As we apply these tools and patiently work with our wayward children, we must maintain our perspective of where and when they are living. This world is possibly the most corrupt among God's creations, and our children are living in the most wicked phase of its existence. Agency and truth are choked by such vile conditions, and God will mercifully take this into account. President J. Reuben Clark Jr. said, "I believe that in his justice and mercy, [God] will give us the maximum reward for our acts, give us all that he can give, and in the reverse, I believe that he will impose upon us the minimum penalty which it is possible for him to impose."[762]

We must remember that our children were among the noble and great ones, whose fall rendered them exceptionally disempowered physically, spiritually, and emotionally. They are *asleep* as to their true identity and to things "as they really are."[763] Nevertheless, in His wisdom, God foresaw these conditions, and with the redemption of all His children in mind, He created a plan to organize families into saving relationships, where strong parents nurture spiritually weak children, and strong children bless spiritually weak parents.

We parents were prepared for our mortal redemptive missions. Despite our temporary amnesia, we carry within us vital instruction and skill to become saviors on Mount Zion to our children. As we perform our missions, we will develop essential godlike characteristics that will propel us into the celestial kingdom. Central to our being able to hone the invaluable skills of working redemption among God's children, we will be introduced to "the heart of the gospel message," which Jesus described in the parables of the lost sheep, the lost coin, and the prodigal son. We will observe firsthand the Savior's ability to rescue those who have wandered, who have become lost from view, or who have rebelled and traveled to a "far country" to live like the Gentiles. We will be invited to follow His example. We will also observe the work and glory of God as He sets His hand to reclaim

---

762 J. Reuben Clark, Jr., *Conference Report*, October 1953, 84.
763 Jacob 4:13.

His wayward children. In the process we will recognize angelic ministrations as the powers of heaven are loosed to answer our prayers in behalf of our children and to assist us in our mission.

To ground us in faith and to provide us with strength to persevere when all might seem lost, we can rely on the many prophetic promises that assure us of a positive outcome. Central to these promises is our obligation to sanctify ourselves and to offer service in the temple that blessings might more easily flow from heaven.

Parents and spouses can have confidence and power to *gather* in the name of Jesus Christ as we call on the powers of the priesthood—the powers to bind our children to us, to turn their hearts to us, and to claim them forever through the eternal weld that is represented by our sealing.

In the end, we know that the worth of our child's soul is great in the sight of God. Our Heavenly Father anticipated and prepared for the difficult situation that we are now facing. He sent His Son, Jesus Christ, to rescue the child through the power of the infinite and eternal Atonement. The work of the Father and the Son is fully adequate to snatch our children from the deepest abyss, break down every obstacle, and place them on a throne.

Let us, therefore, ascribe to our Heavenly Father and Jesus Christ the perfections of character They are due: mercy, love, power, knowledge, compassion, grace, truth, and so forth. When we attempt to impose upon Them constraints of time or imagine that a difficulty is beyond Their reach, we discount the testimony of prophets, who have said nothing is too hard for the Lord.[764] Therefore, we should be careful when we pass immutable judgments on wayward souls, even when they sin grossly or remain unrepentant even until death. A veritable tome of evidence testifies that, with the help of the Lord, parents can be equipped with immeasurable ability and resources to rescue their wayward children from any location, time, or situation. Clearly, our covenants take on an added dimension when viewed in this light, for great power is given to those of us who sincerely make and keep covenants.

As we sanctify ourselves in the covenant, we reach out to Jesus, who extends "the arm of mercy towards them that put their trust in

---

764 See Genesis 18:14.

him."[765] We become *one* with Him in every way and thus have access to His saving power. No statement of understanding could be more comforting as we persist in the work of redemption.

We end with President Monson's counsel on gaining peace over the care of our families. He shared these sentiments with faithful members in leadership positions, but considering the broader context of the prophets' promises regarding all worthy parents who are sanctifying themselves and serving the Lord, these words clearly apply to all of us: "You are not alone," President Monson promised. "We pray for you." He goes on to remind us of a scripture from the Doctrine and Covenants: "'Verily, thus saith the Lord unto you . . . your families are well; they are in mine hands, and I will do with them as seemeth me good; for in me there is all power.'"[766] May we always have faith in the Lord's power to work in and through us. May we always remember the love He has for each of us. And may we never forget that with God *all* things are possible.

---

765 Mosiah 29:20.
766 Thomas S. Monson, "News of the Church" *Ensign*, September 1994, 76.

Note

286. Regarding the Lord's perfect timing in disseminating light on an individual, so as not to condemn them or require more than they can yet bear, Orson Pratt taught, "If you were, within one week from this time, to be let into all the visions that the brother of Jared had, what a weight of responsibility you would have upon you; how weak you would be, and how unprepared for the responsibility; and after the vision had closed up in your minds, and you were left to yourselves, you would be tempted in proportion to the light that had been presented before you. Then would come the trial, such as you never have had. This is the principle upon which the devil is allowed to try us. We have a circumstance in relation to Moses' being tempted; when the vision withdrew, and the heavens closed, the devil presented himself and said, 'Moses, son of man, worship me.' Moses replied, 'Who are you?' 'I am the son of God,' was the answer. Then said Moses, You call me son of man and say that you are the son of God, but where is your glory?' Could Moses have withstood that terrible manifestation, if he had not practised for many years the principles of righteousness? A mere vision would not have strengthened him, and even to shew him the glory of God in part would not have enabled him to combat with the powers of darkness that then came to him. It was by his knowledge of God, by his perseverance, his diligence and obedience in former years, that he was enabled to rebuke the devil, in the name of Jesus Christ, and drive him from him.

"So it will be with you, whether you have the necessary preparation or not, for the Lord will say to the powers of darkness, you are now at liberty to tempt my servants in proportion to the light that I have given. Go and see if they will be steadfast to that light; use every plan so far as I permit you, and if they will yield they are not worthy of me nor of my kingdom, and I will deliver them up and they shall be buffeted. You, Satan, shall buffet and torment them, until they shall learn obedience by the things that they suffer.

"Hence the propriety of preparing for these things, that when they come you will know how to conquer Satan, and not want for experience to overcome, but be like Michael, the archangel, who, with all the knowledge and glory that he had gained through thousands of years of experience, durst not bring a railing accusation, because he knew better. And when Moses withstood Satan face to face, he knew who he was and what he had come for. He had obtained his knowledge by past trials, by a long series of preparation; hence he triumphed.

"So it must be with Latter-day Saints, and if we prepare ourselves we shall conquer. We must come in contact with every foe, and those who give way will be overcome.

"If we are to conquer the enemy of truth his power must be made manifest, and the power which will be given of the Lord through faithfulness must be in our possession. Do you wish to prevail—to conquer the powers of darkness when they present themselves? If you do, prepare yourselves against the day when these powers shall be made manifest with more energy than is now exhibited. Then you can say, the evil powers that have been made manifest, the agents that came and tempted me, came with all their force, I met them face to face and conquered by the word of my testimony, by patience, by the keys which have been bestowed upon me, and which I held sacred before God, and I have triumphed over the adversary and over all his associates" (George D. Watt, ed., *Journal of Discourses*, Volume 3, 353–54).

SELECTED BIBLIOGRAPHY

American Heritage Dictionary. Cambridge, MA: Softkey International, Inc., 1994.

Babbel, Fredrick. *On Wings of Faith: My Daily Walk with a Prophet.* Springville, UT: Cedar Fort, Inc., 1998.

Benson, Ezra Taft. *The Teachings of Ezra Taft Benson.* Salt Lake City, UT: Bookcraft, 1988.

Brown, Hugh B. *An Abundant Life: The Memoirs of High B. Brown.* Salt Lake City, UT: Signature Books, 1999.

———. *Continuing the Quest.* Salt Lake City, UT: Deseret Book, 1961.

Brown, Matthew B. *The Gate of Heaven: Insights on Doctrines and Symbols of the Temple.* American Fork, UT: Covenant Communications, 1999.

Burton, Alma P., ed. *Discourses of the Prophet Joseph Smith.* Salt Lake City, UT: Deseret Book, 1977.

Clark, E. Douglas. *The Blessings of Abraham: Becoming a Zion People.* American Fork, UT: Covenant Communications, 2005.

Clark, James R., ed. *Messages of the First Presidency of The Church of Jesus Christ of Latter-day Saints 1833–1964* [6 vols]. Salt Lake City, UT: Bookcraft, 1966.

Cowley, Matthew. *Mathew Cowley Speaks: Discourses of Elder Matthew Cowley of the Quorum of the Twelve of the Church of Jesus Christ of Latter-day Saints.* Salt Lake City, UT: Deseret Book, 1976.

Dalrymple, G. Brent. *The Age of the Earth.* Stanford, CA: Stanford University Press, 1991.

Dressler, David. *Youth in a Troubled World.* Brigham Young University Speeches of the Year, 2 May 1960.

Durham, G. Homer, ed. *The Discourses of Wilford Woodruff: Fourth President of the Church of Jesus Christ of Latter-day Saints.* Salt Lake City, UT: Bookcraft, 1998.

Ehat, Andrew F. and Lyndon W. Cook, eds. *The Words of Joseph Smith: The Contemporary Accounts of the Nauvoo Discourses of the Prophet Joseph.* Salt Lake City, UT: Bookcraft, Inc., 1980.

Ellsworth, Sterling. *Latter-day Plague: Breaking the Chains of Pornography.* Provo, UT: Maasai Publishing, 2002.

Encyclopedia of Mormonism. New York: Macmillan Publishing Company, 1992.

Goddard, Wallace C. *Drawing Heaven into Your Marriage: Powerful Principles with Eternal Results.* Fairfax, VA: Meridian Publishing, 2007.

Hafen, Bruce C. *Covenant Hearts: Marriage and the Joy of Human Love.* Salt Lake City, UT: Deseret Book, 2005.

Hafen, Bruce C. and Marie K. Hafen. *The Belonging Heart: The Atonement and Relationships with God and Family.* Salt Lake City, UT: Deseret Book, 1994.

Hinckley, Gordon B. *Teachings of Gordon B. Hinckley.* Salt Lake City, UT: Deseret Book, 1997.

Holzapfel, Richard Neitzel and Thomas A. Wayment. *The Life and Teachings of Jesus Christ,* Vol. 2, Salt Lake City, UT: Deseret Book, 2006.

Hymns of the Church of Jesus Christ of Latter-day Saints. Salt Lake City, UT: The Church of Jesus Christ of Latter-day Saints, 1985.

Kimball, Edward L., ed. *The Teachings of Spencer W. Kimball.* Salt Lake City, UT: Bookcraft, 1982.

Kimball, Heber C. *President Heber C. Kimball's Journal.* Salt Lake City, UT: Juvenile Instructor Office, 1882.

Kimball, Spencer W. *Faith Precedes the Miracle.* Salt Lake City, UT: Deseret Book, 1972.

———. *The Miracle of Forgiveness.* Salt Lake City, UT: Bookcraft, 1969.

LDS Bible Dictionary of the Standard Works of the Church of Jesus Christ of Latter-day Saints. Salt Lake City, UT: The Church of Jesus Christ of Latter-day Saints, 1979.

Lee, Harold B. *Decisions for Successful Living.* Salt Lake City, UT: Deseret Book, 1973.

Maxwell, Neal A. *Lord, Increase Our Faith.* Salt Lake City, UT: Bookcraft, 1994.

———. *That Ye May Believe.* Salt Lake City, UT: Bookcraft, 1992.

———. *Meek and Lowly.* Salt Lake City, UT: Deseret Book, 1987.

———. *But for a Small Moment.* Salt Lake City, UT: Bookcraft, 1986.

———. *Even as I Am.* Salt Lake City, UT: Deseret Book, 1982.

———. *Wherefore, Ye Must Press Forward.* Salt Lake City, UT: Deseret Book, 1977.

McConkie, Bruce R. ed., *Doctrines of Salvation: Sermons and Writings of Joseph Fielding Smith* [3 vols]. Salt Lake City, UT: Bookcraft, 1999.

———. *Sermons & Writings of Bruce R. McConkie.* Salt Lake City, UT: Bookcraft, 1998.

———. *A New Witness for the Articles of Faith.* Salt Lake City, UT: Deseret Book, 1985.

———. *The Mortal Messiah.* Salt Lake City, UT: Deseret Book, 1979–1981.

———. *Mormon Doctrine.* Salt Lake City, UT: Bookcraft, 1966.

McConkie, Joseph Fielding and Craig J. Ostler. *Revelations of the Restoration: A Commentary on the Doctrine and Covenants and Other Modern Revelation.* Salt Lake City, UT: Deseret Book, 2000.

McConkie, Joseph Fielding and Robert L. Millet. *Joseph Smith: The Choice Seer.* Salt Lake City, UT: Bookcraft, 1996.

———. *The Man Adam.* Salt Lake City, UT: Bookcraft, 1990.

———. *Doctrinal Commentary on the Book of Mormon* [4 vols]. Salt Lake City, UT: Bookcraft, 1987–1992.

———. *The Life Beyond.* Salt Lake City, UT: Bookcraft, 1986.

Millet, Robert L. *When a Child Wanders.* Salt Lake City, UT: Deseret Book, 1996.

Nelson, Russell M. *The Power within Us.* Salt Lake City, UT: Deseret Book, 1988.

Packer, Boyd K. *The Holy Temple.* Salt Lake City: Bookcraft, 1982.

Roberts, B. H. *History of The Church of Jesus Christ of Latter-day Saints* [7 vols]. Salt Lake City, UT: Deseret Book, 1978.

Smith, Joseph. *Lectures on Faith.* American Fork, UT: Covenant Communications, 2000.

Smith, Joseph F. *Gospel Doctrine: Selections from the Sermons and Writings of Joseph F. Smith.* Salt Lake City, UT: Bookcraft, 1998.

———. *Teachings of the Prophet Joseph Smith.* Salt Lake City, UT: Deseret Book, 1976.

Snow, Lorenzo. *The Teachings of Lorenzo Snow.* Salt Lake City, UT: Bookcraft, 1996.

Stuy, Brian H., comp. *Collected Discourses Delivered by President Wilford Woodruff, His Counselors, the Twelve Apostles, and Others, Vol. 3, 1892–1893.* Burbank, CA: B.H.S. Publishing, 1989.

Talmage, James E. *Jesus the Christ.* Salt Lake City, UT: Deseret Book, 1983.

———. *The House of the Lord.* Salt Lake City, UT: The Church of Jesus Christ of Latter-day Saints, 1979.

———. *Sunday Night Talks.* Salt Lake City, UT: The Church of Jesus Christ of Latter-day Saints, 1931.

Taylor, John. *The Government of God.* Grantsville, UT: Archive Publishers, 2000.

Thomas, M. Catherine. "Alma the Younger, Parts 1 and 2." Neal A. Maxwell Institute for Religious Scholarship, Provo, UT.

Tvedtnes, John A. *The Church of the Old Testament.* Salt Lake City, UT: Deseret Book, 1980.

Watt, George D., ed. *Journal of Discourses* [26 vols]. Liverpool, England: Samuel W. Richards and Sons, 1852–1886.

Widtsoe, John A. *Program of the Church.* Salt Lake City, UT: Deseret News Press, 1936.

Yorgason, Blaine. *I Need Thee Every Hour.* Salt Lake City, UT: Deseret Book, 2003.

———. *Spiritual Progression in the Last Days.* Salt Lake City, UT: Deseret Book, 1994.

Young, Brigham. *Discourses of Brigham Young.* Salt Lake City, UT: Deseret Book, 1999.

ABOUT THE AUTHOR

Larry Barkdull is a longtime publisher and writer of books, music, art, and magazines. For many years, he owned Sonos Music Resources and published the Tabernacle Choir Performance Library. His published works have received a variety of awards: the American Family Literary Award; the Benjamin Franklin Book Award; and *Foreword Magazine*'s GOLD Book of the Year Award for best fiction.

His books have sold in excess of 250,000 copies and have been translated into Japanese, Korean, Italian, and Hebrew. Additionally, he is the creator and producer of the popular Scripture Scouts musical series to teach children the scriptures. He and his wife, Elizabeth, live in Orem, Utah, and are the parents of ten children and a growing number of grandchildren.

Larry Barkdull can be contacted on his Web site, www.larrybarkdull.com